Not Responsible for Lost Articles

With best wishes —

Klaus G. Roy

December 1993

Not Responsible for Lost Articles

Thoughts and Second Thoughts
from Severance Hall, 1958–1988

Selected Essays, Entr'actes, and
Features from the Program Books
of The Cleveland Orchestra

Published in Honor of the Orchestra's
Seventy-Fifth Anniversary, 1993

Klaus G. Roy
and Numerous Contributors

Frontispiece by John DePol

Illustrations by Melissa E. Roy

The Musical Arts Association
Cleveland, Ohio
1993

Not Responsible for Lost Articles, by Klaus G. Roy
    and Numerous Contributors
Copyright © 1993 in this edition by The Musical Arts
    Association, Cleveland
All rights reserved
ISBN 0-944125-21-2
First edition
Vignette illustrations by Melissa E. Roy (then age
    ten to eleven), published mostly in the 1970–1971
    Key Concert programs of The Cleveland Orchestra
Book design by Roderick Boyd Porter
Typesetting by Delmas of Ann Arbor, Michigan
Printing by The Emerson Press, Inc.
Binding by Forest City Bookbinding of Cleveland
Dust jacket design by Watt, Roop & Co., Cleveland,
    based on drawings of Melissa E. Roy
Manufactured in the United States of America
All proceeds from the sale of this book benefit
    The Cleveland Orchestra
The publication of this book has been made possible
    by a generous and deeply appreciated gift from
    Dorothy Humel Hovorka

Library of Congress Cataloging-in-Publication Data

Roy, Klaus George, 1924–
    Not responsible for lost articles : thoughts and second thoughts
    from Severance Hall 1958–1988 / Klaus G. Roy ; with frontispiece
    illustration by John DePol.
        p. cm.
    Principally essays reprinted from Cleveland Orchestra program
    books, 1958–1988.
        ISBN 0-944125-21-2
    1. Music—History and criticism. I. Cleveland Orchestra.
II. Title.
ML60.R877   1993
780′.15—dc20   92-41977
                                                              CIP
                                                              MN

This book is dedicated
to the memory of my parents
ALBERT ROY
(Vienna, 1893—Boston, 1970)
Poet, Essayist, Book Publisher, Librarian, Philatelist
MARY K. ROY
(Vienna, 1902—Cleveland, 1978)
Painter, Designer, Puppeteer, Potter, Master Teacher

and to the memory of my friend and first "Boss" in Cleveland
A. BEVERLY BARKSDALE
(1913–1993)
Scholar, Singer, and Manager of The Cleveland Orchestra, 1957–1970

Table of Contents

III. PEOPLE AND PLACES

IV. POINTS OF VIEW, SPECULATIONS,
     AND FURTHER SECOND THOUGHTS

"If I had my life to live over again, I would have made it a rule to read some poetry and listen to some music at least every week. . . . The loss of these tastes is a loss of happiness, and may possibly be injurious to the intellect, and more probably to the moral character, by enfeebling the emotional part of our nature."

—Charles Darwin

"I think sometimes could I only have music on my own terms, could I live in a great city and know where I could go whenever I wished the ablution and inundation of musical waves, that were a bath and a medicine. . . ."

—Ralph Waldo Emerson

"Take a music bath once or twice a week for a few seasons. You will find it is to the soul what a water bath is to the body. It elevates and tends to maintain tone to one's mind. Seek, therefore, every clean opportunity for hearing. Purchase some kind of instrument for the home and see that its beneficent harmonies are often heard. Let music be as much a part of a day's routine as eating or reading or working."

—Oliver Wendell Holmes

"Life without music would be a mistake."

—Friedrich Nietzsche

PRELUDE

Silentium! Silentium! Leave all the chatter, idle hum! And now commence; we say, commence!

Richard Wagner
from *Die Meistersinger*

Prelude

BOOKS CUSTOMARILY BEGIN with a foreword, a word before many words. During a tenure of thirty-and-a-half years as program annotator and editor of The Cleveland Orchestra at Severance Hall and Blossom Music Center, the author wrote program notes for perhaps one thousand compositions. What follows is not a compilation of those "notes on the program" (with two exceptions that deal as much with history and ethics as with music). This book is, rather, a collection of the essays and "entr'actes" contributed to the weekly program book, and a selection from the smaller features and addenda that have been scattered throughout the programs for the sake of variety and the possible interest of concert patrons.

The book does not intend to represent fairly the contents of the weekly program book over the years: it does not include the countless profiles of Orchestra members upon their joining or their departure; it does not include biographical material on the soloists and guest conductors; it does not include the many pages of reviews and reports of the Orchestra's national and international tour concerts; and it does not include the regularly printed material on the daily and weekly activities of the Orchestra and of The Musical Arts Association and its many committees that contribute so mightily to its maintenance and functioning. This book is for the most part what its title proposes: "thoughts and second thoughts" on music and the musical life.

Yet the authorship claimed on the cover of the book is somewhat misleading. By the time the reader arrives at the title page, he or she will notice an amendment, a retrenchment, an admission gladly made. Most human enterprises are not the result of individual action alone, but are the outcome of collaboration, interaction, shared purpose and intent. One of the editor's objectives over the decades has been to represent many viewpoints, opinions, styles, even arguments and contradictions. The greater the variety, democratically speaking, the wider the range of views, the greater the opportunity for thought and response. However contrary some of the standpoints may appear, the shared purpose was always to engage the readers' attention and to sharpen their listening experience. It seemed of value, therefore, not only to reprint the editor's own commentaries, but to reflect the cultural milieu of this area from many angles, to highlight some of the personalities who have enriched it, and to let as many stimulating people have their say as space would allow.

All the authors whose contributions here appear had originally given their kind permission for the inclusion of their writing in the program book. We trust that they will not object to finding themselves thus summarily anthologized, and appreciation for their indulgence is expressed to them. Whatever material is not identified otherwise must be charged to—or blamed on—the undersigned.

*

It has been the considered belief of the author that neither program notes nor special essays for a sophisticated concert audience need be "objective", limiting themselves to historical facts and analytical detail. Thus it is that this collection is full of opinions, viewpoints, eccentricities, stands defended and attacked, and—occasionally—polemics delivered. The greatest writer of program notes in musical history, Sir Donald Francis Tovey, held and practiced these convictions, and his disciples everywhere follow him on that path.

The variety of material here contained means to mirror the variety of musical offerings by the great orchestra under whose auspices they were written and for whose seventy-fifth anniversary they contribute a voice in celebration. It is the author's hope that these writings will amuse as well as inform, entertain as well as instruct, pique the interest as well as shed an occasional point of light.

*

A few new corrections from the original have been silently made. Some misprints have been corrected (and, we hope, no new ones added), some facts confirmed or established, some information updated to encompass the present, some word choices made more elegant. And, in one essay, "four billion" has been revised to the more correct "four-and-a-half billion". A minor emendation, surely. (A minor? As the PG-13-rated limerick has it, "A minstrel from North Carolina / Contributed—what could be finer? / With a jarring C-sharp / On his old Southern harp / To the delinquency.... yes, of A minor.")

And speaking of delinquency: if any readers find themselves upset by occasional oddities of punctuation, flying in the face of custom, this particular rebellion is accounted-for in the "editorial confession" at the close. It may not be irrelevant to recount at this point that a German-born secretary working at Severance Hall some years ago referred to this author, in an official letter, as "the Orchestra's program agitator".

*

Because the contents of this book are drawn from the years 1958 to 1988, there is only a regrettably small proportion of material concerning the incumbent music director, Christoph von Dohnányi. This writer had the privilege of working with Mr. Dohnányi for four seasons since he took over the Orchestra in 1984—all too short a time. Yet those years were exceptionally rewarding both artistically and personally. My wife Gene and I admired (and continue to do so) Mr. Dohnányi's sterling musicianship, imaginative and often daring program making, and integrity as an artist and a human being. We have become good friends, sharing experiences and ideas, books, insights in literature, art and politics, and lively conversation. Most treasurable of all, we have enjoyed good companionship, and we value the genuine warmth of both Christoph and Anja Silja Dohnányi (a great and admirable artist in her own right) and their three delightful children. The Orchestra, as we all know, is at this time at an all-time high in the world's estimation, and this continued stature of unsurpassed quality owes much of its maintenance and nurture to the stature and quality of the man who guides and directs it.

I am most grateful to the exceptionally enlightened orchestra administration which has allowed me to expatiate at length on so many subjects—some of them quite controversial—and never made an audible objection to whatever was discussed or to the way it was done. It was "freedom of expression and opinion" at its finest, and I am pleased to have found here an exemplification of what this country has long claimed to be all about.

A. Beverly Barksdale, who shares the dedication of this book, was manager of The Cleveland Orchestra for the last thirteen years of George Szell's twenty-four-season tenure as musical director and conductor. His period of service coincided with and greatly influenced the Orchestra's most dramatic growth and development, and its rise to international eminence. In 1958, Mr. Barksdale supervised the acoustical reconstruction of the Severance Hall interior. Among Mr. Barksdale's many other notable accomplishments were the planning and guidance of the epochal eleven-week tour of the Orchestra in 1965 to Europe and the then Soviet Union—in its extent an unprecedented enterprise for an American orchestra. Mr. Barksdale was deeply involved, with Mr. Szell and the trustees, in the envisioning, construction, and inauguration of Blossom Music Center between 1966 and 1968, and he guided the Orchestra on its first and hugely successful tour of the Orient in 1970. From 1970 to 1980, he served as general manager of The Cleveland Museum of

Art. He retired to his native South Carolina where he served on the board of the Charleston Symphony, was active in the area's cultural affairs, and sang with a local chorus. It had been Beverly Barksdale who, on behalf of Mr. Szell, called me at my home in Boston, in September of 1957, to inquire about my possible availability for the position of program annotator in Cleveland. In the years that followed, it was again Mr. Barksdale who directed, counseled, and, at stressful moments, calmed and protected this fledgling sorcerer's apprentice. Beverly Barksdale last visited Severance Hall in November 1992 to tape some eight hours of his reminiscences for the Orchestra's archives. At that time he was moved and delighted to learn that this book was to be dedicated to him. Regrettably, he did not live to see it in print; he died on April 3, 1993, at the age of 79. He will be warmly remembered by his countless friends and admirers.

Deep appreciation and gratitude are expressed to the author's friend and colleague of more than thirty years, Dorothy Humel Hovorka, whose extraordinary generosity has made possible the production and publication of this book. Mrs. Hovorka has served the Orchestra as a volunteer in a variety of posts, including the presidency of The Women's Committee, the presidency of Lake Erie Opera Theatre, which presented numerous fully-staged operas with The Cleveland Orchestra, and as a long-time Trustee of The Musical Arts Association which she now serves as a Vice President. Among her many constructive and visionary ideas and projects was the initiation of the weekly pre-concert talks or concert previews, begun on a regular basis in 1972 and continued to this day. Dorothy Humel Hovorka's abiding concern and involvement set a splendid example in the never-ending process of supporting and nurturing the arts. I am very touched and grateful.

It was an inestimable joy to work with Roderick Boyd Porter, as perceptive and knowledgeable a publisher and editor as one could imagine. He was, in addition, a perennial enthusiast for the Orchestra's musical offerings. Rod Porter designed this book and advised on its contents, but to our sorrow did not live to see its publication. He died on March 11, 1993, at the untimely age of 45. A book producer of distinction, he was greatly respected in his field for his high standards, impeccable taste and highly cultivated mind.

I am happy to be able to thank my daughter Melissa E. Roy (now Mrs. Neal J. Legger) for allowing us to use her charming drawings, most of them made more than twenty years ago.

Thanks are due Gary Hanson, director of marketing and public relations of the Orchestra, for his editorial and production assistance and his discerning counsel. Special appreciation goes to Carol Jacobs, archivist of the Orchestra at Severance Hall, for her consistent helpfulness with archival material, with the illustrations, and with many aspects of assistance to this complex publication. I am appreciative also of the assistance in proofreading by Timothy D. Parkinson, publicity associate, who was my colleague in the program office from 1971 to 1988, and Eric Sellen, the Orchestra's publications editor, for his design assistance.

*

Although this writer was not obligated by his contract as annotator to produce the vast majority of the pieces here included, he did them almost entirely on "company time", as a natural outgrowth of his functions at Severance Hall. It is therefore his great pleasure to see the proceeds from the sale of this book go to the use and benefit of the incomparable orchestra which it was his immense privilege and honor to serve for three decades and more.

—K.G.R.
Cleveland, September 1993

I. UN POCO GIOCOSO

Say, what abridgement have you for this evening? What masque?
What music? How shall we beguile the lazy time, if not with some
delight?

William Shakespeare
from *A Midsummer Night's Dream*

"What Does One Say to an Artist after a Performance?"
(MARCH 1980)

*

The idea for this essay came to the editor from Mrs. Virginia Kuper of the Severance Hall staff. It attempts to come to grips with a perennial "problem", but is likely to be anything but comprehensive. The article has been several times reprinted in Stagebill *magazine, under the title "After the Applause".*

*

IT SHOULD BE EASY, but it isn't. When the line forms in the Green Room to greet the performer or performers of the evening, the wheels begin to turn in the minds of the greeters. The crucial moment arrives, and what is said? From some, it is a simple "thank you." From others, "I really enjoyed that." And from yet others, a reasonable piece of instant music criticism, like "that was marvelous", or "just superb", or "bravo; magnificent!" One would suppose that no one stands in line to say, "I've heard better."

One possible approach, surely, is to find an aspect of the performance that was important to the hearer; something like, "exquisite playing; you understand the style so well." Or, "I liked especially what you did with such-and-such a spot" in the piece; that kind of thing might actually interest a performer, and show the listener as a connoisseur, not merely as a fan.

The words one chooses are of course important. Lorin Maazel likes to tell the story of an elderly gentleman who came up to him after a concert and gushed, "Maestro, your performance tonight was irreparable!" It was an incomparable encomium. One recalls the lady who greeted the late Adlai Stevenson after an address with the remark, "Mr. Stevenson, your speech was absolutely superfluous! Could I have a copy of it?" "Of course," replied the witty statesman; "it will be published posthumously." "Splendid!" exclaimed the lady; "and the sooner the better!"

It was also Adlai Stevenson who was responsible for one of the all-time great rejoinders. Introduced somewhat too effusively before an address, he began: "You know, ladies and gentlemen, flattery is all right as long as you don't inhale."

In the German language, a woodwind or brass solo is not played, but blown ("geblasen"). It is not advisable in English-speaking countries, however, to tell a soloist on one of those instruments, "you really blew that piece!" This horrifying thought leads us to the possible ways of intentionally saying nothing, when that particular approach seems desirable. One can always tell an artist, "you really played that piece!" Or, "what a performance!" That kind of thing can mean anything, and can therefore be taken by the player as complimentary, when it may not actually be.

"Terrific", "fabulous", and "fantastic" have been for some time devalued verbal currency. Another word that may or may not mean much is "interesting": "It's interesting what you did with the concerto." Now does that mean, "I was interested in how the work was played, in comparison to how I have heard it before", or does it mean, "I don't know what else to say"? Something that genuinely interests a listener, piques his curiosity or critical acumen, is worthwhile, and can lead to probing discussion. As an escape mechanism, "interesting" is creaky. For listeners to new or unfamiliar music, it has long been a staple, meaning primarily "I didn't understand it". Perhaps a moratorium on that term should be declared, unless its original intent can be recaptured.

3

Other safely ambiguous observations that have been suggested for use-as-prescribed include such things as "I've never heard such Bruckner," or "Beethoven must be very happy tonight." Considering the available time for meeting the artist, they may be preferable to "Well, you know, Bruno Walter did the transition to the recapitulation somewhat more slowly, but your way was very individualistic . . ." or "I don't quite follow your *sforzando* at measure 375 . . . whose edition are you using?"

What to do if one has serious reservations about a performance? One may, of course, forego the after-concert greeting ceremony. But if one has no choice, and for one reason or another must shake hands with the artist, there are ways to say something without compromising oneself seriously; something like, "thank you for bringing us that work—we haven't heard it here for a while . . ." or similar generalities.

The nature of an artist's response to praise is important to the congratulator; it tells much about a performer how this is done. The signing of autographs, for instance, admittedly a bit of a chore, can be done brusquely, hurriedly, and without looking at the autograph collector. But when an artist shows his or her appreciation of such a request, and pays at least momentary personal attention to the requestor, one gains an increased awareness of that performer's human qualities. There is little excuse, furthermore, for looking over the enthusiast's shoulder to see who the next person in line might be, or what more important personalities might be there to greet and be greeted. Those others will still be there thirty seconds later; a little counter-courtesy is not too much to ask.

The story goes that Serge Koussevitzky was once assaulted by a lady after a Boston or Tanglewood concert, with the exclamation, "Dr. Koussevitzky, you are marvelous!" "Tenk you," was the answer. "Dr. Koussevitzky," continued the enthusiast, "for me, you are God himself!" "Madame," said the conductor, his smile changing to a serious mien, "I know vot mine responsabilities are!"

For some years, the editor had been telling a story unascribed to a particular person or set of circumstances. After one such example of galloping anecdotage, Josef Gingold took the raconteur aside, and in his quiet and kindly manner said, "I must tell you, that story really happened; I just thought you would like to know." Thus we recount it now as Mr. Gingold vouches for it. It seems that the Bohemian pianist Alfred Grünfeld (1852–1924) finally managed to get an engagement at the emperor's palace in Vienna. Following the concert, the Emperor (Franz Joseph I) came up to the performer and said, gravely: "As you can see, I am already very old. I have heard the greatest pianists in the world. Believe me, I have heard Anton Rubinstein in his prime! I have heard Hans von Bülow at the keyboard! I have even heard Franz Liszt play! But you know," he concluded, placing a benign hand on the pianist's shoulder, "none of them sweat as much as you did!"

The nature, degree, and extent of applause, at the conclusion of a piece or of a concert, is another matter entirely, and may eventually be dealt with in another such essay. Here we are concerned with the verbalization of opinion and feeling, at that moment which in contemporary parlance is sometimes called "one-on-one".

Surely this essay is not intended to make people self-conscious about the customary post-concert observances. Artists, to be sure, enjoy praise and appreciation for what has been accomplished; but they have an instinct for its substance or lack of it. Ultimately, what counts will be the genuineness of the brief sentiments expressed and responded to, and whether that particular moment will linger pleasantly if briefly in the memory of both protagonists in the encounter.

Two-and-a-Half Cheers for Technological Advancements
And Other Acoustical Hazards (MARCH 1982)

ALL MEMBERS of an audience will surely agree that the only relevant sound at a concert is that which comes from the stage, from the performing artists. At the conclusion of works, of course, the opportunity for listeners to make appropriate sounds is happily provided. As Victor Borge once remarked at Blossom Music Center, "Ladies and gentlemen, *if* you are going to applaud, would you please use both hands?"

There has been much discussion in the programs about the unintentional marring of musical works by coughs, sneezes, dropped programs, jangling bracelets, unwrapping of candy, etc. All these extra-musical events, naturally, "are not in the score", and are not only extraneous but disturbing. They may also find their way onto the recording tapes and contribute to the immortality of the noise-producer in ways less than flattering. "Ha, that was *my* cough in that *pianissimo* passage!" Such is fame, of sorts.

With trepidation and apologies, it was mentioned last year that if hearing aids are turned up during soft moments in the music, a high-pitched squeal may be heard by all but the wearer. It is an unfortunate side-effect to a regrettable disability, and those affected were asked very respectfully to keep the potential danger in mind.

Our modern technology has now presented us with a new problem, pointed out to us in several letters and many personal comments. Digital watches tend to tell wearers that the hour has struck; all well and good, but they also tell everyone else. At 9:00 p.m. and 10:00 p.m., there begins a veritable chorus of digital beeps. On television, offending words are "bleeped"; is there a way to bleep the beeps? Perhaps there is. Could wearers of such devices be asked kindly to put them in the non-beeping mode (put the beepers to sleep) during concerts? Appreciation would be wide-spread.

While we are on the subject of concert deportment, one more problem should be mentioned: It may indeed be necessary for some patrons to get to the parking lot as quickly as possible; but one more minute will make no real difference. Thus what one letter describes as a stampede of departing patrons—not only the moment after the conclusion but even before the last notes are sounded—could be avoided. The thoughtful consideration of all listeners is respectfully requested, so that the ambience of the performance may be retained and extended into the closing response itself.

The Severance Hall audience is a sophisticated one, and such long moments of silence as after the recent performance of Mahler's Tenth Symphony prove just how knowledgeable, sensitive, and sophisticated it can be. Visitors from out-of-town, of whom there are many, should leave Cleveland not only with esteem and admiration for its varied cultural opportunities, but also with a sense that here is indeed not only an incomparable symphony orchestra, but an incomparable audience.

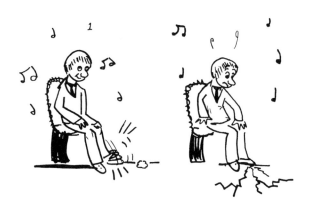

"Coughing" (January 1975),
by Arthur Loesser

*

This article is from Musical Etiquette, *a series of short essays published in booklet form by* The Cleveland Press, *1947.*

*

COUGHING at public musical events is a social error of the first magnitude, a veritable menace. To befoul the delicate web of a musical composition with an irrelevant mess of excretory explosions is to grossly affront all sensitive musical souls. Let no one think that his own little coughing noise is so slight as to be negligible. His bad example will corrupt the restraints of dozens of other people; presently an annoying, repulsive barrage will fill the room and a beautiful nocturne or love song will be converted into a pockmarked torso.

Only one apology has ever been offered for this misbehavior. It is that minor respiratory infections are widespread during certain seasons of the year. With all the colds and catarrhs about, the coughing is inevitable, we are sometimes told.

It is a poor excuse. A person suffering from an absolutely uncontrollable throat irritation ought not to go out in public at all. If the coughing impulse is suppressible, the concert hall is the proper place to suppress it. Normal civilized human beings are expected to inhibit all such urges to the last stage of painful discomfort rather than offend their immediate neighbors. A willingness to cough into music is a mark of disrespect for it and for those who want to listen to it attentively.

However, all this is not entirely to the point. The fact is that most of the petty coughing that bepimples our concerts and operas has no bodily cause at all. It is a reaction to mental, not physical distress. People tend to clear their throats nervously when they are compelled to sit still without having their attention sufficiently engaged. The coughing always increases when the music is long drawn out or difficult of comprehension. But that makes it all the easier to inhibit.

It can be pointed out in this connection that performers themselves almost never cough. A hundred orchestra musicians will go through a sniffly winter and spring, playing several concerts a week, without ever shooting off their throats while working. They are too busy.

The Three Bs on the Sweatshirts

*

This piece was first published in 1962, in Wes Lawrence's Saturday column in The Plain Dealer, *Cleveland, and later reprinted in* The Christian Science Monitor *(which the author had served as a contributing music critic from 1950 to 1958).*

*

"Be cultured! Buy Beethoven, Brahms or Bach SWEATSHIRTS. Be the first on your block to wear a highbrow sweatshirt! It's simple, it's fun . . . and it's classy."

—Advertisement

(Presto agitato, con melancolia)

How to prove your love of art?
Keep the masters near your heart.
Don't just follow; do some leading!
Show your upper crust and breeding:
If you wish to look high-leveled,
Dress distinguished if disheveled.
Nobody would dare insult ya:
It's not shirts you've bought, it's cultya!
You'll be really on the beam
With the classics on your team.

Give us your artistic views:
Which composer will you choose?
Johnny Brahms was in the know,
Seb a real honest Joh.
Why not Reginald de Koven?
Nothing less than Lou Beethoven!
(Friend of ours; dropped the "van"—
Very democratic man.)

Laundering may seal their fate
At a centri-fugal rate:
May not dissonance transpire
In the automatic dryer?
Aren't you at all afeard
For the shape of Brahms's beard?
Have you brain enough to think
"What if all those heads should shrink?"

Fear no more, afflatus seekers!
In the offing: Status Sneakers.

The Charmed Circle, and a Legendary George Szell Story
(MARCH 1987)

THE CLEVELAND ORCHESTRA's broadcast tape of Alexander Zemlinsky's symphonic poem, *The Mermaid* (February 22, 1987, from the performances of February 5 and 7), was severely compromised by a barrage of unstifled coughs: no fewer than twenty-seven in the course of the first movement alone, and many of them erupting during the quietest parts of the music.

Although those extraneous noises emanated from a vanishingly small proportion of the total audience, less than one percent, they still transformed the locally and nationally broadcast performance (and, of course, the concert itself) into what Arthur Loesser once called "a pockmarked torso". To hear it on the air in that way leaves in the minds of listeners worldwide an unfair impression of our audience's degree of attentiveness, involvement, and courtesy. Because of worry about the next possible disturbance, neither player nor hearer can concentrate to the full on the music in progress. The charmed and fragile circle of composer-performer-listener is easily punctured; to paraphrase a saying from Goethe's *Faust*, Part II, "here the irrelevant becomes an event."

On April 9, 1959, George Szell conducted the Orchestra in an all-Tchaikovsky program, including the *Violin Concerto* (with Nathan Milstein) and the *Fourth Symphony*. The concert began with the *Overture-Fantasy, Romeo and Juliet*. Its introductory section, for low woodwinds, is very quiet. After about ninety seconds, Mr. Szell cut off the Orchestra in mid-phrase with a wide sweep of his arms, turned around, said to the stunned audience, "I give you five minutes to clear your throats," and stalked off. He returned exactly five minutes later, greeted by one defiant cough from the balcony, and said: "Ladies and gentlemen, we here on stage are only trying to do our best. Would you please do the same?" He then proceeded to lead a performance of *Romeo and Juliet* nearly two minutes faster than his usual tempo.

There followed editorials in the papers, pro and con; there were special meetings, considering commendation or condemnation; there were public and private arguments, Bronx cheers and plain cheers. But who now remembers the hubbub? No amount or variety of "cough ads" in this program book (or those of other orchestras) seem to make the slightest difference to the eminently vocal one percent. As the famous French proverb has it, "the more things change, the more they are the same."

Corrections: a Note (JANUARY 1983)

MISPRINTS ARE THE BANE of an editor's existence. Either the original error is made by the writer, faithfully reproduced by the printer, and studiously overlooked by the editor, or the sequence begins with a printer's error which is then not caught in time. The numbers 3 and 8 are particularly susceptible to such hazards; it has happened to us before, with Alexander Borodin, whose birthdate should have been given as 1833, not 1838. But it was especially embarrassing—and comical—to have the birthdate of Brahms appear as 1883 instead of 1833. It is, indeed, the one hundred and fiftieth anniversary of the composer's birth which we are celebrating this year, not his one hundredth.

The comical aspect of the matter is two-fold. First, a life of less than fourteen years (1883–1897) is rather brief for a major composer; Brahms was a prodigy, it is true, but not that much of one. And second, since his first symphony was completed in 1876, it evidently came about (according to those dates) before he was born. We have heard of posthumous compositions (published, not written, after the composer's death), but up to now we have not encountered prehumous compositions. The dates of the mythical non-composer P. D. Q. Bach are given by Professor Peter Schickele as 1807–1742; we assume that these new dates for Brahms should give him a new historical (hysterical?) discovery to utilize.

We might also inform our audiences that on the first proof of a recent annotation for the Bach-Stokowski *Toccata and Fugue in D minor* the title was given as *Toccata and Fudge*. It was, luckily for all, caught in time. But there will be, one may be absolutely certain, other disasters to live down. Oh, fudge. . . .

"When the Music Stops . . ." (NOVEMBER 1981)

THE QUESTION OF QUALITY—how good a work of art (and its performance) is considered to be—remains one of the most difficult issues to resolve or even to discuss. It is a matter both personal and universal, both subjective and objective. This is not the time and place to deal with it in a serious way, but let us make a stab at an aspect of it.

The editor has devised an unofficial test to judge the quality of a piece; the method is hardly infallible, but what is? When you drive your car to or from work, to or from an engagement, and your radio is tuned to WCLV-FM, you might try it. You arrive at your destination, and you cannot stay in the car to continue listening. If possible, of course, you will wait until a proper cadence or resolution, to create a sense of at least momentary completion. But in any case, the piece has to be cut short. What is your reaction when the sound suddenly stops? Are you sorry, or are you glad? Are you disappointed not to be able to finish listening, or are you relieved to be done with it? Of course, if you dislike the work or the style anyway, the problem becomes academic; but let us assume you are—for one reason or another—interested.

Now, in some cases the sudden cessation of the sound seems to do violence to the piece, and leaves you dissatisfied and even somewhat angered that the music's proper time-scale cannot be yours as well. In other cases, there may be a feeling of "My, wasn't that a rather poor (or at least pointless) example of note-spinning?" That sense of "good riddance" may be one of the criteria of judgment, or at least of evaluation. Of course, if you know the work well, you can "complete" it in your mind as you step out of the car. There are times when you may wish to stay in for another few minutes just to find out who played or sang it; on occasion, that may tell you why the piece seemed so good, or so mediocre, or so bad: for performances can sometimes make or break a work of music, and you may just wish to escape from one that "breaks it" while desiring to stay with one that "makes it".

In any event, the forcible abridgement of the listening experience is a moment of artistic imbalance, made necessary by circumstances. Yet it may help focus on the issue of quality both of the work and the performance, and thus—in an odd sort of way—it may serve some purpose after all.

"It Sounds O.K., But How Does It Look?" (NOVEMBER 1978), by James Barrett

*

This was the fourth in a series of articles by members of The Cleveland Orchestra, published intermittently. James Barrett received his early musical training in Spokane, Washington and while still in high school there became a violinist in that city's newly organized symphony orchestra. In 1925 he went to Detroit to study with Ilya Schkolnik, and in 1926 joined the Detroit Symphony Orchestra. He was promoted to principal second violinist and later became the assistant concertmaster. In 1949, at the invitation of George Szell, he took a similar position with The Cleveland Orchestra. He retired in 1979, after thirty years of service, and died in 1990.

*

THE RECITAL for voice and piano was over, and Mark Twain was speaking to his future son-in-law, Russian pianist Ossip Gabrilowitch. "Young man, you play beautifully, but my daughter is much better looking than you are."

His judgment proved to be accurate, for young Ossip was soon to become world-famous as the "Poet of the Keyboard". His wife, Clara Clemens Gabrilowitch, a real beauty, musical and well trained, had the wisdom to realize that her voice was not intended for concert halls.

Although Gabrilowitch could not be called handsome, he had a dignified, deadly serious manner and his face revealed the intensity of his feelings. He became the conductor of the Detroit Symphony Orchestra, and my first professional experience was gained there, under his direction.*

Like everyone else, Mr. Gabrilowitch was sensitive to what he saw, as well as to what he heard. During my first season, my desk partner and I were told to report to his room at an intermission. He asked us, "Why were you smiling during the Overture? I looked at you—I wanted a crescendo—you were smiling."

We stood for a moment in puzzled silence. Finally, my partner, who was the section leader, replied, "Oh! I remember. We had worked out a fingering for the difficult modula-

---

*Gabrilowitch conducted the Detroit Symphony Orchestra in a Cleveland concert in 1920, sponsored by the Musical Arts Association. He appeared as piano soloist with The Cleveland Orchestra in 1921 (Rachmaninoff *No. 2*), 1928 (Schumann), and 1934 (Brahms *No. 2*).—Editor.

tion that occurs just before the big climax in D minor. Tonight it came out perfectly clean. Did we give you the crescendo you wanted, Maestro?"

Mr. Gabrilowitch chuckled softly and said, "Yes, you did;" then he continued, "But your smiles were disconcerting—they were quite inappropriate to the mood of the music." Upon reflection, we had to agree. The piece we were performing was the Brahms *Tragic Overture*.

The late Leopold Stokowski was almost psychic in his evaluation of player cooperation. While guest-conducting in Detroit, he pointed out a certain violinist who always played with a poker face. "You, sir—in the third desk on the inside—you don't like me, do you? You can leave the rehearsal if you wish. You can take the week off—I will make sure that there are no penalties for you." The player said later that he had always disliked Stokowski, but didn't think it was apparent either in his playing or in his manner.

An excitable Italian conductor once addressed his first clarinetist as follows: "Why you look at me bad? I don't look at you bad. No! I love you! I am your father—you are my son . . . you are my father—I am your son . . . I love you . . . why you look at me bad?" This same conductor once put down his baton at rehearsal and rushed to the side of a musician who he felt was not emotionally involved in the music. He grabbed the player's hand and thrust it inside his shirt so he could feel the perspiration. As he walked back to the podium he said scornfully, "You sweat not so!"

George Szell liked to see a bit of animation in his players but was against unnecessary motion. One of his remarks at rehearsal was, "You sit there as if waiting for your pensions." Another time, when he had asked for more accent, one musician accompanied the sound with a violent forward motion of his body. Szell said, "Yes. That's the accent I want; but I don't need the demonstration."

An equally famous conductor, still living, called in two violinists who sat together at the same desk and told them, "I know that you are good players, but you seem so uninterested. What can you do about this?" The violinists devised the following plan: as the music got louder they would lean forward; at climaxes their scrolls would touch the music stand. As it got softer they would lean backwards; at the softest point they would be completely erect, violins held higher than normal. After their first tryout of this system the conductor called them in and said, "I don't know what you fellows were doing, but I liked it. Keep it up!"

During his many years of concertizing, Jascha Heifetz was considered by some concertgoers to be cold and unexpressive. His stage manner was one of quiet, courteous, almost aloof dignity. Whether dazzling his listeners with the brilliance of his pyrotechnics, or pouring out a songful melody, he would stand erect, playing with utmost economy of motion, his face displaying only the taut intensity of his concentration. If those who judged him to be cold would listen to his recordings, they would surely discover that his interpretations are actually very warm, and are colored with an infinite variety of expressive tonal shadings.

When an orchestra plays on television, appearance may seem to be more important than the purely musical effect. The sound is never high-fidelity, but the picture is invariably clear and colorful. Skilled cameramen, aided by a musician who knows the score, are able to focus, as in football, on whatever player happens to be "carrying the ball" at any given moment. After a telecast, friends never say, "I heard you on television"; it's always, "I saw you."

In the concert hall, most of what we see is the natural result of the musicians' sincere efforts to bring the score to life. If the visual impressions add to our pleasure and to our understanding of the work being performed, well and good; but if they are distracting or irritating, it might be better to close our eyes and let the music speak for itself.

"Unlikely Predictions":
Department of "Oh, Really?" or "You Have To Be Kidding!"
(JANUARY 1985)

*

If Beethoven was convinced that his symphonies would be played long after his death, and would become standard repertoire, that was a reasonable assumption. Here are some assumptions that would have been quite unreasonable when—and if—they were made.

*

ERNST VON DOHNÁNYI, 1924, when he made his début with The Cleveland Orchestra as conductor, composer, and pianist: "In exactly sixty years, my grandson—who will be born about five years from now—is going to be the music director of this orchestra!"

ANTONIO VIVALDI, *c.* 1715: "My all-girl orchestra at the orphanage needs a new concerto by tomorrow. They have a good *flautino* player this year; maybe I'll write a piece . . . or two, or three . . . for her. Piccolo players a couple of hundred years from now will need that kind of piece. Hardly anyone else but me will write such concertos. . . ."

JOHANN PACHELBEL, *c.* 1700: "There's a young fellow name of Bach who will learn a lot from my church and organ music. Is my own music any good? Come on, now! My organ chorales, motets and magnificats are known wherever music is performed, not only here in Nuremberg. But you know what? I've got a little piece that's going to sweep the world in about two hundred and fifty years. Everybody will play it, sing it, arrange it, sell it, buy it, put it on those funny things they'll call tapes and discs, and make millions from it! What's it called? Well, it's a little *passacaglia* or *chaconne;* they call it a Canon, by mistake. You think I suffer from delusions? Just wait around . . . if you can!"

ANTON BRUCKNER, NEW YEAR'S EVE, 1884: "Now look here, Herr Professor Dr. Hanslick— you must admit that my *Seventh Symphony* had quite a success when it was first done yesterday in Leipzig, by the Gewandhaus Orchestra. It will go well in Vienna, too, and in just a couple of years they'll play it in Chicago! No, with all respect, I can't agree with you that the symphony is 'unnatural, sickly, and decayed', or, as one of your colleagues said in a review, that I compose like a drunkard. Chicago, that's a big city in America. There's a smaller one not far from there; Cleveland, they call it . . . manufacturing town . . . no orchestra of its own yet. In exactly one hundred years the Gewandhaus Orchestra will play the *Seventh Symphony* there. . . . Now don't interrupt, please, Herr Doktor! And the next month the local orchestra—it will be a good one!—is going to play the *Fourth,* and the month after that it will do my *Sixth*. . . . Dr. Hanslick, please. . . . No, no, don't tell the Emperor that I have finally gone over the edge! He's very gullible, you know! Happy New Year 1885, anyway, and take it easy on the Schnapps. . . . Just a little joke, with your permission."

MODESTE MUSSORGSKY, 1880: "Ah yes, those *Pictures* . . . nice set of piano pieces. I'm willing to bet that in the next century there will be at least a half dozen arrangements for full orchestra, and a bunch of popular versions too, for guitar, for something they'll call a rock band, for music by electricity—they'll call it electronic—and whatever else they can find! You think I've had too much? Pass the vodka."

GUSTAV MAHLER, 1911: "My time will yet come." (His spirit, no longer bruised and reviled, floats ecstatically around a plate-sized disc entitled "Mahler's Greatest Hits".)

II. PIÙ SERIOSO

Music without ideas is unthinkable, and people who are not willing to use their brains to understand music which cannot be fully grasped at first hearing are simply lazy-minded. . . . Every true work of art to be understood has to be thought about; otherwise it has no inherent life.

Arnold Schoenberg

"Image into Sound—The Composer Hears a Painting"
(APRIL 1981)

*

All art constantly aspires toward the condition of music.
—Walter Pater (1873)

*

WITH ALL RESPECT to the visual, plastic, and literary arts, was Pater right? Is he saying that music is the greatest of the arts, or is he merely putting his finger on the unique nature of musical expression?

The subject is complex. It has been dealt with by numerous writers, composers, critics, and also by the editor in illustrated lectures. To summarize the issue is difficult and brevity means in this case oversimplification. In simplest terms, music is spirit without substance, time without space. It is a set of sounding symbols which defy verbal explanation. It is not vague, but specific; as Mendelssohn once wrote, "What any music I like expresses for me is not thoughts too indefinite to clothe in words, but too definite." While the plastic and visual arts exist in space, to be touched, observed, and studied at leisure and for a period determined by the viewer, music exists entirely in time, in a duration determined by composer and performer, and necessitating an act of "following". The meaning of a word, likewise, is capable of many more individual interpretations than is a melodic phrase, a chord, an instrumental or vocal color or effect. However different may be the ways to "interpret" such a piece of musical substance, its essential meaning is exact. And while words and pictures are almost always "concrete" in their associations, musical symbols are "abstract", fulfilling their purposes on a level that reaches far below the discernible surface.

What Walter Pater may be saying is that the visual and literary arts are envious of the power of music to reach that deeper level, instantly and—to the musical person—with incomparable exactitude. A musical idea or phrase is understood not so much as to "what it means" but as to "how it means". What are the means by which it goes about meaning? The question is not so much what it *means* but what it *is*. Verbal explanation tends to fail, or at least to confuse. We take the musical "thing" for what it is and what it does. The power of the painting, sculpture, or poem, Pater seems to be implying, lies precisely in the closeness to that exactitude of communication which music innately possesses. One of the glories of "modern" art, abstract or non-objective, is precisely that distance from the verbally explainable subject matter, which forces us to see and take the work for what it is, and no more. The common question, so often heard in museums, "What is it?", is therefore an irrelevancy when it implies a need for representation of familiar objects. And even with classic portraiture, such as Rembrandt's *The Man with the Golden Helmet*, the issue is not "who is this man, and what was his name?" but "what does the painter do with a human face, with light, with the balance of elements, and with the supremely successful shape and form itself?"

*

All of this, in brief and probably inadequate summary, is offered as a series of thoughts related to music which transforms paintings into musical symbols. Gerard Schürmann's *Six*

17

Studies of Francis Bacon is only one of the latest in a growing series of musical compositions which base themselves on the inspiration of visual art. Each sets itself, in its own way, the problem of animating a static image into dynamic sound, or to find in the implied activity of the picture a possible stimulus for actual musical motion. Each meets the challenge in somewhat different ways, but each establishes a kind of correlation between those art forms that are in substance and essence not "interchangeable".

With the composer's implied approval, the annotator for Mr. Schürmann's studies has written that "it would be a grave mistake to assume that the work is merely a sequence of descriptive pieces; in essence, it is an intensely *musical* composition, which is bound together by the subtlest use of thematic ideas in a fully interrelated and almost symphonic manner." In the same way, all the many works that have a similar objective of animating a painting or set of them into musical action must stand or fall on their musical substance and skill; that is to say, a great picture will not rescue a poor piece of music, just as a great story will not make a masterpiece out of a second-rate symphonic poem based upon it. The two art forms must stand on equal terms, must complement each other, must somehow extend or expand the horizons of each through the other. It is not necessary, of course, that each picture so utilized must be an imperishable masterpiece; some of Hartmann's drawings used as stimuli by Mussorgsky are ultimately not so fine as their musical counterparts. But the issues themselves remain: What does the music say that goes beyond the picture, that adds to its enjoyment yet another dimension, that is not merely naïve and all-too-easy "sound-painting", that stands on its own as a composition, and that affords the listener an experience of genuine interest and value beyond the original purpose of "interdisciplinary" transformation? In art, said a famous critic, it is achievement only that matters, not the intent, however admirable.

*

Here is a brief listing of musical compositions that have transformed "image into sound", as performed over the years by The Cleveland Orchestra. Most recently, of course, just two weeks ago, we heard at these concerts Morton Gould's *Burchfield Gallery,* an enchanting set of seven pieces stimulated by the works of the Ohio-born painter Charles Burchfield. Most famous of all such enterprises, surely, is Mussorgsky's *Pictures at an Exhibition,* a suite of musical sketches based on the drawings and architectural designs of Victor Hartmann; originally a piano work, it is best known in Ravel's masterly orchestral version. As an example of the challenge Mussorgsky faced, let us consider the implied motion of the *Ballet of the Chicks in Their Shells* and *Baba Yaga,* against the totally static *Catacombs* and *The Great Gate of Kiev.* How do the latter become dynamic, as music? The composer gives us the magnificent answer.

At these concerts, we have several times heard Gunther Schuller's delightful *Seven Studies on Themes of Paul Klee,* a masterpiece of its genre. There exists another set of Klee studies, by the American composer David Diamond; we have not yet heard it here. Hindemith's great symphony, *Mathis der Maler,* is of course based on the Isenheim Altar of the sixteenth-century painter Matthias Grünewald; the music is a staple of our repertoire. Respighi, always fascinated by the sights and sounds of Italy, turned to art in three remarkable works: *Fountains of Rome, Botticelli Triptych,* and *Vetrate di Chiesa* ("Church Windows"). Italian art also stimulated Martinů to write his *The Frescoes of Piero della Francesca.* The American composer Elie Siegmeister gave us, a few years ago, an "homage to five paintings", *Shadows and Light,* on works by Albert Pinkham Ryder, Paul Klee, Fernand Léger, Edgar Degas, and Vincent van Gogh. Cleveland composer Eugene O'Brien has composed a delicate work several times heard in this city, *Embarking for Cythera,* based on a painting of Watteau. And there are others in the literature, too many to list.

An interesting example of the opposite venture—to make pictures based on sound—occurred here in 1943, when Erich Leinsdorf commissioned faculty members of The Cleveland Institute of Art to make new pictures of Mussorgsky's tonal images, for an exhibit connected with our performance of the work. A splendid and varied series resulted. In recent years, Cleveland sculptor John Clague has devoted himself to making "sounding sculptures", metal works which—when animated by air or hand—produce delicate sonorities. Other artists similarly inclined have included the sculptors Harry Bertoia and Richard Lippold—all disciples of Alexander Calder and his "mobiles".

*

The indebtedness of musicians to their colleagues in the visual arts extends even to terminology. The technical language of music is often incomprehensible to the nonprofessional; that of art makes instant contact. We speak of light and dark in music; of colors and hues; of shapes and designs; of textures transparent and dense; of impressionism and expressionism. A musical work put together from many small elements may be called a mosaic. Architecture has been called "frozen music", while music itself may be conceived as "flowing architecture".

In works of this nature, the boundary lines between the arts become less clearly defined, even if they do not vanish altogether. A synthesis is approached. While the languages of music and of visual art remain autonomous, both strive together toward a kind of ideal order, toward sense and comprehension, toward *form*. Unlike the proverbial two parallels which may meet only in infinity, these art forms occasionally touch, and at rare moments intersect.

In the final analysis, the musical symbol is in itself an image: it becomes a sounding reflection, a sonorous form found for a concept, an idea, a feeling, a mood, an experience. A sensitive nerve is touched, a significant moment captured from our inner life. Thus the composer pays a crucially important tribute to his colleague, the visual or plastic artist: he must put to work a power whose very name is derived from the term that means "image-making"; namely, *Imagination*.

Reproduction of an Original (DECEMBER 1982)

IN THE AUGUST 1982 issue of *Harper's*, Prof. Edward C. Banfield of Harvard University raises once again the question whether a first-rate reproduction of a great painting is not just as valuable—to the viewer—as the original. In an article entitled "Art versus Collectibles", he draws a distinction between the work as an investment and as an aesthetic communication. He asks whether the wide public distribution of great art is not ultimately more important for our culture than the insistence that only the "original" is valuable (as well as expensive). Is a good reproduction really a "fake", or is it a perfectly acceptable version of the artist's intent?

The issue is complex, and full of subtle aspects not easily resolved to everyone's satisfaction. The title given to the controversy on the cover of the magazine, "Let Them See Fakes", is an amusing allusion to Marie Antoinette's infamously elitist remark about bread and cake. But what is of exceptional interest to us are the references to music, and to its comparison with visual art.

"How many people," ask Dr. Banfield, "would not dream of having a 'fake' Rembrandt on their walls, however high its quality, yet own and enjoy record sets of the

Beethoven symphonies?" Observing that not only crude but superb reproductions of Leonardo's *Mona Lisa* are available to millions, he remarks: "It has been suggested that something like this has happened to the great musical classics—that the Beethoven symphonies are degraded, the aesthetic joy of hearing reduced, by too frequent hearings, however excellent the reproduction. But the purpose of encouraging the reproduction of visual-art masterpieces is not to enable people to see them often enough to get sick of them, but to enable more people to see them at all. . . ."

*

It is a truism of art history and aesthetics that the visual arts exist in space, and the musical arts exist in time. The difference is crucial. While the painting or the sculpture or the tapestry are singular objects, with the artist's fingerprints tangibly upon them (though of course in some cases a sculpture may exist in an "edition" of several copies or versions), the original score of a musical work is almost never seen by the public at all. Valuable and emotionally affecting though it may be as an object "handled" by the author himself, it is only a blueprint which must be copied, distributed, studied, and interpreted before it can reach an audience in performance. Even allowing for differences in size, lighting, and general ambiance, a painting—original or reproduced—conveys the same information, the same "message". The musical work, however, is never the same twice, even when performed by the same artists on successive days; it cannot be. A recording, as the great American composer Walter Piston once pointed out, is a "frozen moment": it provides a specific version of the work in a permanent, unchanging form, with all the dangers and advantages "thereunto appertaining". A live performance, on the other hand, is bound to vary from any other in a number of subtle ways, and each time it is attempted there occurs a genuine "re-creation".

A well-reproduced painting, therefore, comes as close to the artist's original intent as possible. There is now a veritable industry of expert copies, produced not with the intent to deceive, but by their very quality creating new problems of authentication and price-versus-value. The interpretive musician, however, operates on a whole series of assumptions of what the composer really wanted, and if the latter is a master long dead he might be very surprised—if not shocked—by the results of those assumptions. A reproduced Rembrandt is still a Rembrandt; a Japanese woodblock print may still be "by" Hiroshige or Hokusai. But a reproduced or re-created Beethoven is Szell's Beethoven, Maazel's Beethoven, Ceccato's Beethoven. They will be similar, conveying approximately the same "information" or "message", but they will still be almost as different in details as Gielgud's *Hamlet* is from Olivier's. We say "almost", because the stage play is capable of a yet wider interpretive range than the piece of music. The instructions provided in and for a symphonic score are specific, and they may be honored in observance as well as in the breach. While it is possible to say, Beethoven wrote "suddenly louder" here, there must be good reason to do so, not to do so, or *how* to do so. The exact emphasis in a speech by Shakespeare is a matter much less clearly defined. Music and drama are "time arts", filling an approximate block of minutes or hours in different ways, while the painting or sculpture stands in space and fills a viewer's time according to the latter's personal decision, not that of a "middleman" or interpreter.

A musical performance, therefore, is always a reproduction, based on an original envisioned (enaudited?) by the composer-author, and differing from it by necessity. What is interesting to an audience at a concert is just that difference in interpretation, from one artist or group of artists to another. Within certain limits, each version may be valid, instructive, illuminating. A painting incorrectly reproduced, however—with color values changed, with higher or lesser gloss, in a size that alters the proportions of the whole work in space—will always be "wrong". In music, "wrong-ness" is much more difficult to prove, unless the composer's instructions are utterly ignored or contradicted; one may take the issue of the "correct tempo" as just one example of how first-rate interpreters may come to quite different conclusions.

*

Prof. Banfield's provocative thesis does not come to grips with the issue of magic—the strange and moving fact that Van Gogh's or Picasso's hand was actually on that original piece of canvas, and no reproduction, however good, can make that claim. But while one may continue to argue with his proposal of making visual art more widely available to the public through acknowledged "fakes", one must accept with pleasure and gratitude the fact that musical art can exist only through that inconsistent, varied, and often arbitrary process called "interpretation". One of the marvels of recordings is that one can compare, repeat, study, live with a composition, come to "own" it in a deeply personal sense. There are currently some forty versions of Beethoven's Fifth Symphony available on recordings; some, surely, are better than others, but none is a "fake". Each attempts to be, if not an "exact" reproduction of an imaginary original, at least an imaginative one.

The Challenge of Public Performance (FEBRUARY 1969), by Arthur Loesser

*

This article was originally written and planned for publication in the program book of February 27, 1969. With his performances as pianist, author, lecture-recitalist and master teacher, Arthur Loesser enriched the musical scene of Cleveland and the nation for more than half a century before his death on January 4, 1969. His lifework continues to do so, as it instructs and delights us.

*

PERFORMANCE is the realization of music, its coming to life; without it music would remain a mere gleam in a composer's brain. The performer is the second member of an inseparable trinity of which the composer and the listener form the other two. It takes all three to make the music.

Of this trinity the listener is the most interesting and the most variable. If you compare the composer to a powerhouse and the performer to a transmission wire, the listener may be thought of as a light-bulb: no matter how strong the power or how perfect the transmission there will be no light if the bulb's filaments are not of the proper material, shape, and position for producing it. Continuing the metaphor we may say that the strength and duration of the incandescence aroused in the listener's mind is the measure of the music achieved.

The filaments in human minds are not made of crudely measurable carbon or tungsten, they are living stuff which changes perpetually with the slightest impulse from the outside, and with the slightest movement of inner process; their make-up cannot be predicted from one moment to the next. The listener's age, sex, condition of health, or fatigue are among the simpler, more fundamental elements of his temperamental state. So of course is his previous musical experience and cultivation.

The associations, favorable or adverse, of a concert's locale also have their profound influence upon his musical receptivity. Some of them are physical, some of them mental. How are the acoustics, how is the air conditioning? Are the seats hard, or too close together, or low enough for short legs? Is it a specially designed concert hall, is it a college auditorium, a private home, a theater, a convention hall or a vast hangar often used for political rallies and poultry shows? Does it exude an atmosphere of upper class luxury distasteful to many persons, or one of careless shabbiness unpleasant to many others? Have people been going there for music for years, or is music a new experiment in the place? The day, the time of day, the season, the weather, all squirt themselves as ingredients into the psychological mixture. Is it an enterprising Saturday night, a sedate Sunday afternoon, is it Thanksgiving Day evening with everyone loaded down with excess turkey? Is there a blizzard outside, or an intoxicating spring night? And how about the world situation: are we brooding over a war disaster, a financial depression, or are we elated over an election result?

Ethical forces also help shape the listener's mind at any instant. Is he present at a musical performance because of a basic, exclusive interest in the precise compositions played, or is he being plucked at by a variety of motives? Is he going through a concert as through a ceremony suitable to his station in life, is he going to please his wife, or is music being thrust upon him when he is defenseless at a social gathering? Does a lady merely want to hear that Prokofiev concerto or does she also want to be in the same room with a fashionable celebrity? Does she have a personal acquaintance and sympathy with the performer, or is he a total stranger? Does she insist on finding him wonderful because she enjoys agreeing with some fancy people who say he is, or does she find it impossible to acclaim him because *The New York Times* has not yet done so?

If every individual is tossed about by these ripples and tides, we must remember that every listener is also affected by every other listener present. Even without talking with one's fellow concert-attendants one can see their faces and their wriggles, hear their coughs as well as the swish or crackle of their applause: they all make their subtle effects upon the mind. Thus a concert is a psychical situation of inconceivable complexity, an insoluble jungle of imponderables, of which the actual tones produced constitute only one element. It is a jungle that never stays still, is always stirring and shifting within itself. We may say that the same tones, the same performer and the same audience will not add up to the same music twice in succession.

*

No performer can dominate all the elements of such a situation. He can adapt himself to some of them. The simplest form of such adaptation is in the suitable choice of a program. When an audience is restricted to a special group a negative choice is sometimes easy: one could play the entire *Well-Tempered Clavier*, or an all-Schoenberg program, for a gathering of advanced music students, but it would not be quite the thing for a Rotary Club convention. A large mixed audience presents the hardest problem. It is probably impossible ever to appeal to all of such a one at any one time: the easiest compromise is to make a variety of offerings, each of which might satisfy a different section of people.

However, the desire to find a lowest common denominator of the greatest number of listeners may have its pitfalls, may encounter some ethical resistance. It is, I firmly believe, a great mistake to play down to an audience. Whether the performer is playing down, however, is not a matter of what he does, so much as of the spirit in which he does it. There can be no moral distaste when a performer presenting vulgar or platitudinous products is nevertheless doing the best and truest that he can. It is the evidence of condescension that is insulting. A listener will not resent being bored or puzzled by something beyond him, he may even feel subtly flattered at having his understanding overrated; yet even where he is being amused he is bound to feel offended at being treated as an inferior.

The effect made by any piece of music is necessarily influenced by the nature of the music which has just gone before it. Consequently the juxtaposition of program numbers is a special problem for performers. It may be said that any piece may seem redundant if it is in the same movement and rhythm as the one immediately preceding. Absolute pitch is not a widespread gift, yet an audience may feel a vague monotony when the key of a piece is the same as that of its predecessor. The audience's custom of applauding after every number has often been regretted, especially when the handclapping comes after the close of some particularly tender or melancholy strains. Nevertheless it has its very positive value: the noise, however perfunctory, provides a clean break with what has just been heard and makes it easier to regard the following number as an independent adventure, as it ought to be. It does a little to lessen the contamination of successive impressions to which we have just referred. It is one of the more active of the audience's contributions to the music.

*

I have found that, in general, an audience's greatest capacity for attention is developed during the second third of a program. Before that period minds and feelings are still somewhat taken up with getting used to being in the hall and being with a lot of strangers. After the second third, fatigue begins to set in. Moreover, after an intermission devoted to conversational din and social smoking the listening potential tends to be lowered. All this ought to influence the performer in his choice of presentations, namely whether music is suitable for a rising, a maximum, or a declining appetite. The selection of an opening number offers a special problem. To begin with a short trifle is easy on the late-comers and the people they disturb; yet it seems self-belittling and does not do much to launch an atmosphere of elation. On the other hand, to begin with a twenty-five-minute sonata is a little overbearing. The best course, if it can be followed, is to open with an impressive composition which involves a fair amount of muscular vigor, of moderate length. There is of course much more freedom of choice before an audience of students and connoisseurs.

The encore custom has its quaint aspects. The original principle was that the listeners were enjoying a performer so much that they could not bear to have him stop, and insisted on his adding to his program. Since then encores have become a kind of ceremony, and a concert is judged incomplete if the performer has not given the audience its obligatory little tip. For certain portions of audiences it appears to have become a challenge; they feel satisfied if they have bullied the artist into playing more than he was scheduled for. Other concertgoers live only for encores; they stolidly endure *Opus 111* and the *Brahms-Paganini* variations in the hope of hearing the *Ritual Fire Dance* or the *C-sharp minor Prelude* after the program is over. Encores are a nuisance, most often a pretense, and are unfair to the body of the offered program. Yet I would not urge anyone to refuse to play one, or at most two. The custom is so entrenched, at least at recitals, that many people actually consider it a piece of calculated malice not to conform to it. Artur Schnabel, it is true, never played an encore; he seemed to have acquired a special audience that did not expect him to. On the other hand I once heard Josef Hofmann play something like seventeen encores at one concert; he would not allow a pair of hands to fall together without giving forth one more piece. Later on his managers boasted of this achievement in an advertisement.

*

Thus far we have spoken of the performer's adaptation to the concert circumstances. We must now take up the way in which he can steer rather than follow the prevailing psychical currents. He may, if he is gifted and skillful, throw a decisive element into the situation by an effort of the will sometimes called "projection". Projection consists largely of the immediate physical vigor of the performer's conviction about his tones at the instant he is making them. He makes himself want certain kinds of sounds so hard, and is so insistent on getting them, that other people cannot help but be impressed with the force of his assertion. In good projection every speed, every least accent and rhythm, every tiny shading, melodic salience and climax, every pause and every pedaling, all must show the evidence of convinced purpose, of intense direct feeling, of premeditation. More vehemence will not do, of course—although vehemence too is, in its proper place, a valuable component of projection. Most persons are incapable of craving anything so hard in such detail and so instantaneously as a performer craves those precise sounds that he strives to bring forth. His concentration of intent can be arresting, almost awe-inspiring to ordinary people; it is his aggressive determination in regard to every least bit of his music that "puts it across"—assuming always that the hearers have the minds to take it. Clearly some kinds of music are more difficult to project than others. Compositions full of sharp contrasts of theme and rhythm, those requiring delicate shading and positive climaxes are easier to deliver than those whose great virtue lies in their unitary logic, such as the fugues of Bach, or in certain emotional neutrality, such as some modern music.

An effective performer must have the projective disposition to begin with; he must be a person who is not only not scared by an audience, but who feels stimulated and expanded by one, someone who loves to assert himself toward others, who enjoys being conspicuous. Introverts, or shy people, are temperamentally ill-fitted to be public performers, no matter what good musicians they may be. The same is true of those who were effectively persuaded early in life that well-bred persons do not show off.

The good projector, as we have said, puts an invincible determination into the sound-values he produces; yet he can do that only if he gives them his fullest, undivided concentration. That means that he must have assimilated the actual sequence of the notes of his music so thoroughly that their reproduction has become nearly reflex. If he has to try to remember what his next line is he will not deliver it with proper conviction; it will be tainted with preoccupation or with anxiety. It is frequently possible to memorize a composition adequately in the quiet of one's room, only to find that the assimilation has not become sufficiently automatic for public projection. Only people who can memorize and fluently reproduce vast quantities of note sequences, practically without seeming to think about them, are fit to become public performers.

But the very fluency, the very reflex quality of memorization, may become a pitfall in itself. Some fine players have memorized their notes so well and have played them so often that they themselves no longer hear them properly as they go by; they cannot dwell on them enough to project them. Inattention to the notes carries over into inattention to their delivery, the tones come out reeled off, whisked away, unconcerned and meaningless, however accurate.

Stage fright is a well-known enemy of good projection; it comes from inexperience in public, as well as lack of confidence often based on a guilty feeling of not having worked or thought hard enough. It may also come from an anticipatory overemphasis upon the performance in question: teachers and mentors may make the event out to take on an exaggerated importance no human being could support without trembling. With players who have the true projective temperament, and who have learned their stuff properly, stage fright does not extend beyond the earlier part of any given performance. The player's consciousness of past success and his growing familiarity with the feel of being on a platform combine to abate his stage fright to a controllable minimum.

*

One more hindrance to good projection, surmountable by the performer, lies in certain entirely nonmusical aspects of his behavior. He may injure the proper transmission of his music to the listeners by untoward facial expressions or gait or other gestures. All feelings are catching and an audience will tend to feel the way the performer looks. If he looks uncomfortable, anxious or unfriendly the listeners will have to share his misery, they will hate him and his music for it. German audiences, and possibly Russian ones, may have admired a performer who wore an expression of tense, dedicated solemnity. That may have helped them to be serious about what they were hearing. But American people do not much appreciate this attitude: an amiable confident suggestion of a smile puts them in the mood they best like to be in. It is true that Rachmaninoff could contrive to render the lugubrious arrogance with which he approached the piano seem attractive to many people—but he was an outstanding exception.

Trifling items of a performer's clothing may have a distracting effect upon the musically less pure-minded listeners—that is to say the majority. I was once admonished by an experienced manager always to be sure to allow a little bit of white cuff to show beyond the edge of my sleeves, because some low-thinking person might otherwise let his mind roam from my phrases to wondering whether I was wearing a real shirt or only a dickie. A young friend of mine hearing me in a concert confessed to me that he could not enjoy my last group because he was too fascinated by the end of the handkerchief which I had imperfectly stuffed into my trousers' pocket.

In the case of a woman player the wearing of attractive clothes—provided they are not too flamboyant or too lascivious—certainly improves her music. First of all it raises her personal morale so that she actually performs better, secondly it establishes a general prejudice in her favor, especially among the feminine portion of the audience, a prejudice which cannot help but pleasantly tint its opinion of her tones.

As we have said, a musical performance is an incalculable psychical complex into which the performer can only thrust one or two decisive factors. Yet if it is a success, he gets all the credit, if it is a failure he takes all the blame. He must deal with unseen powers, so if he is wise, before every concert

He will pray.

STEINWAY PIANO

SEVERANCE HALL

Home of
The Cleveland Orchestra

OP.—K.—ANH.—D.—F.—BWV—WoO—HOB.—POSTH.
and Other Puzzles (NOVEMBER 1981)

*

This article was republished in Stagebill *magazine under the title "Musical Alphabet", and has been reprinted in the program books of other orchestras.*

*

WE ARE OCCASIONALLY ASKED what the peculiar letters after musical works stand for. They serve, basically, as identifying features for compositions, and can be as useful as they tend to be confusing.

Op. has nothing to do with Op Art. It is an abbreviation for *Opus*, meaning *work* in Latin. (Thus "opera" means, quite literally, "the works"!) Composers like to number their works in chronological order or order of publication, from their first acknowledged piece as Op. 1 to whatever is their latest. Beethoven, for instance, composed (or, better, completed) one hundred and thirty-five such works to which he gave numbers. Op. 136, however, was a cantata of about 1814 not published until long after his death; Op. 137 was a fugue for string quartet written ten years before his death but unpublished; and Op. 138 is the *Leonore Overture No. 1* of 1805, discarded by him during his life-time. But lest it be believed that Beethoven wrote only one hundred and thirty-eight works, the complete catalogue of his music by George Kinsky also includes 203 *WoO*, which means *Werke ohne Opuszahl*, "works without opus number".

An additional complication is the fact that Beethoven often put several works under one opus number; Op. 27, No. 2 is the famous *Moonlight Sonata*, while No. 1 has no title. Shall we opt for "Sunlight"? Other such instances are the *"Razumovsky" Quartets Op. 59*, or the *Six Quartets Op. 18*. A further problem arises when a work is published later than one written earlier . . . if that makes any sense. Beethoven's *Second Piano Concerto*, for example, is numbered Op. 19; written before his first, which appeared in print as Op. 15, it was published later, and therefore received a higher opus number. Help!

On the whole, however, if we know approximately how many works a composer wrote, the recognition of an opus number can tell us quickly whether we are dealing with an early, middle, or late composition.

This is particularly useful in the case of Mozart's K. or K.V. numbers. Ludwig von Koechel (1800–1877) was a botanist and mineralogist whose hobby was music. In 1862 he published a chronological and carefully annotated catalogue of Mozart's music, which became known as the *Koechel-Verzeichnis*. A remarkable achievement of early musicology (the "science of music", especially in history), the K.V. was first revised by Paul Graf Waldersee in 1905, and then further enlarged in 1937 by Dr. Alfred Einstein. Since we know that Mozart is credited with six hundred and twenty-six works (the last so numbered being the *Requiem*, actually completed by his pupil Süssmayr), we can deduce the approximate period of a composition from the K. or K.V. number. Thus K. 219 (the *A major Violin Concerto*) would be from his late teens, and K. 551 (the *"Jupiter" Symphony, No. 41*) from a few years before his death. Since no other music was apparently written between that latter work and the preceding one, the *G minor Symphony, No. 40*, is known as K. 550.

So far so good; but Einstein's attempt to be more specific about the chronology of origin than Koechel resulted in some mystifying double-numbering as well as clarification.

There are subdivisions for certain K. numbers in his edition, like 320, 320a, 320b—all the way to 320f, different works of the same period grouped together; only then does one get to K. 321. Thus Einstein calls the famous *Sinfonia Concertante*, K. 320d, which he considers more correct chronologically than the previously accepted K. 364. Trying to find things in the updated Koechel-Verzeichnis is often exasperating. *Anh.* means "Anhang", or Appendix, that which "hangs on", and includes those hundreds of works attributed to Mozart which are either unfinished, lost and rediscovered, copies of music by others for study purposes, spurious or doubtful compositions, etc., a.s.o. and a.s.f.

Another instance of double-numbering occurs in the symphonies of Dvořák. The last three were long known as No. 2, No. 4, and No. 5, the last being the *New World*. The fact is that Dvořák wrote nine symphonies, not five, but that the first five were not published until the last four had appeared. 2, 4, 5 are therefore known today as 7, 8 and 9, and if one wants to be terribly accurate one will identify No. 7 as "Old No. 2" and so on.

D. identifies the 998-plus works of Schubert, in the catalogue by Otto Erich Deutsch, 1951 (revised 1978), and *Hob.* refers to the Haydn Catalogue by Anthony van Hoboken (1957). The *BWV* (not to be confused with VW, BMW, or BVD) is the "Bach-Werke-Verzeichnis" published in 1950 on the 200th anniversary of Bach's death, by Wolfgang Schmieder in Leipzig; it lists 1080 works and an Anh. of 189 numbers. *F.* is the code name for the Vivaldi catalogue compiled by Antonio Fanna. An earlier Vivaldi catalogue, by Marc Pincherle, gives us *P.* numbers, and a more recent one, by Peter Ryom, provides us with *R.* numbers. *Posth.* is of course the indication that a work was not published until after the composer's death, and does not refer to the music reported to have been dictated to the English medium and spiritualist Rosemary Brown by various departed masters.

There exist some instances of musicological chicanery, one might almost say sadism. When Ralph Kirkpatrick made his otherwise admirable catalogue of the harpsichord sonatas of Domenico Scarlatti, he omitted the previous *L.* numbers (for Longo), revised the chronology, and provided a set of . . . *K.* numbers—for Kirkpatrick! Would not S.K., or K.S., or anything other than K., have been kinder to hapless concert-goers?

Some composers, like Hindemith, stop using opus numbers after a certain point (in his case, Op. 50 of 1930); others, like Bartók, disdain them entirely, while their biographers assign them as optional. Other composers, like painters, may only date their works, by day, month, or year. Perhaps we should be grateful for such forbearance. It is not improbable that some time a new way of identification will be discovered or invented by someone, perhaps involving little colored squares or circles.

If the entire subject seems to complicate matters quite beyond reasonable dimensions, at least it testifies to man's unceasing if imperfect quest to put things in order.

Musicians with and without Feathers (SEPTEMBER 1982)

IN 1982, ANTAL DORATI conducted The Cleveland Orchestra in a program which featured pianist Ilse von Alpenheim in Haydn's *D major Concerto* and included that composer's Symphony No. 83, "The Hen", Stravinsky's *Song of the Nightingale,* and Kodály's "*Peacock*" *Variations.* Although no one was brazen enough to claim that the program was strictly "pour les oiseaux", it was evident that three of the four pieces took their inspiration from the aviary kingdom. Of the three birds, however, only one can sing: the nightingale. The hen is not noted for its musicality, and the peacock's beauty resides in the gorgeous plumage of its coda (tail), not its vocal cords. Haydn, whose piano concerto was the only non-aviary piece on the program, dealt with birds in his oratorios, *The Creation* and *The Seasons,* if none too willingly. Mozart owned a pet starling, and taught him the beginning of the finale theme in his *G major Piano Concerto, K. 453.*

A quick glance at "bird music" in its historical setting may be appropriate. There have been numerous extensive studies of the subject, and Roger Tory Peterson's marvelous record album of bird calls and songs is indispensable to the true aficionado. Percy A. Scholes's chapter "Bird Music" in the *Oxford Companion to Music* (ninth edition, 1955), begins by claiming that "but for the humans, birds are perhaps Nature's only musicians." (Recent discoveries prove that some species of whales are magnificent "singers", producing musical patterns of remarkable subtlety and sophistication.) "Bird music," continues Dr. Scholes, "is very varied and sometimes quite elaborate." He quotes a scholar by the name of Garstang to have emphasized that "we are not to regard birds as automatic musical-boxes, but as sound-lovers who cultivate the pursuit of sound combinations as an art as truly as we have cultivated our arts of a similar aesthetic character. To many of the birds 'art has become a real object in life—no less real than the pursuit of food or the maintenance of a family.'"

"The demeanour of birds in song," Dr. Scholes observes, "varies according to their temperament. The nightingale is lost in ecstasy; the pigeon utters its song lazily, like a cat purring. Many birds accompany their songs with some invariable characteristic gesture. . . . Highest of all in rank comes the blackbird, whom Garstang calls 'The Beethoven of the Birds'. He has long abandoned the mere short cries of his ancestors and freely invents continuous and developed tunes, quite comparable with some of those that our human composers have taken as the subject matter of their sonatas and symphonies. The blackbird, thrush, and some others of the artistic aristocracy of the bird community, show, as many must have noticed, an appreciation of the octave and the common chord (doh-mesoh) and introduce these into many of their tunes. There is great variety in blackbird song, and it appears as though an individual will fashion a little tune that pleases him and then somewhat extend it from year to year. Birds can sometimes be observed engaged at something that looks like definite 'practice'. . . ."

The sounds of nature quite "naturally" provide raw material for the imagination of composers, and the material birds provide can be far beyond "raw". Indeed, the transcription or transformation into musical notes of some bird songs has been recently developed into an art of great refinement, immeasurably transcending mere imitation. The master of this art and craft is the Frenchman Olivier Messiaen, whose many "bird pieces" (among them *Réveil des Oiseaux, Oiseaux Exotiques,* and extended sections of other works) are of the greatest scientific as well as artistic interest and value. With his music, we can marvel not only at the skill with which he has made music out of sounds and patterns to which most of us pay only cursory attention, but at the astonishing finesse and variety of the original "music" in the first place.

Messiaen's art, in fact, has little to do with the attractive but largely coloristic use of birdcalls as we find it in hundreds of pieces since the Renaissance. Those works, however, have retained their simple charm, from the amusing choral pieces by Jannequin and Gombert, the harpsichord pieces on birdcalls and bird names by Couperin, Daquin, and Rameau, to Handel's organ concerto entitled *The Cuckoo and the Nightingale*. We would be loath to part, for scientific reasons, with Beethoven's trio of birds in the "*Pastoral*" *Symphony* (nightingale, quail, and cuckoo), with the Forest Bird in Wagner's *Siegfried*, and with Vaughan Williams' *The Lark Ascending*. Mahler's cuckoo can sing the interval of the fourth in his *First Symphony*, while Delius retains the interval of the third *On Hearing the First Cuckoo in Spring*. Boccherini's string quintet, *L'uccelleria* ("The Aviary") is not so well known as Respighi's suite, *Gli Uccelli* ("The Birds"), based on pieces by eighteenth-century composers, and the twentieth-century Italian caused an international artistic flap when he utilized a recorded nightingale in his *Pines of Rome*, skillfully set into the orchestral fabric. "We may yet live to see," cried Mr. Ernest Newman in mock outrage, "the evening when the *Pastoral Symphony* will be given with real running water in the slow movement, nightingale by the Gramophone Company, quail by Messrs. Fortnum and Mason."

The denizens of the aviary realm constitute a delectable "Carnival of the Animals", and Saint-Saëns' witty treatment of some of them continues to delight us quite apart from arguments about aesthetics and scientific accuracy. Perhaps Hans Christian Andersen was right when he extolled the virtues of the real nightingale over those of the mechanical one, but even Stravinsky's "real" nightingale is a musical one, not a creature of flesh and blood, bones and feathers. Whether quoted or transcribed, recorded or classified in tones, imitated or transformed, the song of a bird in a composition stands or falls (better: flies) on the quality of the musical form and the degree of imagination which the composer has found for it.*

---

* In 1985 the writer tried his hands at this genre with a piece for oboe and soprano, using as a text Izaak Walton's disquisition on birds in his *The Compleat Angler* of 1653. The dedicatees, oboist John Mack and soprano Christina Price, premiered the piece in 1986, have performed it about two dozen times since then, and recorded it for the Crystal Records label (released in 1991).

Mahler: "Down with Program Books!
They Propagate False Ideas!" (JANUARY 1985)

"All the arts live on words; and a literature, spoken or written, is inseparable from man's creative drive."

—Paul Valéry

"Music can only be alive when there are listeners who are really alive. To listen intently, to listen consciously, to listen with one's whole intelligence is the least we can do in furtherance of an art which is one of the glories of mankind.

—Aaron Copland

A LITTLE MORE than forty years ago, in the spring of 1943, the newly appointed music director of The Cleveland Orchestra, Erich Leinsdorf, wrote a letter to the then program annotator of the Orchestra, George H. L. Smith. He proposed a brief essay on the subject of program notes, to appear in the first program of the 1943–44 season. As it turned out, the idea was not carried through; but the thrust of the essay remains stimulating and relevant. With the conductor's permission, we quote from the letter:

> During recent years, I have often pondered the disadvantages of doing two things at the same time. This thought came to me each time I saw a concert-goer reading his program notes while the music was being played. I felt that one should either read words or listen to music, but not do both things simultaneously.
>
> The fact that it is done so constantly is no fault of the public. The concert-goers who want to know something about the works on the program have no choice of a suitable time to read their program notes; they receive their program upon entering the Hall; by the time they settle in their seats the music is about to begin, whereupon they start reading. In the attempt to familiarize themselves with the first selection on the program, they may miss it almost entirely.
>
> I came to the conclusion that the best time to read about the concert you are going to hear IS BEFORE you enter the Hall, and therefore arrangements have been made that you may get the program notes ahead of time.*
>
> After having read your program-book you will be in a position to decide whether or not you wish to read still more about the works on the program or the composers. . . .
>
> All this does not mean that any preparation is necessary for the enjoyment of music. It is part of the freedom of music itself that every person who loves music can approach it and receive it in his own way. Therefore, there are as many ways of enjoying music as there are different faces and characters among people. Some like to know all about it before the concert starts, others prefer to experience a purely emotional reaction.
>
> There is no rule for How to listen to—and be influenced by MUSIC.

Mr. Leinsdorf was of course quite right and—as usual—perceptive on the subject. But in his reply, Mr. Smith cogently remarked as follows: "Of course we don't want to do anything that will make the Program Book seem as 'dry as dust' or that will make it

---

* That device was indeed tried, and soon abandoned because of the prohibitive time and postage expenditure, and also because the demand by subscribers was inconsiderable. In more recent years, copies of the season's bound volume have been made available for purchase, so that regular concertgoers might build a veritable library of program notes.—Editor.

lose its authority. A good many people depend on it, you know, for their information about the music and expect to get all they need from it. We don't want to tell them that it only scrapes the surface and make them think they have to go elsewhere for authoritative information."

So the problem remained unsolved, and it does so to this day. Problems, rather, for there are many. In 1964, the editor attempted to deal with the issue in a long essay, parts of which are adapted for the present article.

Writing to a musician who had offered to make an analysis of one of his symphonies, Gustav Mahler replied on May 15, 1894:

Please accept my sincerest thanks for your kind offer. However, it is hardly my intention to confuse the audience at a musical performance with technical remarks—and in my opinion it amounts to nothing else when one stuffs a 'program booklet' into the audience's hands, thereby forcing it to see rather than to hear! Certainly I consider it necessary that the web of motives be clear to every listener. But do you really believe that in a modern work the singling out of several themes is sufficient for this? One must achieve the cognition and recognition of a musical work through exhaustive study, and the more profound a work, the harder it is, and the longer the study takes. At a first performance, however, the principal thing is to give oneself with pleasure or displeasure to the work, to allow the human-poetic in general to affect one; and if one then feels drawn to it, to occupy oneself with it more thoroughly . . .

Elsewhere, Mahler was even more emphatic; in a letter to the historian and critic Max Kalbeck, he wrote:

Beginning with Beethoven there exists no modern music which hasn't its inner program. But no music is worth anything when the listener has to be informed as to what is experienced in it—in other words, what he is expected to experience. And so again: may every 'program' perish! One must bring along one's ears and heart and, not least, surrender willingly to the rhapsodist. A bit of mystery always remains—even for the creator!

Mahler's annoyance was directed particularly toward attempts to "explain" a work in programmatic or literary terms; he wished people, as he said, to be left to their own thoughts about the work being played, "not to be forced to read during a performance, and not to be prejudiced in any manner." He believed that the composer only reached his goal if "by his music he forces on his hearers the sensations which streamed through his mind"; it is the task of the language of tones, he was convinced, to express the language of words, while it is itself "far more capable of expression and illumination." Was he not overly idealistic in his expectations?

In his book on Schumann, Robert Haven Schauffler calls into question the whole issue of appending descriptive titles and programmatic associations to musical pieces, in these provocative comments: "The very core of music is its infinite capacity to transcend any one concrete meaning. So, if the composer rashly imposes a program by revealing the concrete image that is in his own heart when he writes notes (but an image, for all that, none the more true of the music than anyone else's idea about it), he may prevent the listener from independently asking himself what these notes mean to him personally. And thus he will sin against the holy ghost of music by seeking to make its infinitude finite." One may ask, in turn, what's wrong with following the composer on his own paths of extra-musical thought and feeling? One may disagree with them or eventually disregard them, but one ought first to know what they are, if the composer wishes to divulge them. If a musical piece has been stimulated by a picture, a poem, or a specific scene, who has the right to censor that information if the artist gives it out? And furthermore, however different may be the reaction of different hearers to the same phrase, the same melody, rhythm, or harmony, the "infinitude" of music does not mean that its details are vague.

In fact, as Mendelssohn said so emphatically, "What any music I like expresses for me is not thoughts too indefinite to clothe in words, but too definite." It is here that the annotator's or commentator's real problem lies: how to deal "in other words" with the unique and autonomous language of music.

*

Some twenty years after Mr. Leinsdorf wrote his letter, the *Seventh Symphony* by the American composer Peter Mennin (1923–1983) was performed at these concerts. Requested to provide an annotation for his symphony, Mr. Mennin sent a brief outline, but prefaced it with these remarks:

> In recent years I have become increasingly reluctant in making analyses of my works for use in program notes. In a sense, I feel that it is inappropriate for the composer—who has been looking inward during the creation of the work—to have to explain merely the compositional techniques without the emotional involvement with the content of musical ideas that created the urgency to make the work come into being. Compositional techniques are merely tools of the creative impulse and are uninteresting in themselves, except to the musician, who, with score in hand, wants to study the music in detail at a later date. Actually, it is difficult in the extreme for a composer to analyze his work dispassionately—or should be.
>
> Also in recent times it has become prevalent that highly detailed explanations accompany the performances of new works. The practice of analysis and "evaluation" has so increased that one sometimes wonders if the music itself will become obsolete.
>
> To do justice to an intricate structure, a full-length analysis would have to be offered. The device of "hitting the high points" seems to the composer to be somewhat superficial. He feels that the listener should rather concentrate, at a first hearing, on the sound and its expressive development rather than on any elements of compositional technique.

Not long thereafter came a communication from the American composer Leon Kirchner:

> I don't think that an analysis of the type which usually appears in a program note can help the listener to a finer and deeper appreciation of the score. They are usually a highly superficial and linear form of analysis, resulting in the attention being concentrated on thematic recognition rather than on the organic growth of the work as a whole.

Program annotators might, perhaps, come to appreciate these attempts of distinguished composers to save them work, if not indeed to put them out of work altogether. Yet for the sake of the listening public, this is not so simple and clear-cut a matter. This uncompromising viewpoint of music's ability to "tell its own story" takes a great deal for granted in the musical abilities of listeners, which may or may not be wholly justified. Certainly the composer worth his salt will not wish to modify his artistic conception in order to make it more easily and painlessly understood; but what can he—and the annotator—do to make the process of comprehension more focused, to direct the pleasurable effort of active listening to what is most relevant?

Any program book, certainly, is obliged to provide the essential data on what, who, when, where, by whom commissioned, written for what instruments, perhaps how long in duration—in short, the facts. But is that not merely the skeleton, without which the organism could not function but which tells you nothing about the appearance of the whole body, not to mention its personality as a living thing? There is much to be said for the concise program note that gives the reader a few points of orientation, perhaps a sentence or two describing or characterizing each movement, and no more. One finds this method effectively used in programs of smaller orchestras, sometimes at summer music centers, and often in European program booklets. But although it is possible to say "much with little", such summaries cannot really come to grips with many issues of aesthetics, of intent and achievement. What the important program annotators of the past have left us—men such as Donald F. Tovey, Philip Hale, Lawrence Gilman, James G. Heller, John N. Burk, Louis Biancolli, and many others—is a *literature* about music, material not only of immediate but of lasting value. Most of those annotations, incidentally, were much longer than their contemporary counterparts; did people have more time, in the "good old days", to read as well as to write?

*

In essence, the serious program annotator proposes to provide a guide in words to a structure in sounds. It is not here the issue whether this is to be done with complete "objectivity"—that is to say, by simply describing in irrefutably factual terms what happens structurally and technically, or whether there should be added a certain amount of interpretative or "editorial" opinion that may be stimulating though arguable. The issue is whether—in the realization that music always "begins where words stop"—anything can be done at all to aid the hearer in his quest for understanding and, one hopes, enjoyment. If an annotation is to transcend in any way its original purpose as a source of factual "background" information, then how can it help in the deepening of the musical experience without crudely trespassing on the mysteries of artistic creativity? How can the "organic growth of the work as a whole" be illumined without reference to the cells from which the organism grows? How is one to describe a "form" without demonstrating its essential elements?

Both Mahler and Mennin speak of the later occasions when the musician—or the interested layman—may immerse himself further in the work, perhaps with score in hand. But both composers skirt the problem that this opportunity may not so soon arise again, if it arises at all. In the usual course of affairs, a new work is heard once by the same group of listeners; if it is "successful"—that is, exceptionally well received—it has a better chance of being heard again at a later date; it may be broadcast, and even recorded. A few works of rare quality may even enter the repertoire, and be offered at regular intervals— every third season, let us say. But with the vast majority of works, a single hearing may be expected; since they cannot predict the future, composer and annotator may jointly face the problem of how much verbal assistance should be provided for the listener's use.

The annotator must, of course, proceed on the assumption that the audience will make immediate use of the material. Yet he knows full well that this is not consistently the case, and that nobody can be forced—as the old adage has it—to consume the proferred nourishment however conveniently at hand it may be. A large percentage of the observable concertgoing public does not make as efficient use of its programs as it might. Many of its members leave even a glance at the pertinent information to the last moment, and others miss a few minutes of the music while trying to orient themselves. Still others have the booklet open only to the program page during the performance; with a work well known to them, this is not unreasonable, but when the music is new or unfamiliar one would think that sheer curiosity would lead them further before the performance commences. It is to be doubted that all of these listeners are merely accepting Mahler's suggestion to give themselves without preconceptions to the artwork; for in almost all cases there are some "background" data that can focus the direction of the emotions as well as of the intellect. If, for instance, the composer had anything in mind that he wishes to communicate to the hearer before the performance—like a literary connection or a specially interesting relationship to watch for—this will of course be missed unless a little advance preparation is done (hall illumination permitting). Bedtime perusal of the program, though pleasant, will then come too late.

Here again, one may wonder whether a musical performance might not be seen in a wider context than mere entertainment or "enjoyment"; that it might, in fact, have certain educative functions. The composer has done—and the word is meaningful—a "work". How much effort can—or should—the hearer bring to its comprehension, particularly in view of the fact that many a *première* is likely to be also a *dernière*? How can more be achieved than a "first impression"? Music, after all, embodies an intellectual experience as well as an emotional and aesthetic one; how can the listener—without being "forced"—be offered something to see which may help him or her to hear better? Is it not, for example, an opening of doors to further thought when a piece of music is discussed also in its cultural and historical relation to other works and artistic trends?

Writing in 1962 to Edward Downes in response to a request for notes on his new *Eighth Symphony* in the New York Philharmonic program, William Schuman remarked as follows:

> Frankly, over the years I have become increasingly resistant about issuing play-by-play accounts of my own music. Perhaps I'm making a minor protest against the elaborate essays which these days often accompany the launching of new works. Complicated polemics for particular aesthetic creeds or compositional procedures may be of value to scholars, but they confuse laymen. Techniques, after all, are work methods, which, in the mature artist, cannot be isolated from his creative process. Preoccupation with descriptions of techniques bears a direct relationship to the rather absurd lengths we go to in placing composers in categories and often prejudging their work accordingly as though musical vocabulary had something to do with excellence.

> This is not to say that it is not desirable to help an active listener hear more in his first exposure to a new work (passive listeners are not receptive to help, since their particular joy is sound-bathing). Certainly, a writer can supply helpful guideposts and I am all for it, provided he sticks to the music and avoids philosophical meandering. In time, the music will be judged by its inherent worth. Fortunately, no propaganda, however skillfully contrived, can, in the final analysis, substitute for genuine criteria any more than prose explanations can substitute for musical clarity.

> Having divested myself of these gratuitous comments, I had better stop before I write the kind of essay I am complaining about . . . ."

Quoting the above also in his annotation for Columbia Records, Mr. Downes comments: "Mr. Schuman makes it hard for a program note to communicate anything useful beyond objective historical fact, the most pertinent of which he has furnished himself. Perhaps he did not mean it to sound so. And certainly it is not easy for a program note to persuade a baffled (and often embattled) listener to enjoy a thorny new work . . . . With an unfamiliar work, in no matter what art medium, it is often helpful to know what *type* of expression to look for—just as it can help to know what *not* to look for, in order to avoid frustration and irritation . . . ." Where, then, is the boundary line between "sticking to the music" and "philosophical meandering"? Was Mark Twain all too correct when he wrote, "I hate explanations; they mix things up so"?

It was William Schuman, incidentally, who once said that the first requisite for a musician in any branch of art was to be a virtuoso listener. True enough; but in order to close the circle of the musical experience, as his colleague Roger Sessions saw it, does not the listener himself or herself require a degree of virtuosity commensurate with that of the composer and the performer?

*

Hearing and listening are not the same thing. Listening is an activity; hearing may be merely a "passivity". We tend to say, when hurried, "Yes, yes, I hear you!" But in that case, are we listening? Are we *doing* something? Robert Shaw once said that the good listener must be able to do two things: to remember, and to anticipate. The third act of a play may make little sense unless we can remember what happened in the first act. The same is true in music; how can there be a "surprise" in a Haydn symphony if we did not recall the previous context and now expect something else to happen? In a so-called "development section", what is it that is being developed, and why? Even without technical obfuscation, these are things with which a program note could be helpful—if it is used appropriately.

There is no such thing, surely, as an "average listener". Each is an individual, differently prepared, differently conditioned, different in artistic philosophy, taste, endurance, concern, awareness, and state of mental receptivity at the moment. Furthermore, only about ten percent of the concertgoing public—to pitch the figure high—can read musical notation. For these hundreds, however, the availability of a musical example may make an enormous difference. There should be no pretense, as Mahler warned, that the quoting of a theme is "sufficient" for comprehension of the web of motives. But if a hearer is musically trained to some degree, might it not be of immediate aid to him to have the shape of a theme before him so that he could more easily recognize its transformations as they occur, and thereby come closer to the work at the first hearing? If an analysis is provided—and is not *ipso facto* unreadable on account of abstruse terminology, hopeless length or just plain dullness—could not the listener attempt to use its descriptive comments as guides to his own "following" of the music?

One occasionally sees a hearer with the page open to the movement described, on the lookout for whatever facet is mentioned as especially important and worth noting; it only takes seconds to locate oneself in such a commentary, to make the necessary correlation, and then to return to the sound emanating from the stage. There is no doubt that reading about the finale while the slow movement is in progress—to say nothing of studying the performer's biography or a page listing committees—will succeed in thoroughly obliterating the effect of that slow movement. Reading can, of course, be used to escape from whatever is being played, should it be—in the listener's opinion—annoying, soporific, or too well known to retain interest. But in any event, an irrelevant activity will not contribute to the musical experience.

There remains the crucial fact that true comprehension of a musical work depends on acquaintance, familiarity, growing awareness of detail, and ultimately a kind of "ownership" that is akin to love. Each hearing of a genuine masterpiece should offer new facets of experience. It is impossible to grasp a major work in full at the first, second, and even the fifth hearing. There is always more to be learned and discovered. But in the case of an established classic, the opportunity for re-hearing is considerable, and aids to study are abundant. With a new work, nothing can ultimately take the place of hearing it again—if, as Mahler said, one feels drawn to it—and in time coming to "own" it as well. But while on the way to that enviable sense of possession, one may wish to hang onto this straw, lean on that crutch—to keep oneself upright and, as the phrase goes, "stay with it". A quick impression can thus be fortified or validated at once, instead of being possibly forever lost.

Until something better is devised, the analytical program—with all its evident flaws—will continue to remain the means of providing these aids. Donald Francis Tovey once wrote that he had often been "grateful for a dull description that faithfully guides me to the places where great artistic experiences await me." His own guideposts had the further advantage of never being dull—though often complex and challenging; and they were conditioned by the awareness that only the listener's own devotion and active interest can, in the "final analysis", make the musical experience a valuable and memorable one.

"Progress" in the Arts
(FEBRUARY 1983)

"Show me something new; I'll begin all over again."
—Erik Satie

With the addendum incorporated, this article was reprinted in Stagebill *in December 1984.*

*

MANKIND TAKES PRIDE in the concept of Progress. It believes, and with some justification, that each era, each century, even each decade, demonstrates elements of progress over the previous one. It is surely progress when a disease like polio can be virtually eliminated, and a drug like penicillin can control numerous other scourges. It is a progressive achievement when men can land on the moon and explore the solar system. It was progress when anaesthesia made serious operations bearable—indeed possible. Color television is progress over black-and-white television, whether or not the programming shows a comparable growth. It may be argued whether or not the "refinement" of the weapons of war represents progress—if indeed the unlocking of the power of the atom is not rather a step into the abyss, a second consumption of the forbidden fruit from the tree of knowledge.

There can be little question that advances in hygiene represent progress. To be blunt, the flush toilet is a distinct improvement over the bathroom of Louis XIV. Even the highly advanced sanitation of the Cretan palace of Knossos, two thousand six hundred years ago, suddenly swept away in the destruction of the Minoan civilization, was no match for ours. Progress, therefore, appears to be "a good thing"—and there we get into trouble.* If progress means that something new is something better, other than in a purely technical sense, we enter the area of qualitative judgment. Yes, to be able to fly from New York to London in seven hours is "better" than having to do it on a sailing vessel in the course of seven exhausting weeks; but those who objected to the "horseless carriage" only eighty years ago would have had a stronger case had they been able to point to fifty thousand automobile traffic fatalities annually.

There is a price for progress, certainly, and a technologically advanced civilization must accept certain risks not known to its predecessor. One might even claim that the lovely practice of "house music" was compromised by the availability of recorded, i.e. ready-made music, and that it is therefore no longer as necessary to become proficient

---

* As Bob Choate reminded us in a *Signature* essay on Cleveland's TV/25, Louis Bromfield once warned that plumbing should not be confused with civilization.

on an instrument for home-use as it once was. The frozen dinner has not killed off the art of cooking, but consistent reliance on the prepackaged article has some dangers. Wisely used, the Cuisinart is a blessing, most evidently in the matter of time and effort that must be spent; but the slope down the path of oversimplification of life is steep. You can precook a sausage; but how long before you will be able to purchase pre-chewed chewing gum?

*

Older civilizations employed slaves as a matter of course. Even the ancient Greeks, whose culture we so admire, did so. The official elimination of slavery in the United States represents progress, no doubt; yet it remains with us in subtler forms, and quite overtly in many other places in the world today. Social progress has in some ways been dramatic in our century, while in many nations there has been none to speak of—if not, indeed, a downward trend. The idea of "progressive development" of civilizations has been effectively destroyed by what we have learned of past ages and eras, and by the writings of such scholars as Spengler and Toynbee. And the most dramatic proof that progress is not synonymous with quality as such occurs in the arts. Has there been "progress" over the sculpture of ancient Greece, the jewelry of Scythia, the literature of Athens and Rome, the architecture of Karnak and Knossos? Are our cathedrals "better" than Notre Dame and Cologne, St. Peter's and Hagia Sophia? Is our painting an "improvement" on Giotto and Rembrandt, our music "progress" over Machaut, Palestrina, Monteverdi and Purcell? What, in the creative and recreative arts, is meant by progress at all? Does it exist?

Yes and no. In a purely technical sense, we may claim that some things are actually "better". We can build a house more efficiently today, although whether it will last as long as a Trojan wall is doubtful. The painter can buy an astounding variety of ready-made colors to mix, and we can reproduce his picture in accurate color to any size and in any amount we choose. The invention of movable type and its many offshoots has made the distribution of literature—and of ideas in general—an incredibly rapid process. Music can be made, even composed, by machines, and sound combinations never before dreamed possible have indeed become so. Yet, for some reasons not yet absolutely determined, we cannot build a better violin than did Stradivarius more than three hundred and fifty years ago.

Above all, we are an age of reproduction, of duplication. A work of art can be instantly recorded: that is to say retained, made permanent (in a relative sense). The word *record* is meaningful, and its import not sufficiently noted. *Recordari,* in Latin, means to be mindful, to remember, to keep in heart and mind. The German *aufnehmen* is not helpful; the French *enregistrer* is better. The fact that musical history has become available to us in its totality, at the press of a button, and in virtually all its variety and glory, is an absolute revolution in the perception and knowledge of art. Nothing worthwhile need now be lost—and, of course, much that is not worth keeping is also kept, bought and sold. Yet the idea of being able to see a great painter at work, in a television film, to watch the greatest available acting by someone thousands of miles away or now deceased, to hear a voice long gone, to watch an artistic or historical event of decades past—all this is without question Progress.

*

But what, if anything, is progress in the work of art itself? Can there be any reasonable discussion of progress from Mozart to Beethoven, from Lassus to Monteverdi, from Schumann to Brahms? Yes, we may say, the German romantic opera had an example or two in Weber, realized to its fullest by Wagner. Yes, we may say, many minor figures paved the way in the rococo or pre-classic period for the masterworks of Haydn and

Mozart, who perfected the forms handed to them. (Some regard the move from the baroque to the rococo as "re-gress", a step backwards.) Yes, we may say, Beethoven vastly extended the available forms of the sonata and the symphony, their technical possibilities and their emotional scope; but in no way did he thereby invalidate what was done before him. There was no way to "pro-gress" beyond the oratorios of Handel, in that particular design, or the Passions of Bach; something else had to be done. Nor has there been another Wagner, another *Ring* cycle. Monet did not outdate Courbet, Cézanne did not make Delacroix unnecessary. The idea that a new style, an expanded form, a discovery of something not yet seen or heard, is automatically "better" than a previous style or form, is evidently untenable.

Nor is it true that "bigger is better". Vast forces may or may not be more enthralling than the small and perfect; "auch kleine Dinge können uns entzücken", goes a song by Hugo Wolf, on a text of Paul Heyse. That the modern organ can do things Bach's cannot makes no difference whatsoever to his music, and that Mozart did not use the marimba and the suspended cymbal does not make his symphonies any the less *aktuell*. Nor is the complex necessarily an improvement on the simple. This is true even within a composer's own work; we may think as highly of "Bist du bei mir", a modest song by Bach, as of his grandest five-part fugue. Such examples abound.

In the minds and under the hands of truly gifted composers, our recent technological possibilities, such as music actually made on electronic tape, may be used toward genuinely creative purposes, not as merely effective gimmickry. With any technical advancement, it always comes down to who is using it, and toward what ends. Where, then, is the crux of the matter?

*

The solution to the problem is comparatively simple. The law of art, as of life, is change. "Everything," said Heraclitus, "is in flux." Or, in another version, "There is nothing permanent except change." There must be, when a period of art has run its course and achieved its uttermost, something else, something new. An artist, at least one of genius, cannot repeat or duplicate, or imitate, what has been done to perfection already. He must press on, pour old wine into new bottles (or new wine into old bottles), or create both wine and bottle anew. Within his own output, he may indeed pro-gress, *make* progress—without necessarily invalidating the earlier work. He may be, as Beethoven was, dissatisfied with his earlier work and set out to do something that is new for him as well as for everyone else: thus the *Eroica*, after the Second Symphony. But who would then dispense with the Second Symphony? Or the First? Not at all; these works stand fast, superseded only within the master's own canon, and not by "progress" as a term of quality.

"The talented can progress," writes Walter Sorell in his valuable and beautiful book, *The Duality of Vision* (published in the mid-1960s by Bobbs-Merrill). "The talent has the ability to utilize what he absorbs and assimilates; he seeks to expand that which he possesses. The genius transcends his own limitations." And the author quotes Stravinsky's fine remark that it is the artist's task to "insult habit", "to escape old formulae, ever to be ready to exchange today for tomorrow." Yet it was Stravinsky who realized that most ideas and most devices are age-old, and that something really new is rare indeed. "That which lasts longest," he once wrote, "is that which is oldest and most tried." By that token, one can speak of progress only in the sense that the development of a really new form gives us an experience we have not similarly had before. Surely the step from monody, the single-voice unaccompanied song of the Middle Ages, to polyphony, the combination and contrasting of individual lines, represents an element of progress—again by no means invalidating the monodic song. Who would say that a grandiose twelfth-century motet in five voices is *therefore* better than a sublime plainchant melody? Of course not. They are different, they have not the same artistic objective, but they are not comparable qualitatively as forms and devices. "The more things there are," John Cage has said, "the merrier."

There are instances, even, in which a composer's major effort, one into which he pours much sweat and technical skill, may be a much weaker work than one of his earlier and simpler pieces, like a small song. He may have felt that his big work represented progress over the small one; but the artistic measuring-stick works on a different scale.

*

Was there a "golden age" of singing? There always is, and it is now as it was then. It is not possible that there have been better singers than those of our own day. Certain phenomena, like Lotte Lehmann and Lauritz Melchior, do not return; but will not history "record" Pavarotti and Domingo as in a class with Caruso, Martinelli, and Bjoerling? Was there ever anyone who could match Marilyn Horne roulade for roulade, in two-and-a-half octaves? Progress—perhaps: singers are required today to sing more of the right notes.

Symphony orchestras probably play better today than they did one hundred and eighty years ago; those that gave the first performances of the *Eroica* and the *Ninth* are reported to have been pretty miserable. But was not Haydn's orchestra at Eszterháza as good as the English Chamber Orchestra is today? Very likely. Instruments have been improved, technically; a flute and a bassoon work better today than they did two hundred years ago, and so does a French horn. But that's mechanics, a technological matter, in which of course there can be progress.

Un paso adelante—"one step at a time"; that is the motto of composer Alberto Ginastera. PROGRESS: "Pro-gressus", a step forward. Webster's gives us three definitions: 1. a moving forward or onward. 2. development. 3. improvement. The creative artist is interested in all three, and amalgamates them in his own way. As Mozart said, "I am not interested in doing things differently; I want to do them better." In the process, he did them differently as well. And it is those steps toward perfection that mean true progress, in any age, in any style, in any form. The forward step must come from somewhere, and it must go somewhere. Its direction and purpose are what counts. Sometimes, it is even wise to take a step backward, where the view is better, before one decides to take the crucial step forward.

An Addendum (MARCH 1983)

IN AN ATTEMPT to write an essay on so complex a subject as progress in the arts, there always remain things unsaid, aspects not covered, ideas thought of too late. It is an ongoing issue, one with which one may wrestle for years without exhausting it (though readers may give up sooner).

For instance, one should deal with the question what happens when a pathbreaking work of art is produced and widely recognized as "new" in form and content, or even "progressive". When Berlioz wrote his *Symphonie Fantastique* at the age of twenty-seven, in 1830 (only three years after the death of Beethoven!), was not the history of music irrevocably changed? Yes and no. That astonishing composition, to be sure, was a landmark in orchestration, in the use of programmatic devices, in matters of design such as the "cyclic form" in which a single idea recurs in various guises throughout the five movements, and in expressive power. Its influence on later music, such as that of Liszt and Wagner, is undeniable. It represents to us an aspect of "progress" in music, a step into a territory not previously explored in that manner and to that extent.

But what happened in music directly after that piece was first performed? Overtly, nothing. While Berlioz himself continued on the path he had mapped out, most of his contemporaries went their own way. With the exception of Liszt and Wagner, the other masters of the time did not adopt Berlioz's discoveries. Chopin "progressed" in quite different directions; Schumann, a decade later, wrote songs and symphonies as if the *Fantastique* had never happened, and Mendelssohn devoted himself to conducting Schubert and Schumann as well as his own comparatively "conservative" compositions. Nor did Brahms evince any interest in the music of the French iconoclast. It took many years before the pathbreaking, "progressive" work of Berlioz became accepted as a natural step in the evolution of music; and while it still astonishes us today (not only in the context of 1830), it did not automatically make all music after that time "obsolete", "outdated", or "regressive". Musical history does not work that way; it does not go forward in a steady stream, but backtracks, circles, spurts onward, returns, moves in many directions at the same time.

*

The same is true of later years. We are taught to consider Wagner's work as "progressive", indeed the "music of the future" as it was then called. But we are surprised to discover that while his *Tristan und Isolde,* harmonically and expressively the most "advanced" of music dramas, was completed in 1859, it was *followed* between 1861 and 1867 by the profoundly "classical" and "conservative" *Die Meistersinger.* It would lead us too far afield to discuss whether or not Wagner's music, so enormously influential at the end of the last century and the beginning of this, really was "futuristic" in nature, or represents the close of an era rather than its beginning. In 1933, on the one hundredth anniversary of the birth of Brahms, Arnold Schoenberg wrote a long essay entitled "Brahms the Progressive", in which he sharply contradicted the generally held belief that the Hamburg master was entirely a "conservative" without a future, merely the antidote to Wagner; and he showed us how "advanced" was much of Brahms's musical thinking, and how many of his methods have retained a lasting validity and influence into our own day—while most of Wagner's have faded.

Schoenberg himself represents an example of "progressivism" which, while followed and learned from by many hundreds of gifted composers, was by no means adopted by all men of genius. Stravinsky, Bartók, Hindemith, Chávez, Copland, Prokofiev, Shostakovich, Britten—all went in quite different directions. If Pierre Boulez claims that the twelve-tone method and serialism itself make all other new music obsolete and essentially pointless, the existing literature emphatically contradicts him. If Schoenberg's discoveries were indeed a "historical necessity" (and there is some argument about that even now), they were not the only possible path. And today, the use of electronic devices to produce music, so evidently an outgrowth of technological progress, is not the method used by all creative musicians; it is there, but not every composer feels that he *must* employ it to be "up-to-date". But that the art of sound recording represents technical progress at its most astounding—from Edison's cylinder to the laser disc in a century!—is undeniable.

Stravinsky's *The Rite of Spring* of 1912–13 was without question a "revolutionary" piece, and all music thereafter was in one form or another influenced by it, positively or negatively. But it is remarkable that the composer himself did not continue in that particular line of extreme dissonance-tension and folkloristic transformation, but only a few years later changed his approach to what we now know as the "neo-classical" style, which became ultimately a much stronger influence than had the *Rite.* Thus the "progressive" piece turned out to be a milestone which no one could ignore and which everyone had to take into account; but it could not be followed or imitated, not even by the composer himself. Instead, Stravinsky celebrated the first of his "many happy returns", the revitalization of classical and baroque principles and devices in twentieth-century garb.

We might compare the situation to the discovery of electricity and its practical applications. Its immense usefulness is obvious; our civilization could not do without it. But that does not prevent many of us from returning as often as possible to situations where we must use lanterns or even candles, where there is no telephone, and where we must only be sure that we have a flashlight to go down the path to our primitive cabin in the woods where water is drawn from a well. It is the same in art; the "last word" is there for us to use, but we enjoy the frequent return to the simple, the unsophisticated, the "old ways". We even can, if necessary, do without modern plumbing—at least for a while. And we can cook on a wood-burning stove, though we hesitate to give up the convenience of canned food, and of the microwave oven. The unadorned song has not lost its magic, even when "progress" has made it possible for us to conjure up yet unheard sounds on electronic tape. The new and the old can co-exist, not in bitter opposition to each other, but as options for the mind and hand to explore, as complementary aspects of the infinitely varied and incomparably fruitful human condition.

*

NO COMPOSER *worthy of the name has ever written anything merely to be 'as great as' or 'better than' some other composer. He writes in order to say something of his own—to put down some expression of his own private personality. . . . Each artist of quality has, in art, a* raison d'être *of his own. . . . Bach, the master of masters, cannot substitute for his predecessor Buxtehude any more than Stravinsky can substitute for an American composer. . . .*

All past musical history shows us that our art cannot remain static. Whether it is moving forward well or badly can only be determined from a greater perspective than we now have. Fortunately there is no one way to which we are committed. With open minds and a good amount of forbearance the musical challenges of the future will have to be met. As Marc Wilkinson has written: "We have inherited new worlds, and part of our work is to chart these, to explore and cultivate them, and to grow new fruit."

—Aaron Copland

On the Quandary of Wagner in Israel (NOVEMBER 1982)

FOR A PROGRAM which includes music by both Wagner and Mendelssohn, it might be appropriate to muse about a matter much in the news during recent weeks: Zubin Mehta's decision to perform excerpts from *Tristan und Isolde* at concerts of the Israel Philharmonic Orchestra.

It appears to be one of mankind's least endearing characteristics that issues which are complex and even ambiguous (like some social-moral problems afflicting us today) are treated in a manner that is simple to the point of being simplistic. In the Wagner-in-Israel case, that kind of reasoning—or rather emoting—goes like this: "Of course not—it's disgraceful!" or "Why, what intolerance! Music is just music." The matter is much less clear-cut.

That Mendelssohn was of Jewish background is well known. His father was Abraham Mendelssohn, a banker in Hamburg; his grandfather was the great philosopher Moses Mendelssohn. Felix was baptized as a Christian, and there is in his music very little attention to his roots. That the Jews are not a race but a cultural and religious community is a fact known to all civilized human beings. Nevertheless, his music was banned by the ghastly one-thousand-year Reich, which lasted from 1933 to 1945.

Wagner was a rabid anti-Semite, a paranoid condition the "roots" of which are not easy to trace. The first and most likely diagnosis points to the strong possibility that his real father was not Friedrich Wagner but Ludwig Geyer, whose background was partly Jewish. Richard himself so believed, and even admitted it. Thus he may have spent much of his adult life in a process of overcompensation. How all this affected his music and his voluminous—as well as often nonsensical—writings, needs extensive studies. In the immense Wagner bibliography, we find such in at least three books at hand: *The Truth About Wagner*, by Philip Dutton Hurn and Waverly Lewis Root (Frederick A. Stokes Company, New York 1930); *The Racial Thinking of Richard Wagner*, by Leon Stein (Philosophical Library, New York 1950); and *Richard Wagner: The Man, His Mind and His Music*, by Robert Gutman (Harcourt, Brace and World, New York 1968).

Again, it is unfair and unsound to simplify so complicated an issue, as it would be to explain Wagner's detestation of the composers to whom he owed a great deal, namely Mendelssohn and Meyerbeer. What is crucial is that Wagner's ideas, especially those expressed in *Das Judentum in der Musik* ("Jewry in Music", 1869) became for the Nazis a kind of Anti-Bible, used and abused in their characteristic manner of repeating a lie so many times until it appeared to be the unarguable truth.

It is extremely difficult to prove the idea that Wagner's music itself was conditioned by his racial thinking; the literary material, of course, extols the glories of Germany's past, and it is possible to find some subtle caricatures of Jews in the music dramas, if one looks for that. The music itself—that is another matter entirely, and there the unquestioned genius of the composer stands forth in works of extraordinary power and beauty. What counts is that Hitler and his gang found a likely candidate while searching for an artistic and philosophical patron saint. While Wagner's writings and usually despicable behavior gave them plenty of "role models" to follow, they managed to distort the works themselves toward their own ends, and made even such an artistic document as *Die Meistersinger* an example of German superiority. (There are, admittedly, some hints of this in Hans Sachs's final monologue, but that's not what the opera is about.) Bayreuth became a shrine not only for the cultivation of Wagner's works, which it long had been, but a temple of worship for the Führer and his henchmen. The festival became totally politicized, and came to stand not so much for the marvels of the music but the glorification of the arrogant doctrines of racial purity and "Aryan" supremacy.

*

Human beings deal most easily in symbols and in slogans. Thus it is not hard to understand that the newly formed State of Israel would recall with painful vividness that "its" composers such as Mendelssohn and Mahler and Schoenberg had been banned in 1933–45, while Wagner was made the musical super-hero. There is here, of course, a reverse intolerance, for Mendelssohn and Mahler and Schoenberg belong to everyone, not to one national or religious group. But when one puts together the use made of Wagner by the Nazis with the indelible memories of what happened during those horrible twelve years, the operas themselves become symbols of all that was detestable, inhuman, and for many unforgivable. To refuse, therefore, even to listen to Wagner's works seems a gesture of respect to those who suffered and died virtually to the strains of that music. It is a terribly sad and saddening situation, but it is surely understandable on human grounds.

There was, in Israel, no official ban on Wagner's music. That would have been playing the Nazis' own and vicious game. But there was a general acceptance of the idea that the new and struggling state would prefer to have no reminders of that symbol, and those slogans. Thus when Zubin Mehta announced that the Israel Philharmonic would now play excerpts from *Tristan und Isolde*, the submerged pain and fury broke into the open. Surprisingly, the orchestra itself, with extremely few exceptions, agreed to play the music, and with deep feeling, even though a part of the public and the government objected. In fact, soon thereafter Mr. Mehta was elected music director of the Israel Philharmonic for life. That too tells us something. It was realized also that Wagner's music had long been a part of the cultural life of many Israeli citizens, at least those who had settled in the new state after leaving Central Europe. Every cultivated and cultured citizen of Germany, Austria, Hungary, etc., had virtually drunk the music of *Lohengrin, Tristan, Meistersinger,* and *Walküre* with mother's milk, and to experience it again was also a kind of return to one's roots.

In light of the life-and-death problems faced by the beleaguered state, is this an issue of real importance? Of course it is. Cultural concerns often express the deepest feelings of a people, become the most meaningful symbols.

*

There are "side effects". Who could forget that Toscanini brusquely refused Hitler's urging to continue to conduct at Bayreuth, but programmed Wagner's music with regularity elsewhere? That Bruno Walter, Otto Klemperer, and George Szell, exiled from Germany, never abandoned the music of Wagner? That the young Erich Leinsdorf was specifically engaged for the German repertoire at the Metropolitan Opera beginning in 1938?

Wagner himself, in his usual hypocritical and self-serving fashion, finally allowed a Jewish conductor, Hermann Levi, to conduct the premiere of *Parsifal*. He seems to have had no choice, since without Levi he could not have obtained the Munich Orchestra. Here is Wagner's letter to King Ludwig II, on September 19, 1881:

> Notwithstanding that many amazing complaints reach me as to this most Christian of works being conducted by a Jewish Kapellmeister and that Levi himself is embarrassed and perplexed by it all, I hold firmly to this one fact, that my gracious King has generously and magnanimously granted me his orchestra and chorus, as the only effective way of achieving an exceptional production of an unusual work, and consequently I accept gracefully the head of this musical organization without asking whether this man is a Jew, this other a Christian.

On October 11, the King replied:

> I am glad, dear Friend, that in connection with the production of your great and holy work, you make no distinction between Christian and Jew. There is nothing so nauseous, so unedifying as disputes of this sort; at bottom all men are brothers whatever their confessional differences.

This, writes Dr. Leon Stein, was too much for Wagner. In his reply to the King, "as rancorous and malevolent an expression that had ever come from his pen, he excoriates those very Jews who had done him service . . . . The Jewish race 'is the born enemy of pure humanity and everything that is noble in it. I am certain that we Germans will go under before them, and perhaps I am the last German who knew how to stand up as an art-loving man against the Judaism that is already getting control of everything . . . .'" History was to provide a "final solution" that Wagner might not have disapproved. It is no wonder that the citizens of Israel, knowing this, cannot listen with total equanimity to music by so overt a racist and bigot. It is fascinating also to read in Dr. Stein's book that "the anti-Semitism of Wagner was very closely bound up with an anti-Christian, and more specifically an anti-Catholic animus. Ultimately these combined with a rejection of and opposition to liberal and democratic concepts. . . ."

Could some of his anger have stemmed from the fact that his music (not his philosophy) was attacked with a bitterness and lack of understanding almost unparalleled in musical history, and that he needed a convenient target to counterattack? The Jews, as we know, have for millenia been the victims of such disturbed motivation.

*

What happened to the Wagner family, and to the children and grandchildren of the composer and his even more rabidly anti-Semitic wife, Cosima, makes astonishing reading. The older daughter of the four children of Siegfried and the English-born Winifred Wagner, Friedelind, was the one person in the clan to come to reject Hitlerism entirely; she fled the country in 1938—with Toscanini's help. Her book of 1945 (with Page Cooper), *Heritage of Fire* (Harper and Brothers, New York, published in German as *Nacht über Bayreuth*) tells the story vividly and unsparingly. Among the treasures of that book is a letter written by her father in 1921(!), when he had received a request from a man who "wanted him to exclude not only Jewish artists from Bayreuth but also Jewish visitors." We quote the larger part of Siegfried Wagner's reply :

In answer to your letter, which I found here on my return, I feel bound to tell you that I do not agree with your views at all. Among the Jews we count a great many loyal, honest and unselfish adherents who have given us numerous proofs of their devotion. You suggest that we should turn all these people from our doors? Repulse them for no other reason than that they are Jews? Is that human? Is that Christian? Is that German? No! If we wanted to behave like that, we Germans would first have to become quite a different sort of people and have consciences clear as a mountain stream. But we have nothing of the kind. The lives of all great Germans prove that they have been treated with meanness, indifference, malice and stupidity by the German people. . . .

If the Jews are willing to help us, that is doubly meritorious, because my father in his writings attacked and offended them. They would therefore have—and they have—every reason to hate Bayreuth. Yet, in spite of my father's attacks, a great many of them revere my father's art with genuine enthusiasm. You must be well acquainted with the name of former Jewish adherents. Who at that time carried on a press campaign for my father? George Davidsohn and Dohm! You must have heard too of Taussig and Heinrich Porges. Josef Rubinstein arranged *Parsifal* for the piano, and Levi conducted the first performance of *Parsifal*. And if among a hundred thousand Jews there should be no more than a single one who is devoted heart and soul to my father's art, I should feel shame if I were to turn him back just because he is a Jew.

On our Bayreuth hill we want to do *positive* work, not negative. Whether a man is a Chinese, a Negro, an American, an Indian or a Jew, that is a matter of complete indifference to us. But we might learn from the Jews how to stick together and how to give help. With envy and admiration I see how the Jews assist their artists, how they pave the way for them. If I were a Jew my operas would be performed in every theatre. As things are, however, we must wait till we are dead.*

---

* Even after his death in 1930 at the age of 61, Siegfried Wagner's eleven operas were not widely performed, and are now almost forgotten. They really should be looked at again.

No, my dear sir, it is we who must bear the blame for the hopeless state of affairs in our fatherland because we have no national pride, because we leave our own men in the lurch. Are we now to add intolerance to all our other bad qualities and reject people of good will? Are you really prepared to deny that among the Jews there are people whose enthusiasm for Bayreuth is genuine? They are a people that I will not and must not offend. I am in a position to show you that you are wrong and even to give you the names of a very large number. In selecting our artists we have never taken the racial question into consideration. We have been guided solely by voice, talent and appearance suitable for the part in question, and that is a principle by which we shall continue to abide in the future.

I hope that you will grasp my meaning. Bayreuth is to be a true work of *Peace.*

Can we imagine Richard Wagner's reaction had he known that in 1981 a black American, Simon Estes, would reap a phenomenal success at Bayreuth in the title role of *The Flying Dutchman?* And that James Levine would become one of Bayreuth's favorite conductors—especially in *Parsifal?*

*

Should Wagner be played in Israel? It is not a question that can be answered simply. Perhaps it is symbolic of the slow process of reconciliation that may make of the world's peoples again a civilized society. We do not imply approval of the Soviet system when we listen to and applaud the work of a Soviet composer or a Soviet performer. There does come a point where art goes beyond politics and ideology, and delivers its message without associations that are not really relevant to the work itself. This course will take time, and it will be painful; what is needed are sympathy, empathy, and a deep awareness of what humanity is all about.

Aware musicians and music lovers have always known what kind of person Wagner had been. They found it possible to separate the man from the work; finding the former wanting, they could still admire the latter. It was history that made such a division more difficult and—for some—impossible. In the majority of Wagner's music dramas, sin, guilt and the search for redemption play major roles. He knew his subject matter well. As in the man, the texts show us a juxtaposition of grandeur and pettiness, passionate love and bitter hatred, a vision of human fulfillment and revolting meanness. Wagner's work lives on the greatness of its music, not on his social theories. Is it still possible to keep them apart, or is the overlap inevitable?

Nothing of what has been offered here should be taken as conclusive, authoritative, and least of all "official". These are musings, a look at some evidence, an approach to a rational—though hardly dispassionate—dialogue. Let it be stressed that there is much more to be said on both and all sides, and—as in the case of so many human problems— there may be no solution at all, but only an adjustment, an accommodation, a step in the "peace process". Some wounds heal slowly, if at all.

*

There remains to be related an ironic sidelight. While in Lucerne on the 1981 WCLV European Music Festival Tour (which also encompassed Bayreuth), the editor and his wife visited the Wagner House and Museum at Tribschen. There we learned that Bayreuth is no longer owned by the Wagner family, but by the Bavarian State, and that the family itself is currently embroiled in a bitter internecine battle over Wieland's inheritance. "Ah," said this writer; "it's just like *The Ring*, isn't it? Who owns the gold, and how long until *Götterdämmerung?*" "Precisely," was the answer.

A Postscript

IT IS EXACTLY ten years later, and the problem is unsolved, the emotions as raw as ever. The Israeli conductor Daniel Barenboim announced a concert of Wagner's music in December of 1991, but as a special event, not a subscription concert. The Israel Philharmonic musicians voted thirty-nine to twelve, with nine abstentions, in favor of the plan. "Those who feel that they don't want to come into contact with this music," said Mr. Barenboim, "simply don't have to come to the concert." The arguments that broke out in the press and in Parliament were tense and close to violent. A politician and survivor of Dachau said, "One can forgo a pleasure. But one has no control over pain." An abstaining musician said, "There is a connection and responsibility between the person and his compositions, and it cannot be ignored." Within a few weeks, the concert was postponed, and the decision was made to poll the thirty-six thousand subscribers if they wished the ban on Wagner's music (in force since 1938) to be lifted at this time. An expert on Holocaust literature at Hebrew University in Jerusalem, Sidra Ezrahi, was quoted in *The New York Times* (January 12, 1992) to have observed, "Israel's is a symbolic culture. Symbols have people in their grips well beyond the social movements that were supposed to change them."

Amadeus
Fact vs. Fiction, Biography vs. Theatre, Truth vs. Imagination
(MARCH 1981)

THE "BIG NEWS" in Mozart bibliography during the last few years has been not a book, a rediscovered score, a set of recordings. It is a play. And what a play! Controversial, brilliant, infuriating, illuminating, full of insight, full of distortion, sensational, shocking, beautiful, perhaps exploitative—it may be all of these.

Peter Shaffer, the British playwright who had previously astonished us with *Five Finger Exercise, The Royal Hunt of the Sun, Equus,* and several other works for the stage, has now turned to the intriguing story of Mozart's relationship with Antonio Salieri (1750–1825), the much-esteemed court composer of Vienna in the late eighteenth century. Mr. Shaffer, who studied music and for a time served as a music critic, has examined his sources with care. For the theme of his play, he has returned to the idea already dealt with by Pushkin in his play of 1830, *Mozart and Salieri,* according to which Mozart may have been poisoned by his jealous rival. (Rimsky-Korsakov later used that play for an opera libretto.) Shaffer comes to the conclusion—not new, but reasonable—that the nature of the poisoning was not physical but professional and psychological. There is ample evidence that the Italian exerted much negative influence on the Austrian's career, and exacerbated the younger man's personal foibles and irresponsible actions in subtle ways.

Moreover, and again like Pushkin, Shaffer sets up the dramatically striking moral dilemma of a competent but mediocre composer who is consumed by jealousy of an incomparable genius, whom he feels compelled to destroy. In the play, Salieri comes into direct conflict with God, who, he is convinced, has given His own voice to an ill-mannered, disagreeable lout instead of to His willing and devoted servant. Thus the play becomes a three-way battle: Salieri against Mozart, Mozart against his own failings as a man, and Salieri against his God. It is a big theme, and Shaffer has dealt with it in a stunningly "operatic" fashion.

"What the play is trying to do," Shaffer says, "is to give an interpretation of history. . . . Of course I have taken some liberties. This is a play, not a biography of Mozart. But almost everything in it can be supported by historical fact." In the process, the playwright has devised—for dramatic purposes—a kind of "double character assassination". Salieri is not only jealous and manipulative: he is a pious hypocrite, a would-be seducer of Mozart's wife, and an individual driven by both rage and guilt. (That, after Mozart's death, Salieri befriended the Mozart family and even taught one of the surviving sons, Shaffer conveniently fails to mention.) Mozart himself is not only depicted as weak and unlucky in all his relationships, but as a foul-mouthed, sex-obsessed, foppish and quite distasteful buffoon. In fact, the New York production—revised and expanded from the London original—depicts Mozart as a kind of punk rock star bucking the musical establishment. (Cleveland lawyer Albert Borowitz, noted author long involved with the Mozart-and-Salieri poisoning controversy, described the character in that way after recently seeing the play in New York.)

Now the documentation for that kind of image of Mozart exists, if one wishes to slant it in that direction. The sublime composer was not in all respects an admirable man; he was prone to alienating prospective patrons, he loved to gamble, he was careless with money, he was feared for his sharp and merciless tongue, and he may have been free in dispensing his sexual favors. But there is a sharp contradiction between the perceptiveness of what he has to say even in the play (based on his letters and reported statements) and his image as a pitiful clown.

The problem for the viewer is at least twofold. On the one hand, it is obvious that the characterization of Mozart is largely that of Salieri, his arch-rival—who also serves as the narrator in the play. And on the other, there is the danger that playgoers may accept such an image of Mozart as "fact", and come to believe that such a man could indeed have written such music.

No, he could not, and he did not. Our own study of Mozart's life and numerous letters produces a vastly different conclusion. That his failings were many does not alter it. That he was a tease and a punster, full of comedy both high and low, does not change it. Mr. Shaffer hints at this when he has Mozart say, at one point, "My tongue is stupid. My heart is not." The playwright—or at least the figure of his Salieri—does not allow for the nature of eighteenth-century verbal expression. Alfred Einstein explains that at the time "All human and animal functions took place more publicly than in our own more civilized and hygienic days, and unembarrassed reference to matters of an intimate nature was not confined to the lower or middle classes." One should not forget that it was a highly esteemed privilege in the late seventeenth and early eighteenth centuries to attend the daily bathroom functions of Louis XIV, the "Sun King". Eric Blom, similarly, understands Mozart's occasional scatological language as "merely the relic of a time that had no sanitation, either technically or metaphorically; a time, however, that was artistically more fastidious than our own." It is that fact which explains why even Mozart's "dirty canons"—with extraordinarily scabrous texts to amuse his circle of friends—are musically so "pure" that later generations could put sacred texts below the notes.

*

From Mr. Shaffer's play, one is left with the impression that the contrast between so worldly and flawed a personality as Mozart's and the God-inspired perfection of his music is inexplicable. There is here a serious error. It fails to comprehend or demonstrate the fact that there has been no really great artist in history whose work is not a direct and incontrovertible reflection of his essential personality. We find this true of Beethoven, of Wagner, Bach, Shakespeare, Michelangelo, Stravinsky, Picasso, Dylan Thomas, and so on. Mozart never wrote a vulgar bar of music, except when he occasionally wished to depict the vulgar; he himself explained this in his letters. Most of his music is of an unearthly purity and genuine spirituality; no boorish lout could possibly have put it on paper, much less conceived it. The essence of the man, with all his outward failings, was loving, wise, and deeply sympathetic. His range of dramatic expression was Shakespearean. This is what we hear in the music, and the caricature that Peter Shaffer's Salieri conjures up for us may make effective theater, but it is seriously misleading. It is true that the Salieri of the play is overcome by Mozart's genius; he admits it, and suffers from it. But nowhere does he seem to understand the source from which it evidently sprang; to describe it as a bitter joke on the part of the divinity—as a silk purse made of such sow's ears—does not touch the essence of what Mozart must have been really like as a man. The play, one feels, would have been stronger if that issue had been honestly dealt with.

The old aesthetic maxim, "the style is the man", has been much misunderstood. Beethoven's music is often eccentric, but it is always controlled; as a person, the composer was not only eccentric but uncontrolled and uncontrollable. Brahms was known to be laconic, often rude, and personally uncommunicative; his music is expansive, warm, and deeply communicative as well as complex in detail and form. If Mozart's music approaches absolute perfection, it does not mean that the man did also; it means that the inner core was pure and inviolate, and what the style expresses is not the surface but the essence. The personal character of Bartók—the one hundredth anniversary of whose birth we celebrate this week—shines forth with utter integrity from every measure of his music. A work of art symbolizes the personality at its integrated best. It is orderly, even when the individual may be outwardly disorderly. But when an essentially vulgar and shallow person produces music, it will be essentially vulgar and shallow. As for Mozart—consider the evidence.

Whether or not Shakespeare fairly depicted his Hamlet, his Macbeth, or even his kings is not a comparable issue; these are characters too far back in history to trouble our sense of veracity. But about Mozart we know too much. Mr. Shaffer has loaded his dice. Even for so remarkable a dramatic effort as *Amadeus* it was not necessary to distort available history, to slant it toward a characterization that is essentially impossible. Of course, Mozart's music will survive the play; Mr. Shaffer, who adores the music, would be the first to agree. For this master, however sorrowful his short and turbulent life, was truly "beloved of God", which is one of the meanings of the Latin name *Amadeus* (*Gottlieb* in German, *Theophil* in Greek, or, as Mozart himself exclusively signed it, in the French way, *Amadé*). The name, of course, could mean also "lover of God", which is what Salieri wished to be before—in his view—the divinity so utterly betrayed him.

It remains to be said that this writer has not seen the play, but has only read it complete, and has studied the annotated program as well as numerous reviews and discussions of it. There is little doubt that actually seeing the play might confirm its qualities as a piece of stagecraft, the power of its conception, the remarkable sweep of its language; the characterization of the minor characters is sharp, the description of artistic and court intrigue remarkably vivid. But while Mozart's music no longer stands in need of defense— if ever it did—his personal character does, as it relates inescapably to the music which must be a reflection of his deepest essence.

Once More—*Amadeus* (MARCH 1983), by Charles W. Lovy

*

The following essay by the late Charles W. Lovy is included in this collection for two reasons: (1) it was stimulated by the preceding essay on Amadeus *and a subsequent discussion of the issue with Mr. Lovy, and (2) it is a splendid piece of writing which can stand as an example of the many essays by other authors which appeared regularly in the pages of The Cleveland Orchestra's program book.*

*

Mr. Lovy, the distinguished author of Constanze, Formerly Widow of Mozart *and other books, died untimely in 1984.*

THE FLICKERING will-o'-the-wisp triplets rising, at the opening of the *D Minor Concerto*, out of the tumultuous, demonic threat of the orchestra, and, shortly thereafter, the emergence of the divine second theme as the key changes and serenity spreads, put us in touch with the innermost feeling of man, though our reason is unable to state in words what we hear. It is difficult to believe that it was once thought a rococo Mozart, infatuated with minuet dance tunes, could thus have probed fate; as such he appears in white marble, with a coquettish twist of the hips, on his pedestal in the garden of the Imperial Palace in Vienna, where his musical epiphany, passion, and doom came to pass. Shall we now assume that a vulgar, boorish bore could write such music? As such he is represented in Peter Shaffer's *Amadeus*.

The play has raised so much controversy among admittedly sincere and knowledgeable partisans and adversaries that the issue may warrant re-examination.

Let us differentiate between the play as a theatrical event, the historical representation of Mozart's world and personality, and of his adversary Salieri, who emerges as the central character in this work entitled *Amadeus*. Salieri has, in his youth, made a childish deal with God, in Whom he believed then, promising to serve Him if He would grant him in return fame and success as a musician; foiled and threatened by the appearance of the young genius Mozart—although, given Salieri's personality, worldly success should be all he desires, and he continues to enjoy it—he curses God for denying to him what He has so lavishly bestowed on a godless Mozart, whom Salieri relentlessly persecutes and destroys.

The play is not a tragedy, for it lacks the catharsis which, in a celebrating mood, would let us view individual tragedy *sub specie aeternitatis*, as an absolute. It is not drama, for we can identify neither with Salieri, the intrigant and Patron Saint of Mediocrity, nor with his rival, the very dull, vulgar, and verbally uninhibited denizen in the land of anal eroticism called Mozart. Our emotional involvement being thwarted, we remain cold observers from afar of a *Lehrstück*, a didactic theatrical event in the Brechtian manner. However, if Brecht teaches us on occasion that the true owner of a field is he who tills it rather than he who owns it, *Amadeus* teaches us nothing, though it does entertain us. Shaffer raises a valid question, the question how a silly young nobody could write heavenly music, but he fails to answer this question. Thus, his *Lehrstück* implies that, through a fortuitous though fortunate constellation of connections between brain cells, which may occur at random in any living creature, however obnoxious, a musical genius may come into being. The suggestion is to be expected in a naturalistic-scientific age such as ours. We will, of course, never understand the genesis of genius any more than the nature of the boundaries of our universe, but by presenting a genius as a churlish troublemaker of diminished mental capacity, Shaffer has turned a question unanswerable in itself into an absurd one, and has in the process made things very difficult indeed for himself.

He has, nevertheless, done theatrical pioneer work by creating a variant of the Brechtian melodrama. As a melodrama, the play is stunning: theatrical effects abound; the thunder of eloquence overawes us; the wit is exhilarating; the dizzying swirl of scenes, events, moods, characters, elegantly disguised hypocrisy, and foul-mouthed impudence titillates us; the Mozartian musical intervals are well chosen. Shaffer is a consummate master of stage manipulation, which he has learned from virtuosos of the art such as the French writer Jean Giraudoux and our own Arthur Miller: we travel back and forth between Salieri's old-age reminiscences and their forty-year-old roots; we hear Mozart's scores as Salieri, flabbergasted, reads them; we smile as Salieri, having pronounced an invocation to posterity, turns around to face the audience as the lights go up, and says drily, "It has worked."

Yet, we can accept anti-heroes on the stage only if their compelling veracity, as that of Camus' repulsive Caligula, is conveyed by their act of speech rather than by a hi-fi system, however brilliant. Shaffer's melodramatic world remains unreal, two-dimensional, flat, and bookish, as does the young boy in his *Equus*. Can we accept a Salieri, the honored musician, the respected music-manufacturer and efficient superintendent of Joseph II's musical and operative establishment, mediocre musician that he is, yet able to recognize genius when he meets it, thirsting to destroy a rival of genius, as the boy in *Equus*, in sexual turmoil, blinds stabled horses? Can we, indeed, believe that Mozart, when in a frenzy of exasperation, spews out a cascade of four-letter words as the most adequate expression of his feelings?

*

This question brings us to Shaffer's historical interpretation. He has claimed, as other authors do, the right to poetic—or unpoetic—license in treating historical themes. The German Romantic poet—and historian!—Schiller has his Joan of Arc die on the battlefield; it would be patently foolish to accept this as evidence that she was not burned at the stake. The point is that the playwright, by giving play to fantasy, forfeits the right to claim, or to imply, that his interpretation is historically valid—which is precisely Shaffer's claim.

Mozart's letters and the testimony of contemporaries, most intelligently sifted and interpreted (though some of his conclusions are questionable) by Wolfgang Hildesheimer in his recent Mozart book, suggest indeed that Mozart was human (except for his music). He liked good food, pretty clothing, horses, billiards, genius in others, on occasion mindless recreation, punch, especially in his twenties pretty women, all his life women with a soul and a mind, music worth its name, money and success, dancing, cheerful parties; he was an impeccable musical craftsman divinely inspired; the perfection of his work is such that the language has no words adequate to describe it; he knew this, was proud of it, and treated charlatans with undisguised contempt; he was impatient at undeserved success; he knew how to make enemies; he was kind to friends, to those in need, and inclined to forgive even his enemies in the long run. Concrete evidence has brought our image of Mozart from the rococo heaven down to earth. Vulgar words crop up in his letters, although less often than one now claims. Intimate erotic allusions, though rather rare, do occur in letters to his wife, and there may have been more in letters she and her second husband destroyed.

All this will, at the Last Judgment, make it impossible for Mozart to deny that he was human. However, since a play is an object made of words and actions, these become on the stage symbolic; when a stage Mozart at a party throws himself on Constanze and shouts a four-letter word, he is thereby forever characterized as a vulgar lecher; in real life the incident would merely suggest that he had partaken of a stalk of celery (or some other doubtful aphrodisiac), had had one glass of punch too many, had looked too intensely at Constanze's décolletage, and was in general apt to disregard conventions. Yet, we know that he moved comfortably in respectable middle-class and aristocratic society.

*

It may help us to understand why Mozart did not talk as his rococo statue would, if we realize that Austrian German is today, and was in the eighteenth century, a vernacular in love with scatology. Those born in Vienna can even on occasion muster some nostalgic fondness for the habit. Emil Kuh, a prewar literary figure famous for his witty improvised lectures, once produced a text consisting of nothing but verbal variations on the theme of a shocking command (not meant literally, however) which Goethe used in his play *Götz von Berlichingen,* to satirize this Viennese propensity to be both naughty and decisive. Mozart talked like everybody else in Vienna, including his own mother, who was of Salzburg peasant stock. It may be of interest that another German dialect, Swabian, is also in love with scatology, and that Mozart's cousin, the "Bäsle", was from Swabian Augsburg. Much has been made of the incriminatory nature of the letters Mozart exchanged with her as a young man. Their owner, the writer Stefan Zweig, submitted them to Sigmund Freud as if they contained classified material, and a previous owner had left them on his death to a friend, adjuring him to destroy them eventually so that Mozart's image could never be smudged. Could it be that Bäsle's loose talk so excited young Wolfgang that he, admittedly somewhat childish for his age, full of sexual repression through his strict Salzburg education, responded with an orgy of scatological suasion, natural between an Austrian and the Swabian girl, who became perhaps his first love? Later, when he wrote *Voi che sapete* he knew nevertheless how to express convincingly seething young sexuality. Shaffer does not. It would be a pity if we accepted his image of a subhuman Mozart instead of a very human one.

A Postscript (MARCH 1983)

IN HIS ESSAY, Charles W. Lovy refers to the new book entitled simply *Mozart* by Wolfgang Hildesheimer. First published in Germany in 1977 and very successful there, it was translated into English by Marion Faber and published in 1982 by Farrar Straus Giroux, New York. Provocative, stimulating, arguable, illuminating, infuriating, and altogether valuable, this book forces us to rethink at least some of our traditional ideas about Mozart. In a recent program book of the Boston Symphony Orchestra, annotator Steven Ledbetter has concisely and perceptively summed up its nature:

> This challenge to the received tradition of Mozart studies comes not from a musicologist but from an artist and novelist who has studied all the primary sources (especially the composer's letters) for over a quarter of a century. His book is not a chronological survey of the composer's life but rather a 366-page essay built up out of many short sections dealing primarily with Mozart's character, personality, and genius. The cumulative effect of the author's observations and penetrating criticism of the old "haloed" Mozart is to provide an entirely new view of this composer.

One would question only the words "entirely new"; careful readers of Alfred Einstein's book of 1945, *Mozart—His Character, His Work* (Oxford University Press) will hardly be surprised at most of Hildesheimer's conclusions. Particularly applicable to the *Amadeus* controversy are comments such as these by Hildesheimer:

> Characteristically, Mozart consistently failed in every attempt to transfer his silliness, often forced as it was, into music. Wherever his words lack the appropriate tone, his music corrects it. . . . The slightest touch of vulgarity is alien to Mozart's music, even when the words seem to dictate it; here [in the so-called "dirty canons"] he has composed against his own text. We wonder if the seeming evidence about even ignoble things deceives us, too. In other words, Mozart always composed against his own texts—against the texts of his letters, his bearing, his behavior. Or vice versa: his true language, music, is fed from sources unknown to us; it lives from a suggestive power which rises so far above the object of its suggestion that it evades us. Its creator remains unapproachable.

Mozart in Rome, "Doing as the Romans Do" (MARCH 1981)

*

This piece was written with a program note on Mozart's Symphony in D, K. 97, *which he wrote at age fourteen in Rome.*

*

WHILE IN ROME in the spring of 1770, Wolfgang and his father were exceptionally busy as performing musicians. From mid-April dates the extraordinary occurrence so often reported, when the boy heard a performance of Allegri's *Miserere* in the Sistine Chapel. (How many of the millions of visitors to that incomparable chapel have thought, "Mozart was here too"?) Allegri's piece was so prized by the Vatican that it could not be copied or allowed to be circulated. By an astonishing feat of memory, Wolfgang wrote down the music after hearing it once, and took the "pirated" score back to Salzburg with him. "Since it is one of the secrets of Rome," wrote Leopold in a letter, "we do not want to let it fall into other hands and so incur ecclesiastical displeasure."

However busy the Mozarts were with musical pursuits, the boy at least had time for other pastimes as well—"when in Rome, doing as the Romans do". In a letter to his sister, he reports that he had just learned the game *boccia* (bowls), and that he would teach it to her as soon as he got home. Games in fact, were Mozart's passion for all of his life; he became especially adept at billiards, but unfortunately for his economic health learned to gamble as well. Yet at least in those early days, composition and game-playing were not too far removed from one another; nor should one forget that a musical piece and a musical instrument are not "worked" but "played".

The Mozarts' need for secrecy, as in the case of the Allegri *Miserere*, extended also to this set of symphonies. In the same letter to Marianne, dated April 25, 1770, Wolfgang tells her of writing these works, and that the copying was being done by none other than his father, Leopold: "We do not wish to give it out to be copied—it would be stolen." That at least two of these symphonies existed in Leopold's hand may account for the supposition, held by some, that they were actually compositions by the elder Mozart. This idea has long been contradicted, on the basis of all evidence; yet there remains one facet that would speak for the earlier assumption: namely that this set of symphonies is a cut below most of the earlier ones in inspiration. Was young Mozart perhaps a bit more concerned with *boccia* than with score paper, and might the excitement of the Roman experience have distracted him a little?

Even if this were so, and the production of the boy in his early teens is quite miraculous enough, he was not capable of writing something really poor. Mozart's second-rate is still on a very high level of craftsmanship, and the music is everywhere alive. The minuet-and-trio, incidentally, was apparently composed a good deal later; in symphonies of the Italian type, three movements (fast-slow-fast) were customary, but for Austria (especially Vienna) the inclusion of a minuet movement was *de rigueur*.

*

Mozart Writes to His Mother and Sister—Rome, April 14, 1770
God be praised and thanked, I am sound and well from top to toe, and miss my Mama and Nannerl a thousand (or 1000) times. My one wish is that my sister were here with us in Rome, for this town would certainly please her well, the Church of St. Peter's being regulair *and many other things in Rome being* regulair *also!.... Now I have been drawing Saint Peter with his keys, Saint Paul with his sword, together with Saint Luke and my sister, etc., and I have had the honor of kissing Saint Peter's toe in St. Peter's, but because I have the misfortune to be so little, someone had to lift up the undersigned old rascal*

Wolfgang Mozart!

Mozart's use of the French term *regulair* may be taken as a parallel to the American teen-ager's "cool" or "keen" or "neat".—Editor.

Mozart Writes a Wedding Poem

*

This was written by Mozart in a letter to his sister Maria Anna ("Nannerl") congratulating her on her marriage, August 18, 1784 (English translation by K.G.R., March 1981)

*

. . . Und nun schicke ich dir noch 1000 gute
Wünsche von Wien nach Salzburg, besonders
dass ihr beyde so gut zusammen leben
möchtet als wir zweye; drum nimm von
meinem poetischen Hirnkasten einen kleinen
Rath an: den höre nur:

Du wirst im Ehstand viel erfahren
was dir ein halbes Räthsel war;
bald wirst du aus Erfahrung wissen,
wie Eva einst hat handeln müssen,
dass sie hernach den Kain gebahr.
Doch Schwester, dieses Ehstands Pflichten
wirst du von Herzen gern verrichten,
denn glaube mir, sie sind nicht schwer;
doch jede Sache hat zwei Seiten:
der Ehstand bringt zwar viele Freuden,
allein auch Kummer bringet er.
Drum wenn dein Mann dir finstre Mienen,
die du nicht glaubest zu verdienen,
in seiner üblen Laune macht:
So denke, das ist Männergrille,
und sag: Herr, es gescheh dein Wille
beytag—und meiner bey der Nacht.

. . . . And now I send you 1000 good wishes
from Vienna to Salzburg, especially that you
both may live together as well as we two;
therefore take from my poetical skull
["brain-box"] a little advice: hear it now:

Much will you learn in matrimony
that somewhat puzzled you before;
soon will you know from real life
how Eve had to perform as wife,
so that, soon after, Cain she bore.
But, sister, duties conjugal
you gladly will discharge withal,
for, trust me, they're not hard a bit;
yet every matter has two sides:
while the estate will bring delights,
some sorrows go along with it.
You'll see your husband fiercely glower—
which you believe you don't deserve—
while he is in a mood right sour:
So chalk it up to male caprice,
and say: O Lord, your will be done
in day-time—and mine, comes the night.

The Memoirs of Shostakovich—An Extraordinary Controversy
(APRIL 1980)

IN RECENT DECADES, no publication in the field of music has caused a stir comparable to the appearance of the "posthumous autobiography" of Dmitri Shostakovich. It is understandable that much less widespread interest was aroused by a recent "psycho-biography" of Pierre Boulez; and even the continuing argument about the exact authorship of the Igor Stravinsky-Robert Craft collaborations has engaged the public interest less actively. The reasons are not difficult to discern: in the case of the Shostakovich book, our entire image of the composer as a man is in the process of being revised, indeed overthrown; and further, the implications of that "revolution" concern not only art and matters of musical style, but are inextricably interwoven with politics and international relations both diplomatic and cultural.

Published in the fall of 1979, the book is called *Testimony—The Memoirs of Dmitri Shostakovich, as related to and edited by Solomon Volkov* (Harper & Row, New York). Volkov is a Soviet-born musicologist now thirty-six years old, who came to the United States in June of 1976 and has been working as a research associate at the Russian Institute of Columbia University in New York. Acquainted with the composer since 1960, he gained the aging master's confidence and friendship in the early 1970s, and in an extended series of conversations taken down in shorthand the two men created the raw material of this book. The chapters were edited and typed, read and signed by the composer, and surreptitiously smuggled out of the country. It was agreed that the book could not be published until after the composer's death, which he anticipated as only a matter of time. In the United States, the manuscript was translated into effective American English by Antonina W. Bouis, and given to the public.

The first dramatic result—at least the connection seemed evident—was the cancellation of the planned United States tour by the Moscow Philharmonic Orchestra. Its conductor was none other than Maxim Shostakovich, the gifted son of the composer, who—it was said—did not wish to be in this country at that very moment. Within weeks, outraged denials of the book's authenticity came from the Soviet Union, and more recently there have been official attacks on the publication by Shostakovich's family and by Boris Tishchenko, a highly talented young composer and protégé of Shostakovich frequently and favorably mentioned in the book. In New York, Volkov stated, "my friend has betrayed me." It is now clear that Tishchenko had been the very person to whom Volkov expressed appreciation at the close of his Preface, in these words: "And finally, I thank you, my distant friend who must remain nameless—without your constant involvement and encouragement, this book would not exist." The frontispiece photo of the book, moreover, inscribed to Volkov by Shostakovich, includes four people: Mrs. Shostakovich, the composer, the musicologist . . . and Boris Tishchenko.

One can, knowing the nature of the system, draw only one conclusion, namely that the official word to both Tishchenko and Maxim was clear and unequivocal: "If you value your positions and privileges, you will call the book a fake and revile its editor." And in order to retain Shostakovich's music itself as a performable commodity, which would be certainly in the interests of the Soviet Union, his standing as an irreproachable adherent to the party line had to be re-confirmed.

This conclusion is drawn with one prior assumption: and that is that the book is indeed genuine, and apart from some necessary editing the actual words of Dmitri Shostakovich. Having read it with care as well as amazement, we have no doubt that it is just what it purports to be. As Robert Finn wrote in *The Plain Dealer* (following up on his previous and extensive coverage), the book "has the ring of truth about it. The voice of

Dmitri Shostakovich in its pages—colloquial, irreverent, undisciplined, unsparing of itself—is that of a real person. The book is gloomy, often downright depressing. But it rings true." One might add to this that there is no imaginable way in which a young Russian musician could possibly have invented what is told here, in general and in particular. If the book is a fraud, it is an astonishingly brilliant one. There is no way that a young writer—lest he have the gifts of a Chekhov, Turgenyev, or Pasternak—could have created monologues of such profound insight, withering sarcasm, bitter denunciation, and shattering tragedy.

Moreover, from what we know, Volkov must have been reluctant to include certain statements by Shostakovich, such as the rather petty and jealousy-induced attacks on Prokofiev; but he did so on the basis that Shostakovich said it, and no editor had a right to suppress it. It testifies to Volkov's integrity that he did not omit passages with which he himself might have disagreed.

*

Reviewing the book in *The New Yorker* (March 24, 1980), George Steiner takes note of the tone of loathing that runs through the ailing composer's view of things and people; but he fails to account for the growth of that increasingly negative attitude in the very history he describes. Shostakovich himself admits to "self-loathing", for having managed to survive by regularly denying his true feelings. And in discussing the remaining doubts about the authenticity of the book, Mr. Steiner mentions an article signed by six Soviet composers and published on November 14, 1979, in which Volkov's book is denounced as a forgery. "They did so on grounds of style as well as of content. Even in polemic, they said, Shostakovich's idiom retained a characteristic courtesy and finesse." But what were those polemics? Written for Soviet consumption, they never could come to grips with the crucial issue, namely the ultimately demeaning relationship of the creative artist to the state. The composer's political pronouncements, as we have known them for decades, are indeed subtle and understated; but it would seem that in this book he could at last unleash all his long-suppressed resentment and fury. And when Mr. Steiner writes that "Shostakovich's family has apparently never seen Volkov's document; according to Soviet sources, the composer's son . . . believes *Testimony* to be a slanderous fabrication . . ." he misses the impact of the words, *according to Soviet sources*. So the shameful trade of self-abasement for professional survival begins all over again. It may be just a question of time before we have one or more defectors to tell us what was demanded of them.

It is an interesting aspect, not yet widely discussed, that while Shostakovich deals largely with the Stalin era and says comparatively little about the decades since the death of "the great leader and teacher" in 1953, the present Soviet government cannot see its way clear to join the composer in his denunciation of the previous regime. While the memory of Stalin was for a time dishonored, there has been a gradual reinstatement of his standing; the pendulum is swinging back toward a mind-set of absolutism that has no choice but to disavow any attack on the system as such. If Stalin was totally wrong and his methods brutal, then saying so today would invalidate the bulk of what his successors are doing today. An Andrey Sakharov may not be shot, but he is still exiled for speaking out; dissent on ideological grounds has no place in the system, even if it is no longer "classically" Stalinist.

Mr. Steiner's questions how Volkov's own involvement and passion over such matters as the treatment of Jews (discussed at great length by Shostakovich) may have colored the final version of the book are interesting, but they alter nothing. And he quite ignores the constant "gallows-humor" of the composer's words, as well as the fascinating insights into musical creation that abound in the book—and which could have come only from a master composer. Nor does the "enigmatic protection" angle stand up under scrutiny;

Shostakovich was much too famous, far too valuable a "product", to be utterly silenced even when temporarily disgraced.

*

In *The New York Times* of Sunday, March 23, 1980, Harlow Robinson reports that at least one copy of *Testimony* is "circulating unofficially from the Moscow headquarters of the Composers' Union." One assumes it is in English, and no Russian version has been published. "According to one young composer, a Union member, only those 'with enormous influence' . . . can hope to obtain that copy." Now if the book were such an obvious fabrication, whose incorrectness could be demonstrated item for item, why is it being kept so much out of sight? "One leading Shostakovich specialist," writes Mr. Robinson, "who has managed to read *Testimony* told me he has questions about the alleged closeness of the Volkov-Shostakovich relationship, but nonetheless recognizes much of the book as coming from the composer's mouth." The photograph there reproduced is inscribed to Volkov in a trembling hand, but in such a way as to authorize and confirm that very closeness: it says: "To dear Solomon Moiseyevich Volkov in fond remembrance. D. Shostakovich. 13 XI 1974." And there is another sentence; as Volkov tells it: "As I was about to leave, he said: 'Wait. Give me the photo.' And he added: 'A reminder of our conversations about Glazunov, Zoshchenko, Meyerhold. D.S.' and he said: 'This will help you.'" It is clear, furthermore, that Harper & Row has put its prestige behind the veracity of this book, in the conviction that it is in all respects genuine.

From Mr. Harold Ticktin, a noted Cleveland lawyer, we have received a remarkable essay relating the Shostakovich book to the trial of Nikolai Bukharin in 1938. Like Volkov, Ticktin refers to the Russian device of speaking in "Aesopian" terms, a veiled or hidden way of saying things in parables. Bukharin, says the author, couched his defense in those symbolic garments, hoping to have his message understood abroad—just as Shostakovich did in his music, which is filled with wordless hints and allusions. Only in *Testimony* does Shostakovich finally say in words what had remained obscure and puzzling in his music; and he explains that decision in several striking passages of the book.

Again and again, throughout the symphonies, Shostakovich symbolized the regime of which he was supposedly a supporter and exponent. The scherzo of the *Tenth Symphony*, for instance, is "a musical portrait of Stalin, roughly speaking". The composer said that he wrote it right after the dictator's death, "and no one has yet guessed what the symphony is about". It took him some time to discover that only when he combined music with words it became harder to misinterpret his intent, and there were many times when that intent could not be made explicit.

We have long wondered whether or not the obituaries were right; Volkov quotes them with sorrow: "One of the greatest twentieth-century composers and a committed believer in Communism and Soviet power" (London *Times*); "A committed Communist who accepted sometimes harsh ideological criticism" (*The New York Times*). It is clear from this astonishing and unsettling book in Shostakovich's own words, brutally frank and deeply painful, that from the grave he calls out his status as a *refusenik*, a man who—had he not been so shy, awkward, and ridden with health problems—might well have joined Pasternak, Solzhenitsyn, and Rostropovich in disgrace and exile. And what now? Will his music be banned in his own country, or at least re-examined for subversive implications?

An Addendum (APRIL 1981)

IN APRIL OF 1980, the program featured a long essay on the controversy swirling about *Testimony, the Memoirs of Dmitri Shostakovich, as related to and edited by Solomon Volkov*. I believed this book to be essentially authentic. That the composer's son, Maxim, "according to Soviet sources", regarded the book to be "a slanderous fabrication", was easily enough explained in the article; what other choice did the family have, under the circumstances? "The shameful trade of self-abasement for professional survival begins all over again," said the essay; "it may be just a question of time before we have one or more defectors to tell us what was demanded of them." On April 11, 1981, Maxim Shostakovich, the conductor, and the composer's grandson Dmitri, the pianist, defected and sought asylum in the United States. The statements by these artists in Washington, last week, speak for themselves. There is now little doubt that the veracity of the Shostakovich-Volkov collaboration will be convincingly confirmed.

An Addendum (DECEMBER 1984)

RARELY IN RECENT YEARS has a musical composition stimulated so much thought and ongoing discussion as did the *Tenth Symphony* of Dmitri Shostakovich, performed here under Simon Rattle's direction. There were three performances in Severance Hall, one at Wooster College, and one at Oberlin College. Dr. S. Frederick Starr, president of Oberlin College, gave a sweeping historical panorama of Soviet cultural and political issues, stressing Shostakovich's increasing failure to adapt himself to the requirements of "Socialist Realism" with serious results to his own moral stand and veracity. Starr emphasized that in music Shostakovich remained honest and even combative, while hiding his messages in a variety of musical codes. Now that his memoirs have been published, the code has been broken; yet Dr. Starr feels that ultimately the symphony must be judged as a work of art, not as an ideological (or "anti-ideological") tract.

Harold Ticktin referred to the Russian literary tradition of the "Aesopian fable", in which subversive thoughts may be ironically implied without being stated outright. He commented that in the Soviet Union there are three categories of artistic expression: the available, the forbidden, and the inconvenient; and he proposed a possible scenario for the future of Shostakovich's art. Now that the party knows what the composer's real feelings were, he might in time join Boris Pasternak and others in the "inconvenient" category and be increasingly ignored in his own country.

In the program notes as well as the lectures, it was pointed out how many hidden messages were to be found in the *Tenth Symphony* of 1953, the year of Stalin's death. Among these, of course, is the insistent use of the composer's own initials to symbolize his regained identity as an individual. Of course, the notes in question take on in time a life of their own, becoming musical patterns with autonomous functions; yet their implications are inescapable, and one can hardly hear the symphony any more without being reminded again and again of matters that have nothing to do with "music as such", with abstract and purely aesthetic sounds and forms. Shostakovich believed (and often said) that there could be no music without ideology, and in this symphony he seemed to demonstrate Gustav Mahler's famous statement that "the most important part of music is not in the notes".

That Shostakovich admired and loved Mahler's music and was much influenced by it has long been known; for a Special Student Association program by The Cleveland Orchestra on September 30, 1974, Lorin Maazel wrote a script entitled "Shostakovich:

President of the Mahler Society", and led excerpts from Mahler's *Fifth Symphony* juxta-posed with excerpts from Shostakovich's *Tenth* conducted by James Judd. Upon repeated listening and further reflection on the *Tenth Symphony* this year, another striking connec-tion to the music of Mahler was discovered. Something about the first phrase of the long clarinet solo melody, soon after the introductory measures, sounded strangely familiar:

In Mahler's *Second Symphony*, known as the *Resurrection*, the great fourth move-ment contralto solo, the *Urlicht* or "Primal Light", begins with an invocation: "O Röschen rot!" ("O little red rose!"), and continues:

The words, in translation, are these: "Man lies in direst need! Man lies in greatest pain!" Mahler designates the music as "solemnly but simply"; Shostakovich indicates "Semplice". In the course of the first movement, the phrase recurs numerous times, repeated exactly or in various transformations; it is heard at climactic points as well—pathetically—in the strings just before the close.

If it is true, as Shostakovich is reported to have said to more than one astonished friend or acquaintance, that this symphony symbolizes the Stalin years—with the brutal, frenetic second movement a virtual portrait of the late dictator, and the first movement a lament or threnody—then it cannot have been a mere coincidence that these themes so resemble each other, and that the text of Mahler's song is so strikingly appropriate to Shostakovich's intent. Here again we may have a coded message, and Shostakovich—gleeful until his death that "no one has yet guessed what the symphony was about" (except for those whom he chose to let in on the secret) once more had made a subtle symbolic point of poignancy and deep significance. But is it possible that in the extensive public discussions and symposia about this work, held not long after the premiere, no Soviet musical expert discovered that meaningful "Mahler quote"?

Certainly, our erstwhile "music appreciation" division of music into "absolute" and "programmatic" has long since become an irrelevancy. All music, to a certain extent and in a profound sense, is autobiography; whether or not the symbols are explicit, the artist's inner life is expressed in the sounding forms. This is as true of a Bach fugue as it is of a Strauss tone poem; yet one must remember that musical meaning is not the same as verbal meaning. It is when the two sets of meaning are combined, as in a work with a text, that the "concrete" experiences of human beings are more overtly symbolized; but when there is an unspoken or unsung text, as in the *Tenth Symphony* of Shostakovich, we may respond to the work on a variety of levels and hear it also as part of living history. As Dr. J. Bronowski wrote in *The Ascent of Man*, "History is not events but people; but it is not just people remembering, it is people acting and living their past in the present."

Reflections on Immortality in Art
(NOVEMBER 1980)

*

"Life is short, art is long."
—Quintius Flaccus Horatius

"The main function of the artist . . . is to preserve the
history of mankind as if it were in a time capsule."
—Leonard Bernstein

*

TO THE BEST of our scientific knowledge, the earth is some four-and-a-half billion years old. Four-and-a-half billion! We find it difficult enough to conceptualize one hundred thousand years, or even ten thousand. But four billion is four thousand million years, a figure quite beyond our grasp.

It is likely that even the manlike stages before *Homo sapiens* made tools and vessels that were not only useful but attractive. It is probable that with the growth of the brain there arose an instinctive need to make images of what was observed or "imagined". That some of the higher apes "paint" and "draw" when given the materials is well known; but that may be a motor function of no particular artistic intent. The first actual art we possess is from the caves of Lascaux and Altamira, some twenty thousand years ago. Scientists believe that those astonishing representations of hunters and their prey had ritual and educational functions in preparing young men to face the "real thing" in the wild. Nevertheless, they are art, and admirable in their power of communicating images, actions, and ideas. Whether they were meant also to be "beautiful", to satisfy an aesthetic sense, we have no way of telling. Perhaps "form followed function" in that a practical purpose found shapes that pleased for their own sake. Closed and hidden, those cave paintings acquired a sense of permanency as well.

Permanency! Twenty thousand years, in the context of four billion, is a vanishingly small fraction. When we now consider the next oldest purposeful art we possess, from the long-lost civilizations of Egypt, Sumeria, Mesopotamia, Palestine, China, and Greece, we come yet closer to our own time, perhaps five to ten thousand years ago, and the fractional proportion diminishes further.

We are told that within four or five billion years, the sun will expand and heat up beyond imaginable degrees, and the planetary system will be incinerated. Nothing we know, see, or feel will be able to withstand that ultimate catastrophe. One moment, please: it is not the ultimate; for the universe itself, whether closed, open, oscillating, or whatever, is bound either to grow cold or re-form itself for another "big bang". In any event, there is an end, and what the new beginning is to be can be at best a vague hypothesis.

What is certain, however, is that sooner or later "all must pass". The works of man, like the works of nature itself, will either die or be altered in ways we cannot really conceive. As galaxies collide, taking with them uncounted possible civilizations, so will our tiny part of the universe be transformed—and perhaps, "in the twinkling of an eye".

But when we consider that twenty thousand years is to us an amazingly long time, we can see that a survival "grace period" of several billion more is an enormous time span, and so-to-speak "nothing to worry about". Humankind simply cannot afford to fret about such eventualities, however certain; it ought to be more concerned with the short-time prospect of incinerating or poisoning itself. Stupidity, arrogance, and greed will then have vanquished this creature's constructive and creative qualities; a Pyrrhic victory indeed. Having discovered the means of duplicating some of the nuclear processes of nature itself, humanity utilizes that Faustian knowledge at its own peril. We may not need to wait a billion or even a few million years to see all we know and cherish destroyed or irreversibly damaged. We can imagine nature saying to us, at that time, "What's your hurry? If you wish to die of heat or radiation, be patient a while. It is your fate, in any case."

*

Let us assume that humankind will somehow muster the wisdom not to commit nuclear suicide, and to "let nature take its course". Perhaps the earth as we know it will survive another twenty thousand years before man's conceit brings it down, or perhaps millions or billions of years will pass before life will change beyond our contemporary recognition. What then of art? We have no choice but to see history in the light of these extremely brief fractions of the total life of the universe. To us, twenty thousand years is very long; one thousand years is very old, and so is two hundred and fifty. When we stand before a thirteenth-century cathedral, those seven hundred years since its construction seem like a very long time, and we cannot be blamed for forgetting how relatively brief it really is. But our entire knowledge of history is conditioned by those remnants of civilizations and eras of the past. It is not the battles that are vivid to us today, not the inconceivable suffering undergone by those who were in the path of Alexander the Great, Genghis Khan, or the Crusaders. All we have today are the written or transmitted stories of those days, that is to say their literature, and the images they left us, in pictures, stones, metals, costumes, and buildings. The music is younger still, hardly more than fifteen hundred years; we know almost nothing of the music of the ancients beyond some inconclusive fragments. Not until the early Middle Ages did anything like decipherable notation evolve. But from then on, and especially from about the year 1000 A.D., examples multiply, and a "literature" of music becomes a part of our cultural property and heritage.

"Great periods of history," said the architect Edward Durell Stone, "are great only because of the art they produce." Can one go that far? The Phoenicians, after all, developed navigation; the Babylonians, law; the Arabs, mathematics; the Romans, law as well as warfare, aqueducts as well as governments. But what now belongs to us most vitally is that part of a nation's work which is expressed in figures, letters, sounds. So-called barbarian races, long extinct—such as the Scythians and the Etrurians or Etruscans—are alive for us today because of the extraordinary works of art they left. And Ancient Greece! The very name means art—literature, temples, statues, pottery, designs. And also *mores*, customs, philosophy. But most important, the concept of the "classic". Greece "changed the world."

Corroboration for Mr. Stone's dictum comes from a surprising source. "In the long history of man, countless empires and nations have come and gone. Those who created no lasting works of art are reduced today to short footnotes in history's catalogue." The author, at least the man who spoke those words? President Lyndon B. Johnson, in dedicating the National Endowment for the Arts some fifteen years ago. "Art," Mr. Johnson continued, "is the nation's most precious heritage. For it is in our works of art that we reveal to ourselves, and to others, the inner vision that guides us as a nation. And where there is no vision, the people perish."

The technology, production, and material possessions of any era are of course essential to its survival. Even Michelangelo required the services of the butcher, the baker, and the candlestick-maker; but we cannot imagine our existence without *his*. The Napoleonic era was a "great" one in the changing fortunes of history, and the Napoleonic code of laws is valuable still, long after the devastation wrought by his military career has been replaced by later examples of that "ambition that o'erleaps itself". But to us, is not Beethoven's *Eroica Symphony* a more lasting part of that heritage? Virgil said, "Let others mold the breathing stone, plead causes and tell the motions of the stars. Your task, O Romans, shall be to govern nations, to spare the conquered, and defeat the proud." Yet, as a recent writer put it, "Rome fell; the Pantheon stands." It is exactly the stone and the bronze that still breathe, and Virgil's poetry, and Ovid's. The late Loren Eiseley has spoken of "the weary disillusionment of the archeologist as he stands amidst the toppled columns that housed the gods of other years." Toppled or standing, the columns are there. It is the columns, in stone, in letters, and in sounds, that bear lasting witness to man's creative urge.

> *Tout passe. L'art robuste*
> *Seul a l'éternité,*
> *Le buste*
> *Survit à la cité.*
> —Théophile Gautier
> (1811–1872)

> *All passes. Art alone*
> *Enduring stays to us;*
> *The bust outlasts the throne,*
> *The coin, Tiberius.*
> Version by Henry Austin Dobson
> (1840–1921)

We set much store by the concept of lastingness. Leonardo da Vinci's *Last Supper* in Milan is fading, perhaps irreparably. No matter; it has been reproduced so well that it is "owned" by millions, even if the original were to disappear. The autograph scores of many Mozart and Haydn symphonies are lost; but if we have contemporary copies, we know the music; it is ours. A hundred years is long in the light of the Biblical three-score and ten; but that most of J.S. Bach's music was forgotten for nearly a hundred years after his death is but a moment in history itself. One may hope, with some justification, that almost everything of artistic value created in the last thousand years has been found and documented, or will be. We rediscover as much as we discover, and our image of cultural history is fluid, changing, and constantly renewed. In music, the invention of the phonograph has been epochal; the idea that it is possible to put on turntable or tape machine a composition—let us say—from the mid-fifteenth century, and have it speak to us directly, is staggering. No age before ours has enjoyed so panoramic—and instantly accessible—an overview of the existing art of sound.

The artist does not know whether or not his work is destined for what we so blithely call "immortality". He cannot delude himself that what he creates will endure for that space of time we call "forever". In fact, he knows that only about five percent of any art that has been made stands a chance of entering the living repertoire, be it in museums, the stage, or the concert hall. No matter; he must create, must contribute his share to the enormous treasury. He knows that there are few mountains, and many foothills. To reach the heights, the ground must gradually rise. The lesser artist takes part in building that landscape, tills that kind of fertile soil from which the great trees and miraculous flowers may spring. That must be enough reward for him. "Talent does what it can; genius does what it must."

History has found the artist not a frill, not an ornament, not a luxury; he is an absolute necessity to meaningful life and human survival itself. Without the artist, and the art he makes, a people dies of a disease we might call aesthetic attrition. The German poet Friedrich Schiller wrote, in an ode to the Muse: "What I would be without you, I know not; but I shudder when I see what without you hundreds and thousands are." Today, we could speak of billions so afflicted.

A "folk-rock" song by Bob Dylan had this text: "I would not want to be bach, mozart, tolstoy, joe hill, gertrude stein, or james dean. They're all dead." We may not be sure about Joe Hill and James Dean (as we are not about Elvis Presley), and there may be argument about Gertrude Stein. But Bach, Mozart and Tolstoy are tangibly alive today; the light they throw is bright. Like certain stars that are so far away that we cannot be sure they still exist physically, they still provide a light on the way to earth; to us, they are not dead. And is not the current Saturn exploration the most astonishing illumination and extension of our vision, "science as art"? Our space scientists, moreover, are surely among the most brilliant of "interpretive artists".

*

Finding a reason for public support of the arts, Roger L. Stevens said, in the 1960s, "In two hundred years nobody will care about our television sets. Art is the only permanent thing that comes out of a civilization, and we must stop shortchanging it in this country." Permanent? Yes, however relative the term in the light of the earth's existence, past and future. We see and experience the sense of history only in a context relative to the length of our own lives, and a few hundred years are indeed an example of permanency. Antal Dorati recently quoted the Italian composer Goffredo Petrassi: "Anyone who has succeeded in composing one lovely bar has not lived in vain." That sense of sharing, however modestly, in the vast pageant of art over the millenia, must be a sufficient reassurance of immortality. And sharing, also, in the miracle of continuous creation. Something is made where there was nothing before. The images thus made by human beings reflect, not so much objects and subjects, but the mysterious and awesome processes of life itself.

Addenda (NOVEMBER 1980)

ART IS NOT ONLY an adventure and an exploration: it is an act of faith. A start has now been made in the direction suggested by Dr. Lewis Thomas in the quote below. The gold record traveling with Voyager I is reported to contain some music by Bach and Mozart. It is a fine symbolic gesture; let's hope "they" have a diamond stylus.

"Let us assume that there is, indeed, sentient life in one or another part of remote space, and that we will be successful in getting in touch with it. What on earth are we going to talk about? . . . Perhaps the safest thing to do at the outset, if technology permits, is to send music. This language may be the best we have for explaining what we are like to others in space, with least ambiguity. I would vote for Bach, all of Bach, streamed out into space, over and over again. We would be bragging, of course, but it is surely excusable for us to put the best possible face on at the beginning of such an acquaintance. We can tell the harder truths later. . . . Whatever we offer as today's items of liveliest interest are bound to be out of date and irrelevant, maybe even ridiculous. I think we should stick to music."

—Dr. Lewis Thomas
In his book, *Lives of a Cell—Notes of a Biology Watcher*

ART IS NOT ONLY an expression of the artist, but a communication between people. The artwork "speaks" to others—either directly, as in a picture, book, sculpture or building, or through a middleman, as in music and the theater. Over the centuries and millenia, it continues to make contact with those ready to see, to listen, to think, and to feel. Once made ("created" is sometimes too pretentious a word), it becomes a living entity that can be ignored, damaged, misinterpreted; but it cannot be destroyed as a concept.

Art as an "act of faith"? This can be—but need not be—taken in a religious sense. It means, rather, that the artist believes his work to be of value, and perhaps of lasting value. He or she fashions an object or a subject in the conviction that it has something to say, to communicate. The artwork symbolizes not only another object or subject, or an idea, but the process of life itself. Its coming-about becomes a part of that "continuous creation" and "re-creation" which we see about us in nature, expressing that optimistic "willing and working" of which Albert Schweitzer spoke, however pessimistic may be the artist's empirical view of the world.

The artist knows, perhaps more keenly than most, how narrow and dangerous is the dividing line between pessimism and hopelessness, between skepticism and cynicism. To recognize the difference, even if only subconsciously, is of crucial importance to his creative drive.

Isamu Noguchi remarked on the lasting qualities of stone, the immensely long "life" of rocks. That characteristic of endurance, he said, was especially attractive to the sculptor, who—like every artist—wants his work to last.

Carl Sagan has spoken of man's urge to explore as instinctive. So has Jacob Bronowski. And so has Aristotle: "Man by his nature desires to know." Norman Cousins has said that we explore the universe not because our technology makes it possible, but because our imagination makes it necessary.

The gold record traveling with Voyager I contains not only music, but messages in many languages; most touching are the words spoken from "the Children of Planet Earth". What the record contains is a set of images that may show other civilizations what is the best of us. At the conclusion of a stunning *Nova* program, the narrator ended by saying that the Voyager will travel through space for a billion years after it leaves the solar system. And "long after no more music is heard on earth, long after no more records are being played, there will be a record of who we were."

And now, as we explore "The Invisible Universe" (again a *Nova* program on the amazing *Iras* satellite) and probe the almost unimaginable vastness of space, we are forced again to see the works of art on our planet as "our marks", as small as atoms or their even smaller constituents, but as crucially important to the entire structure. The more we consider these efforts in the light of cosmological science, we may take the art work as a never-ending battle against entropy, as an attempt to make order against encroaching disorder. For the time being—in the truest sense of the word—art wins. Until such time as our universe comes to an end, art will give light in chaos, speak for the best we have to offer.

The scientist, however (even if he is, as in this case, an ardent music lover), may take a somewhat different view of what can make "a work of art". In his great book (and TV series), *The Ascent of Man,* the late J. Bronowski remarks that the discovery of atomic structure at the turn of the century was "the intellectual breakthrough with which modern physics begins. Here the great age opens. Physics becomes in those years the greatest collective work of science—no, more than that, the great collective work of art of the twentieth century. I say 'work of art', because the notion that there is an underlying structure, a world within the world of the atom, captured the imagination of artists at once. . . . Modern art begins at the same time as modern physics because it begins in the same ideas."

Dr. Bronowski, toward the end of his chapter "World Within World" emphasizes the concept even more forcefully: "Immortality and mortality is the contrast on which I end this essay. Physics in the twentieth century is an immortal work. The human imagination working communally has produced no monuments to equal it, not the pyramids, not the *Iliad,* not the ballads, not the cathedrals. The men who made these conceptions [in physics] one after another are the pioneering heroes of our age. . . ."

In 1923, Pablo Picasso wrote: "To me, there is no past or future in art. If a work of art cannot live always in the present, it must not be considered at all. The art of the Greeks, of the Egyptians, of the great painters who lived in other times, is not an art of the past; perhaps it is more alive today than it ever was."

Thoughts on the Creative Spirit in Music and Art
(NOVEMBER 1979)

"We are not trying to break anything. We are trying to make what does not yet exist."
—Carlos Chávez

"Exactly herein lies the achievement of genius, that in the finished work there shall nowhere be perceptible the torment and sweat of the creative process. The final result still possesses for the hearer the dewy freshness of first inspiration. Haydn, who clung to nature and all earthly things more fervently than almost any other composer, succeeded in reflecting here the youthful purity of the first day of its own creation, and so produced a work the influence of which endures unbroken through the centuries."
—Karl Geiringer
(in the closing paragraph of the annotation
for the first long-playing recording of Haydn's
The Creation, The Haydn Society, Inc., 1949)

NO ASPECT OF THE ARTS is so fascinating, and ultimately so mysterious, as the creative process. To make something out of nothing, to produce an entity where there was none before, is that ability which most closely relates the human being to the divine.

When we see a tree, a flower, a bird, an ocean, we have little hesitation in discussing the aesthetics of those created or evolved entities; we can observe them, classify them, describe them, evaluate them. But when we try to move from the *what* and the *how* to the *why*, we are caught up short in our own lack of comprehension. Why is it that these things exist? In due course, we arrive at the simple and at the same time overwhelming conclusion that they exist because they were not there before, and had to be made. "And God saw that it was good"; there you have the first recorded instance of criticism. To ask of an artist *why* he made a thing is to inquire of him or her the very thing we are unable to glean from the story of creation itself.

Let's look, for a moment, at words. To call the creative spirit, or God, if you will, "the maker of heaven and earth", has always struck me a little as if we were talking about the maker of such-and-such a product, be it an automobile or a brand of soap. But there is nothing intrinsically inferior about "making" things; once we are not dealing with more or less mechanical substances that must merely be reshaped into this-or-that object, like cars or soaps, an artwork is indeed "made" out of a mysterious substance. The artist utilizes for his process two things: first a "gift" to make things (and "gift" means that he is "given" something, whether it is to a talent or to a genius); and second, "imagination", the ability to shape an "image", either from a model as in all forms of representation, however abstract, or from an inner conception that may have no conscious parallel in nature (until much later we may discover one, as in microphotography or aerial mapping).

To *shape* an image? *Shaping* is perhaps a finer word than *making*. For as Susanne Langer has written, the artist's duty is not primarily to express himself, but to find for his conception a "significant form". Interestingly, in the German language, the word for creator is not the equivalent of maker; the word *Macher* means, unfortunately, busybody. The correct word is *Schöpfer*, which means *shaper*, but also comes from the word *schöpfen* which has to do with dipping one's hands into a substance hitherto formless, whether it be water, or oil, or clay, and to make it useful or beautiful, or both.

The universe is orderly, if on a scale beyond our feeble grasp. The artwork, too, strives for order, for logic, for completeness; even Haydn, calling the overture to *The Creation* "Representation of Chaos", knew at once that he could not do so by writing chaotic music. He could be bold harmonically, could suggest through free modulation the strangeness of the primal world, could thereafter symbolize the "void" by open octaves; but he had to make a shape that is the very opposite of chaos, a convincing, rounded form that speaks more for the shaping power of the Creator than for the shapeless substance at his disposal. To represent "chaos", therefore, in musical terms, becomes for the artist a contradiction in terms, and Haydn was not ready to tell his performers to play whatever came to their minds, or even to countenance a texture arrived at by "controlled chance".

No term is more misunderstood by the non-artist than *inspiration*. To inspire means to endow with breath, and thereby with life. Inspiration, physically, means breathing-in; expiration means that something has ended, and to expire, quite graphically, means not only breathing-out but to breathe one's last. What is little comprehended, however, is that artistic inspiration is not always a directly received idea, an *Einfall* (the German term for something that "falls in" to the artist's lap or consciousness), but also implies work. Many a musical inspiration, as we now hear it, is really the result of much effort over an original shape that was rudimentary, insignificant, and essentially "formless" or "shape-less". But was this not so, "from the beginning"? As we learn from Genesis, even the Omnipotent, the all-powerful, had to rest on the seventh day. For the first six, He had not only created, but He had worked. To labor and to bring forth a mountain is a noble thing, but to bring forth a mouse, in the history of creative evolution, is even more astonishing.

Whether the stimulus to make something comes from an inner or an outer need or experience (or both), the artist is required to work on the basis of the inspiration, the gift, the concept, the vision; he or she must shape the formless into the formed, the in-significant into the significant, the vague into the specific. He or she may ascribe the original gift or concept to the divine; but from then on, the responsibility for completion rests on the individual. How that is done, we can trace. Through his remarkable sketch-books, we can follow an idea of Beethoven's from its early stages to the final version; we are certain that even Mozart and Schubert, who worked quickly and rarely sketched, accomplished their labor in their heads and were usually able to put on paper the nearly completed object, in need only of ultimate polishing and refining. Yet in Schubert's case, we know that many an "inspiration" of his owes its final shape to a last-moment discovery, one that had not occurred to him until the product was virtually complete, and one that transforms the artwork from acceptability to sublimity. It is possible to follow the process: to think along with the composer as he works, to see the painter's brush strokes, to find the sculptor's hand and chisel marks on the statue, to compare the versions of a poem as it grew (Dylan Thomas, that most spontaneous-appearing of poets, is said to have made some two hundred versions of his "Fern Hill"). But there always comes a point where our ability to explain, to account for an artistic decision, runs up against the proverbial stone wall, and we are faced with mysteries as ultimate as those of creation itself.

Composers, painters, sculptors, poets (and of course scientists who deal with abstrac-tions and concepts), have left us countless documents discussing their methods of work. These have been collected in books and documentaries, and possess a remarkable unanim-ity of approach despite all outward differences. Just as evolution proves to us a profound *evaluation* of what may best survive, of what changes must occur in the shape and function of organisms for long-term growth, thus the individual artwork undergoes similar devel-opment to become hardy enough for survival. Art styles, in their adaptability and unity-in-variety (like the numerous species of birds), show us a similar inner wisdom which leads some to professed religion, others to amazed humility and awe before the ultimate myster-ies of creation. The work of art which we call great (a designation that should be used with care and economy) is without question a reflection on a human level of the inconceivable power and beauty and significance of natural creation.

Let's Have an Understanding, Symphonically Speaking!
(JANUARY 1986)

*

This essay was originally written for Stagebill *magazine, and is here reprinted with its kind permission.*

*

HARDLY A WEEK passes that someone is not overheard to say, after a concert in which a comparatively new piece is performed, "Well, I didn't understand that at all." It would be easy enough to reply, "There is no reason why you should, since the piece was complex and new to you. Had you lived in New York in 1884, would you have 'understood' Brahms's *Third Symphony* at its United States premiere? The critics certainly didn't."

But then, one might continue, how well did audiences and critics of 1884 understand a much older piece, Beethoven's *Ninth*? Were people really ready at that time to "speak Beethoven", to know his language so well that even his most complex and challenging works were fully received and absorbed? Did not Bizet complain that in Paris fifty years after Beethoven's Ninth was first performed, listeners still "understood nothing", and applauded only because it was fashionable? Was even that composition still "new" or "modern" to most, far from an accepted classic?

Where a work of musical art is concerned, "understanding" is not an unchanging condition but a process. There are certain stages or levels of reaction to a musical experience, and they do not necessarily occur simultaneously or at once. The first, perhaps, is an aesthetic one: Does the musical style or language appeal to me, or does it not? Second, what is my emotional response? Do I or do I not derive a set of feelings from the music that is positive? Third, does the work reach me in a communicative way—does it, in short, say something to me? Can I, should I, verbalize to some extent what it does say? More importantly, do I respond to the music as a progression of "events in sound"?

Fourth, is it possible for me to follow the musical discourse without getting lost or confused? And if the latter, whose fault is it—mine or the composer's? Is my listening an activity or merely a "passivity"? Am I concentrating and participating, physically as well as mentally? Fifth, assuming that the composer has made some verbal comments about his work and I have taken the time and trouble to acquaint myself with them before (or sometimes in the course of) the performance, can I then comprehend "what he had in mind" and make the appropriate associations? What is the historical and social context of the piece? How well is its intent realized? If texts for a choral-orchestral piece are provided in the program, why not follow them? The lights will be up! Does the structure work? How are the themes related and contrasted and elaborated? How is something that happens in the finale conditioned by something that happened in the first movement?

Now it is obvious that from stage four on, a considerable degree of musical sophistication is called for. Are these later stages necessary to "understanding"? One would have to answer, yes; but that does not mean that without them enjoyment is impossible or even, in its way, incomplete. An artwork can be enjoyed, and intensely so, on the three basic levels; assuming the presence of musicality as such, quite without technical or professional preparation, listeners can derive keen satisfaction from the nature of the "organized sound" alone. One can be an ardent music lover and "know nothing about it." This enjoyment is in itself a form of understanding, and perhaps—when all is said and done—the most important kind.

Countless opportunities are provided to us for getting to know what instruments and voices can do, and to become familiar with a wide repertoire. Books on music, on composers, and on the existing literature, are counted in the hundreds and thousands, and the genuinely interested music lover has everything at his or her disposal to build or enhance a musical education. In this city, weekly broadcasts over WCLV of at least five major orchestras are in themselves a gift of "free concerts", extraordinary when compared to what was available on the air even twenty-five years ago.

If the conditions are right and the receptive listener is willing and able to go beyond the first three stages of contact with the work, it will soon be realized that the later ones take time and a certain amount of effort. Everyone, of whatever degree of musical sophistication, has to work at the process of understanding—and pleasurable work it can be. The more complex and demanding a composition, the longer the process takes beyond the first hearing. And if the work is of exceptional stature and richness of content, the process can never be really complete. We may find, for instance, that after five decades of listening to Beethoven's *Ninth Symphony*, there is still more to discover and to learn, and each different performance will provide us with new insights. We may discover a counter-line here, a sonority there, a phrasing that subtly alters the meaning of a shape, a new rhythmic emphasis, an unexpected treatment of a tempo—and sometimes, the entire approach to a section or a whole movement.

Of course it can be useful to have heard other performances of the same work, and over the course of time to establish for oneself a kind of "ideal version" against which to measure the present one. Yet one must remain open to the possibility of differing approaches and of new and valuable revelations. Every individual performance by a significant artist will provide such new insights. In the arts, comparisons are not odious but exceptionally instructive and illuminating.

One does not need to be a professional musician to hear and comprehend the structural aspects of a composition. One must merely be "musical", and totally attentive. Just as in the theater, certain things that occur in Act III only make full sense if one has paid attention in Act I; musical "following" works similarly. Robert Shaw once said that what is primarily required from a good listener is the ability to remember and the ability to anticipate. If one cannot remember (after considerable listening to the same work) what has been said, then there is no way to anticipate what may happen to the material, and (with the exception of sudden loud chords or other such obvious events) there is no likelihood of being surprised. Haydn's music, for one, depends greatly on this method of the "inevitable unexpected", in Donald Francis Tovey's phrase.

*

Unless the musical work is a poor one, or so obvious in its material (however attractive) that a second hearing tells one little more than did the first, familiarity does not breed contempt but greater awareness and deeper knowledge. The opportunities for rehearing are almost always available—whether in a second performance, a broadcast, or a recording. If a piece is fundamentally appealing or in the true sense "interesting" to a first-time hearer, then it may be lived with, re-examined, and even studied—on whatever level of technical competence that can be mustered. When one meets a person, one does not really know him or her: one has made an acquaintance. Only repeated contact can reveal or determine whether the relationship can ripen into friendship or even into love. With a new piece whose premiere may also be its derniere, that kind of continuing relationship may be hard to achieve; all will then depend on getting the utmost out of a single hearing. This is a problem not easily solved.

So what about "new" music? The immediate counter-question is, new to whom? It is now 1986, and Stravinsky's *Rite of Spring* is more than seventy years old. To large numbers of hearers, it is still "new", and even "modern". The word *contemporary* surely makes no sense in this context. The proverbial forty-year lag has long since been passed, but unless there is some awareness how music changed at the beginning of this century, and why it had to do so, the *Rite* may still be shocking to some. The famous riot attending the world premiere in 1913 was caused not so much by the music but by extra-musical and social circumstances; very soon, the stature of the work became evident, and we have been learning it ever since, with amazement, admiration, and—quite often—affection. Beethoven's *Eroica Symphony* took decades to be accepted and assimilated, after its early and apparently dreadful performances.

The more adventurous and pathbreaking a composition, the longer it takes for it to find its place in the repertoire and in the esteem of general audiences. Was it not said by some, a century ago, that "Wagner's music is not so bad as it sounds"? When "new" music has become "classic", then is the time to get to know it even better. Perhaps Stravinsky overestimated even the professional's capabilities when he made the following statement in 1960, but the issue is clear: "When I compose something I cannot conceive that it should fail to be recognized for what it is, and understood. I use the language of music, and my grammar will be clear to the musician who has followed music up to where my contemporaries and I have brought it." A "good listener" is also a musician, albeit a receiving rather than an executant one; and such a listener's active interest is taken for granted by every composer.

The criteria of "good listening" that must be brought to new music (new in any sense of the word) are the same as those for any music, and the "stages" of understanding also are no different. To "tune out" at the first sign of difficulty means that contact will be lost, and potential communication breaks down. No one, of course, is forced to like everything; but there is the honorable obligation to listen, and to listen knowledgeably. The composer has made an honest effort; no less should be expected from the person to whom he is speaking and with whom he hopes to communicate.

One of the problems with a listener's relationship to "new" music is that the "language" or "idiom" in which it is written may be unfamiliar. If it is true that music is a form of communication akin to language, with its own autonomous rules and principles, then it becomes necessary to learn that language over a period of time; but the sheer sensuous appeal (as in hearing an unfamiliar foreign language well spoken) can provide the first stage of contact. That in our era of "instant communication" across the globe we are forced to learn new musical languages more quickly than in the past—that there is in fact no longer a "common language" (as Mozart and Haydn, and even Brahms and Wagner, spoke it)—adds to the challenge. But music, essentially, is still "organized sound in motion"; and it is our pleasurable task to respond to the sound, discover its organization, and follow its motion through time—whatever the nature of the idiom employed.

*

Our society stipulates many of its actions and reactions on "immediate gratification", whether it is "instant breakfasts" or the granting of privileges to young people. The comprehension of art does not work that way. Understanding tends to be slow, demanding, and sometimes mysterious. K. C. Cole, in a superb article entitled "The Essence of Understanding" written for an issue of *Discover* magazine, reminds us that even scientists do not yet fully understand the theory of relativity, although they see it in action at every moment. She cites Isaac Newton's admission that the law of gravity, which he discovered and codified, remained in essence incomprehensible to him.

At the close of her article, Ms. Cole tells the story of Werner Heisenberg (author of the *Uncertainty Principle*) asking Niels Bohr in 1922 "how anyone could understand the atom, given the lack of an appropriate language or imagery." Bohr replied that "understanding the atom would first require a fresh look at what understanding really means." At that point, the author might well have quoted Bohr's beautiful phrase quoted by Jacob Bronowski in his *The Ascent of Man*: "When it comes to atoms, language is not describing facts but creating images."

"Understanding," writes Ms. Cole, "goes far beyond knowing, in that it requires a certain degree of acceptance. To say you 'understand' something implies a sympathetic point of view." How interesting that the German word *Verständnis* means not only "understanding" but "appreciation" and "sympathy"! Ms. Cole continues: "Indeed, what people understand to be self-evident and what they dismiss as absurd are often matters of faith. . . . . Quantitative understanding (like raw historical facts) is rarely satisfying. Knowing that gravity decreases by the inverse square of the distance is important; yet it tells you no more than knowing how many bricks it takes to build a cathedral tells you about the essence of Notre Dame."

It is the same in musical understanding. Beyond technical knowledge, acoustical facts, formal analysis, and even associative suggestion, we take certain things on faith; and this is most true of the greatest and richest compositions, whose mysteries are of an infinite depth, and whose qualities are not directly demonstrable by "scientific" description. True understanding also means to be able to stand in awe of a Beethoven *Ninth*, a Bach *B-minor Mass*, a Stravinsky *Sacre*—as we do when we stand below Michelangelo's Sistine Chapel ceiling. Stravinsky was not overstating the case when he said that he was "the vessel through which *Le Sacre* passed." And perhaps the French poet Paul Valéry was hardly exaggerating when he wrote, in 1938: "A work of art that does not strike us dumb is pretty poor stuff."

Words, explanations, analyses, criticism (in its best sense of elucidation)—all have their place; but there comes the moment when everything must yield to the sheer impact of the work of art on the receptive ear, mind, and heart. When that happens, and it may not happen at first or all at once, then we can speak of having "understood" more than through the glass darkly.

Second and Third Thoughts on "Understanding" Music (APRIL 1986)

AS IF "Let's Have an Understanding, Symphonically Speaking!" had not already been quite long enough, the author quickly found himself dissatisfied with it, and increasingly aware that a number of important issues had been slighted or even omitted.

There was no mention, for instance, of the ability to remember a piece of music so vividly that one can hear it (or at least major parts of it) long after the actual performance. Ideally, one should be able to "play" for oneself, in one's mind, a composition that belongs to the regular repertoire. When that can be done, the piece will have become a part of one's inner life—as we carry about a favorite poem or the image of a certain painting or sculpture. That kind of "mental performance" is surely a part of understanding, on an intimate and deep-going level.

Conductors, of course, can hear a score (or most of it) when they look at it, and their live rehearsal of it brings that inner image to sounding life. For a listener, it is not at all necessary to be able to read a score, or even musical notation, to conjure up sonorous images of well-known musical works.

When the essay discussed comparisons of various performances, it mentioned the process of measuring them against each other for their specific differences and qualities. But of course that process also makes possible an informed evaluation: how good was the performance, at least in relation to the "ideal version" that the experienced listener may have developed? This may be not only a subjective judgment, but an objective one, close to an assessment of actual facts. In our own different ways, we are all music critics; if we can evaluate everything in life, from automobiles to food, from clothes to spouses, the arts are equally if not more susceptible to value judgments.

The more we understand the issues of style, musical history, tradition, performance practice, and so on, the better we are prepared to account for the difference between a great conductor and a "merely" competent or very good one. What is it that makes a piano recital by X so extraordinary, while Y and Z provide a pleasurable but not a great experience? Why is it usually unprofitable to compare the greatest performers by way of a rating sheet, as if they were race horses a nose ahead of each other? Rather, can we tell what makes them different, and therefore interesting in the truest sense?

And if we fancy ourselves—as we should—capable of evaluating performances, what about the works themselves? As our knowledge of the literature expands and deepens, in the orchestral music of more than three centuries, we become more secure and well-grounded in our opinions of what makes a piece of music good or great, mediocre or poor, or whether there may be splendid moments in a piece for the most part weak, or weak moments in a piece for the most part splendid. What do we mean by such terms, and how could we defend our opinion beyond merely liking or disliking something? What are the reasons why we may like one Brahms piano concerto better than the other? How does a certain piece by Stravinsky "fit" into his total output of sixty years, discounting irrelevant comparisons with *The Firebird*? What is it that makes *this* new piece so appealing, and *that* one so appalling—at least to us? What are our criteria of evaluation, and how have we arrived at them?

*

True understanding has little to do with knowledge of musical terminology. Of course it is useful to be acquainted with basic terms like *allegro, pizzicato, coda*, etc., since there is not always time in a program to translate and explain them. These matters belong to fundamental musical literacy, and should be as much a part of an educated person's intellectual baggage as rudimentary math, science, psychology, spelling, and punctuation. But such familiarity with terms does not yet guarantee that one will recognize a subtle or even a striking modulation in the harmony, that one will be able to follow an important counter-line to the main melody, and that one can join the composer of classical works on the crucially important level of tonality. That is to say, should one not at least be able to *feel* that when Mozart gives us the main material of the *Jupiter Symphony's* first movement in the key of F, it is not yet the "true" recapitulation but a "false" or "deceptive" one, and that he does not really come "home" to the key of C until a minute later? This is not a matter for professional musicians only, nor is it necessary to have "perfect pitch"; but one does well to develop a *relative* sense of keys, of their colors, of their very nature. The so-called "sonata form" as a dramatic device makes full sense only when one has learned to follow the progression and effect of those devices, just as in a play one is asked to sense such subtle fluctuations of the action.

Ideally, at least, a listener's "head and heart", intellect and emotion, structural and aesthetic sensibility, work best when they are in balance and become virtually indivisible.

*

If the shape of a theme as the composer first presents it is not clear to us, and mentally remembered as such, how can we take note of—and delight in—the ways he varies it when it returns? Of course, pieces called "theme and variations" are based exactly on that kind of following, but every good composition will contain aspects of variation, different and often unexpected treatments of ideas stated before. This is as true of the music of Bach and Mozart as it is of every later master. When one comes to know a piece well after hearing many performances, many kinds of new discoveries become possible, many new relationships become apparent. How remarkable, for instance, is the counter-line by the bassoon to the "Ode to Joy" theme in Beethoven's *Ninth Symphony*, after its first and unadorned statement! It took at least one listener many decades of hearing the work before he discovered it—having up to then always paid attention only to the great tune itself. And is it not interesting, not merely a look into the composer's workshop, to recognize the jaunty march tune preceding the tenor solo in the *Ninth* as a variation of the "Ode to Joy" theme itself? One may have sensed subconsciously *that* it fits into the overall structure, but now one realizes *why* it fits. To stay with Beethoven, and a recent Severance Hall performance of the *Emperor Concerto*—what is the sleight-of-hand magic trick by which the composer leads us back to the home key of E-flat major for the finale, from the "distant" B major of the slow movement? Does it become any the less magical if we know how he does it? Music is a series of "events in sound", and to follow them actively and perceptively can only heighten and deepen the enjoyment.

*

We have been speaking here, of course, almost entirely of the orchestral concert—live, recorded, or broadcast. It is clear that there are many other kinds of music; the mother who sings her baby to sleep may be intensely musical, though she may not be a concertgoer at all. The craftsman or worker or businessman who plays an instrument "for fun" may have no desire to involve himself in the world of concert music or to question his relationship to its repertoire. Some members of a church choir may or may not be interested in music of other forms and types. All those activities are valuable and to be respected. In this essay, we have addressed primarily the regular patron of symphony concerts who wishes to examine more closely the nature of his or her response to that repertoire.

Yet even here there is no absolute standard, no compulsion, no "ought". When all is said and done—and it never can be, quite—we are all individual, different in our degree of musicality, education, likes and dislikes, state of mind at the time, needs for and demands on the arts, and even potential for growth. Ultimately, everyone will enjoy and understand a piece of music in his or her own way; and as long as there is an awareness that the horizons are vast and unlimited, that is as it should be.

An Addendum (FEBRUARY 1979)

IN AN ANNOTATION for Lutoslawski's *Concerto for Orchestra*, it was observed that "its varied materials are strikingly cohesive and interrelated." The extent of that interrelation was emphasized in repeated hearings by a fact that should have been included in the subsequent analytical outline: the theme of the third movement passacaglia is quite clearly foreshadowed by a passage in the first movement (pages 11 and 15ff of the score). This shows us once again that works of substance do not give up all their secrets at first hearing, and that complete "understanding" of a complex composition is a process that takes time and familiarity, and should not be expected at a first or even a second hearing.

"Those in Darkness . . ." (DECEMBER 1981)

What Karl Weigl and Ernst Lévy have in common is not so much a musical style, or an anniversary year of birth or death. Primarily, they are colleagues in a condition deserved by neither: comparative obscurity. What follows is not a set of conventional biographical sketches, but some observations on the strange and often cruel ways of musical history.

> *"There are those who are in darkness,*
> *and the others are in light.*
> *And you see the ones in brightness,*
> *Those in darkness drop from sight."*
>
> —Bertolt Brecht

KARL WEIGL assisted Gustav Mahler as an opera coach in Vienna; he later taught at the Vienna Conservatory and at the University of Vienna. In his city, he won many notable prizes and awards. In 1938, he immigrated to New York with his wife Vally, a pianist and herself an accomplished composer. After his death, in 1949, his chamber music and exceptionally beautiful songs continued to be performed, and in 1968 Leopold Stokowski conducted the fifth of his six symphonies with the American Symphony Orchestra in Carnegie Hall, to much acclaim. There exist five recordings of his music, and the Karl Weigl Memorial Fund at The Mannes College of Music in New York promotes the composer's work through its distinguished roster of members, which includes many devoted former pupils. Among those who have spoken and written warmly of Weigl's music are Richard Strauss, Bruno Walter, Gregor Piatigorsky, and George Szell—who conducted his *First Symphony* and *Piano Concerto* in the 1930s. His one hundredth anniversary in 1981 stimulated many performances in the United States and Europe.

The clue to Weigl's comparative obscurity is not difficult to find. It stands out vividly in remarks by Arnold Schoenberg and Pablo Casals. In 1931, Schoenberg wrote from Berlin: "I have always considered Dr. Weigl as one of the best composers of this older generation, one of those who continued the dignified Viennese Tradition. He truly preserved this old culture of a musical spirit which is one of the best parts of Viennese culture." Implicit in this statement is the observation that in order to make a stir in the world composers must do more than "continue a dignified tradition"; they must, like Schoenberg himself, shake things up. And in 1941, Pablo Casals wrote from New York: "Karl Weigl's music will not be lost; one will come back to it when the storm will have passed. . . . One will come back to all those who have written *real* music. . . ." It has been a long storm, and Casals's prophecy has not been fulfilled. To the great cellist, unfortunately, the music of Stravinsky, Bartók, Schoenberg, and others was not "real", and that we are now at least one musical generation beyond further dims his brave hope.

One *did* return to Mahler, it is true; but was he ever really lost? To be a Mahlerite, to write in Mahler's idiom without being him, is one of the causes of the problem. The lot of the epigone, the follower-disciple, is never enviable, however sincere and even beautiful the product. In musical history, the "minor masters" are of considerable importance; they are the foothills from which the mountains rise. But the foothills "on the other side", when one has descended from the mountains, are almost invariably regarded as of less importance than those which show the way to the summit. This, perhaps, is the problem of all those excellent and admirable creative musicians who are "in-betweeners", whose works are valuable and attractive but not pathbreaking, unlike the peaks in the mountain-chain of a great composer's output. But let us listen to music by Karl Weigl; there are many rewards to be found in its fine-grained and romantic measures.

*

The case of Ernst Lévy is more saddening still. For here was a man of such striking individuality that ignoring him was not easy. Born in Basel, he studied the piano with Huber and Petri, and in Paris with Pugno. Between 1941 and 1966 he lived in the United States, teaching at the New England Conservatory, Bennington College, the University of Chicago, the Massachusetts Institute of Technology, and Brooklyn College. He appeared as pianist with the Boston Symphony Orchestra, and the Chicago Symphony Orchestra played his Fifth and Twelfth Symphonies. This writer heard him in recital in Cambridge, Massachusetts, and after all these years recalls him as one of the greatest Beethoven pianists of the era. What he had to offer in illumination as well as transcendent virtuosity was hardly excelled by anyone. (Some recordings, on the Unicorn label of Boston, are extant.) Lévy was in addition a master carpenter and ardent alpinist, a superb chef, a mathematician and philosopher, and the author of such treatises as "On the Proportions of the South Tower of Chartres Cathedral" (M.I.T., 1956). With his friend Siegmund Levarie, he wrote *Tone: A Study in Musical Acoustics* (Kent State University Press, 1968). He died in 1981, at the age of 85.

Why did Lévy not become a lionized virtuoso? He refused to. The concert circuit was not for him. He would rather prepare incomparable steak and endive salad for his friends. Along with all this, he wrote fifteen symphonies, and a vast amount of chamber music and piano music. Having conducted the Philharmonic Choir in Paris many years before, he found conducting no longer necessary for himself. He did find composing necessary, and the lack of interest in his works by major conductors intensified his sense of the sardonic. His symphonies tended to be large; the thirteenth, a magnificent work, spans an hour. That too militated against them. Their style owed more to the Middle Ages than to the twentieth century; can one imagine a mixture of Perotinus and Bruckner? His music, often complex, often astonishingly simple, could also be witty and charming; his last work, *Sonata for Ten* (recorded by Dr. Levarie) is a portrait of the man in virtually all his facets. His musical idiom, both "modern" and timeless, was as eccentric as Janáček's, and perhaps as remarkable.

In 1966, Robert Shaw conducted several movements of Lévy's *Third Suite* in a special concert at the Temple on the Heights. We know of no other performances of his music in this area. There is not a single commercial recording (there is one of a piece by his son Frank, a cellist and composer)*.

One would like to be able to look back from—let's say—the twenty-third century, and see what light musical history will have to shed about Ernst Lévy—and about Karl Weigl.

*

And then there is the visionary Englishman Havergal Brian (1876–1972), with five operas and thirty-two symphonies (and not a single entry in the Schwann Catalogue); the Austro-American Frederick C. Schreiber (born 1895 and living in New York), with seven symphonies—not one of them recorded; the Frenchman Jean Barraqué (1928–1973), none of whose extraordinarily adventurous music is now available on records; the Russo-American Leo Ornstein (born 1892), once hailed as a major figure and almost totally ignored today); the immensely productive and influential Austro-American Ernst Křenek (born 1900), once a meteoric figure of twentieth-century music but now inexcusably neglected; the Hungaro-American Tibor Serly (1900–1978), an excellent composer but known to the world at large mainly as a disciple of Bartók and dedicated editor of his uncompleted

---

* Since this was written, a few recordings of Lévy's music have been issued, including the Fifteenth Symphony.

music; and so on ad infinitum. Composers, ultimately, write music not because they seek recognition, but because they must write music.

Even the greatest geniuses among composers may not be spared "darkness" toward the end of their lives. We know the stories of Mozart and Schubert. When Bartók died in 1945, he was to all intents and purposes a pauper, recognized by comparatively few, paid for his work by much fewer. Now, thirty-six years later, as we observe his hundredth anniversary, his estate—from royalties, recordings and publications—is counted in the millions of dollars. For him, it was too late; but is it not written that "their works shall follow after them"?

For some two hundred and fifty years, only organists, historians and lexicographers knew of the music of Johann Pachelbel (1653–1706). Isn't it delightful to realize that his "Canon" is probably the best known, the most widely arranged, and the most lucrative composition in classical music today? Hope springs eternal.

Spoken Epilogue to a Pre-Concert Talk (DECEMBER 1979)

PERHAPS it would not be inappropriate to reflect for a moment on an issue that may have troubled some of us.

As we begin to celebrate our holiday season, we may ask ourselves a fundamental question: What are we doing here? What right and justification have we, at a time when the world seems to be coming apart all around us, to enjoy a concert of music largely unrelated to what we tend to call the "real" world? Is it fair to call us "escapists" as well as "elitists"?

Many of us, I suppose, have had occasional twinges of conscience about such things, at least momentary "guilt feelings" about supporting an event and an institution that does not seem to contribute directly toward solving the world's problems of hunger, poverty, violence, terrorism, racism, extreme nationalism, war, and other such perennial and for the most part avoidable idiocies.

But is that fair? From the purely economic standpoint, we know that the continued existence and soundness of artistic institutions such as a great symphony orchestra are of vital importance; there are some one-hundred-and-fifty highly skilled people here whose living depends on the institution's survival, and the economy of the entire area would be adversely affected if it did not exist.

Beyond that, however, there may be an even more important point. The world around us, as we have said, is marked by disorder, disorganization, virtual chaos. Almost everything seems to be going wrong in one way or another, and in some areas the rules of conduct have broken down entirely. Now the work of art, both in creation and in performance, is in its essence the exact opposite: order, form, and sanity.

The creative artist strives to make order out of chaos, to organize his conceptions and his visions into a viable whole; if he is successful in that endeavor, his work acquires in addition a sense of permanence, at least of stability: consider the music you are hearing tonight. The executant artist, in turn, seeks to transform that orderly concept into actual sound, to do justice to the composer's intent. Thus a fine performance confirms for us certain principles and values, some "eternal verities" that cut across the generations, across the changing fads and fashions, across the disorderly or chaotic conditions that mark or mar our daily lives. Here we find symbols of the real quality of life, in the face of pervasive superficiality and cheapness. If "elitists" are those who know what quality is, perhaps we should have more of them.

As listeners, you now join in the total artistic enterprise and complete the magic circle of composer-performer-hearer. Far from being unreal or escapist, this joint effort begins to reflect the ideal order, logic, and beauty of the natural universe, before which any sensitive person stands in such awe. Yes, there are earthquakes and blizzards, hurricanes and floods; but we can also count on the changing seasons, and on the unfathomable checks and balances of the solar system. A great performance of a great work can give us a sense of unity, of security, of the feeling we all need so desperately today: that, when everything is said and done, perhaps all's right with the world. This is a hope we must retain and nurture if we are to survive at all.

Thus we leave a fine concert not only with the sense of "wasn't he good" or "what a marvelous piece", but also with a feeling of reassurance that we have experienced a portion of what the world, at its best, could be. To the question whether he was an optimist or a pessimist, Albert Schweitzer replied, "My knowledge is pessimistic; my willing and working are optimistic." There is no act of man more optimistic than the making of a work of art.

And there is one more thing. Life is short, but art is long. The current event is only a moment of the present; the work of art has the potential of life for hundreds if not thousands of years. Ultimately, only art survives. All we really know about the distant past is through its art, its poetry, its books, its painting and sculpture, its architecture, and its ideas whether descriptive or narrative, philosophical or religious. We care very little about so grandiose a figure of history as Napoleon; but we care passionately about Beethoven and his *Eroica Symphony*.

Through this evening's program, Beethoven speaks to us today, and so do Dvořák and Bartók. Above the last measures he was able to complete of his *Third Piano Concerto*, Bartók wrote, rather prematurely and in evident anguish, "the end". It was not. Characteristically, that is when the life of the music began.

Thank you—and enjoy this evening's concert with as merry a heart as you can muster.

III. PEOPLE AND PLACES

We cannot fully understand the history of a period if we do not know anything of its music. . . . For there is a layer in the realm of human emotions and thoughts that can be expressed only by music, and by nothing else.

Zoltán Kodály

Many young composers make the mistake of assuming that they can be universal before they have been local.

Ralph Vaughan Williams

And as imagination bodies forth
The forms of things unknown, the poet's pen
Turns them to shapes, and gives to airy nothing
A local habitation and a name.

William Shakespeare
from *A Midsummer Night's Dream*

Haydn's 250th Anniversary: Some Thoughts on Chronology
(JANUARY 1982)

WHEN JOSEPH HAYDN was born in March of 1732, Handel's *Messiah* was still ten years in the future. And when Bach died in 1750, the young Austrian—then eighteen—may not even have heard about it. He was gifted, but no prodigy; and had he himself lived only thirty-five years, like Mozart, he would have been known by musical history as a composer of great talent and accomplishment (some thirty of his one hundred and four symphonies having been composed by that time) but not as the major master we now know him to have been.

Musical epochs, of course, do not begin and end in such-and-such a year; it takes a few decades to mark a crucial shift. What counts is the nature of the overlapping. The baroque period, for instance, found itself "phased out" around the middle of the eighteenth century, and when Handel died in 1759, the twenty-seven-year-old Haydn was still straddling the fence between the baroque, the rococo, and the pre-classic. The writer recalls a lecture by the eminent musicologist Curt Sachs, in the 1940s, in which he reminded his listeners that "those terms are useful only because they are so vague." Musical styles are not watertight compartments, and musical history moves in circles, curves, spurts, backtrackings, and constant interactions of the tried-and-true and the yet-to-be-tried.

But when Mozart was only ten years old, in 1766, Haydn was already regarded as "the darling of our nation" by a leading Viennese newspaper. Engaged as the music director of the princely estate of the Eszterházys, he officially served in that position until 1790. The security of that post was exactly what Haydn needed; restrictive (and sometimes demeaning) as it was, it still gave him the opportunity to "try things out" with his own orchestra, and to compose music in an immense variety of media as a "steady job", not as a free-lancer (a concept hardly known in those days and—where known—regarded as quite undesirable).

Twenty-four years older than Mozart, Haydn became acquainted with the music of the incredibly endowed youngster in the 1760s and the two composers in time became fast friends and mutual admirers. Mozart learned all he could from Haydn's music, and soon began to influence him in turn. The artistic relationship of these two geniuses is one of the fascinating aspects of musical history; they spoke the same language, but said different things in it. It is foolish to claim that one was superior to the other, except in certain media; Haydn thought Mozart's operas were better than his own, and as a performing virtuoso Mozart was certainly more attuned to the solo concerto. In fact, it is fair to say that Mozart "invented" (that is to say, refined to an incomparable degree) the medium of the piano concerto, while Haydn taught him how to write string quartets and showed him new paths of symphonic development. In popular literature, Haydn is often called "the father of the symphony" as well as of the string quartet; and that is not untrue. He was; and Mozart became his musical son as well as his match as a composer. The later quartets and symphonies by both masters cannot be compared qualitatively; each is *primus inter pares,* first among equals. While Mozart's works for the stage are surely incomparable, he never wrote an oratorio to match his older friend's *The Creation* and *The Seasons.* Separately and together, they shaped the "classical style" of the second half of the eighteenth century, and brought it to a perfection that could (like all things perfect) not be bettered.

Thus when Beethoven entered the scene in 1770 (with Haydn at age thirty-eight and Mozart at fourteen), he must soon have realized subconsciously that he would in time have to do something else. Until he was in his mid-twenties, he was a flower in the garden

81

planted by Haydn and Mozart. Only toward the close of the century did he transplant himself and become the extraordinary master we know today. He is the perfect example of Goethe's maxim: "That which your forebears have bequeathed to you, now earn it so you may possess it."

Brief studies with Haydn were useful for Beethoven; but more useful yet was studying Haydn, not *with* him. It is probable that in 1802, when Haydn was seventy, the older master could not always follow his young disciple's musical adventures; and when Haydn died in May of 1809 (while Napoleon's troops were occupying Vienna), Beethoven had already written his first six symphonies and the Op. 59 string quartets, and was at work on his *Emperor Concerto*. The "post-classic" period was well under way, and what we so loosely call "romanticism" was in the air. In that same year, 1809, Schubert was twelve (he was to write the *Erlking* at seventeen!), and Berlioz was six. A few months before Haydn's death, Mendelssohn had arrived on the scene; Schumann was to make his appearance in 1810, Liszt in 1811, and Wagner and Verdi shared the year of 1813.

The memorization of dates is regarded by most students of history (and of musical history) as the bane of their existence, as dry and fruitless. But if dates of birth and death, of meetings between artists and the production of works, are seen as chronology, as the "science of time", they acquire value and vividness, and serve to illustrate the progression of mankind's attempt to leave a constructive mark on history. In the light of four-and-a-half billion years of the solar system's existence, two hundred and fifty years since the birth of a major composer is indeed "the twinkling of an eye"; but by human standards it is a long time, in which almost every decade provides several artistic events that will prove to be of historical importance.

An Addendum (OCTOBER 1982)

THE QUESTION has been raised whether or not Haydn had the perfect right to juxtapose strongly contrasting moods in the first movement of his *Symphony No. 83*. Of course he did; what the "critical" comments in the program implied is that the opening movement of the so-called "classical" symphony is usually more unified and consistent in expression, with the lighter moments not in total opposition to the more serious ones. It was not until the later romantic symphonies, where a much larger time-scale prevailed, that so much variety could be easily accommodated. Haydn surely did not think, as Mahler did, that "a symphony must be like the world; it must contain everything." One tends to assume that Haydn's irrepressible sense of humor was at work here as elsewhere, and that he enjoyed shocking his audiences out of their expectations; as mentioned, the beginning of the development section emphasizes that dichotomy of moods with special impact, and at the close Haydn shows how contrasting elements can be not only juxtaposed but neatly combined simultaneously. It could be technically demonstrated, however, that there are subtle melodic relationships between the principal and secondary themes, whether or not Haydn consciously intended to provide them; in the work of a good composer, that is a common occurrence.

Karl Geiringer's Eighty-fifth Birthday (APRIL 1984)

*

Dr. Geiringer died on January 10, 1989, just short of his ninetieth birthday. His autobiographical memoir of 1988, This I Remember, *was published in 1993 by Fithian Press, Santa Barbara.*

*

ON THURSDAY, April 26, 1984, Karl Geiringer—one of the world's leading musicologists—celebrates his eighty-fifth birthday.

While the functions of the composer and the performer are clearly understood by the concertgoing public, uncertainty is common as to what a musicologist is and does. In essence, a musicologist is a scientist of music, one whose function it is to discover lost or neglected works, edit them for performance, annotate existing scores, do research on past and present musical periods and present his findings in scholarly journals, compile catalogues and collected editions, write articles and books on various technical, theoretical, or historical matters, and in general serve as the scientist whose "basic research" leads to authentic live performance. Without musicologists (many of whom are highly trained practical musicians themselves) we would not know most of the music of past centuries, and would be a good deal less certain how works of any period should be most correctly presented. All concert audiences are in debt to the unsung heroes of the art, the musicologists of past and present.

One such scholar-teacher, active since the 1920s, is Karl Geiringer. Born in Vienna, he studied there at the Conservatory and University with Guido Adler and Eusebius Mandyczewski; the latter was a friend of Brahms, whose complete works he edited. He subsequently studied in Berlin with Curt Sachs. From 1923 to 1938, Dr. Geiringer was curator of the archives of the Gesellschaft der Musikfreunde (Society of the Friends of Music) in Vienna, then moved to London. Between 1941 and 1962 he was professor of music history at Boston University, where the editor of this program had the privilege of studying with him. From 1962 until his retirement he was professor of music at the University of California, Santa Barbara. In 1955, he was elected president of the American Musicological Society, and in 1959 he was designated a fellow of the American Academy of Arts and Sciences. In 1983, the Austrian Government honored him with a major order of merit.

*

Retirement, for Karl Geiringer, has not meant inactivity. Far from it. He has continued to teach, lecture, revise earlier works, and do new research. In the spring of 1983 he produced four lectures on Brahms for the North German Radio of Hamburg, observing the one hundred and fiftieth anniversary of the composer's birth, and also gave the keynote address for the Brahms Congress at the Library of Congress in Washington. Last October he gave two lectures on Brahms in a symposium at the College of Wooster, Ohio, and the college is awarding him an honorary doctorate of music at its commencement exercises on May 7, 1984. He is currently working on new Brahms articles and lectures, stimulated by the recent discovery of manuscripts long believed lost. In the course of next week, he is giving lectures at Boston University and at Harvard.

Dr. Geiringer's books in English, on which this program has so often drawn, include basic studies of Haydn, Brahms (*His Life and Work,* Oxford University Press, New York

1947), and Bach (*The Bach Family, Seven Generations of Creative Genius*, and *Johann Sebastian Bach, The Culmination of an Era*). Both books on Bach credit the collaboration of the author's wife, Dr. Irene Geiringer, who died in 1983. His book of 1943, *Musical Instruments*, was recently (1978) reissued in a completely revised edition as *Instruments in the History of Western Music*. All these are standard sources on their subjects, without which no music library is complete. Many of them, furthermore, have been translated into other languages. He published numerous works by eighteenth-century composers in scholarly editions, and conducted many of these in live performance, occasionally also playing the viola in the ensemble.

*

One of the distinguishing characteristics of Dr. Geiringer's writing, both in German and in English, is lucidity. The editor vividly recalls his astonished delight when, as a student at Harvard in the 1940s, he ploughed through the original German edition of *Adler's Handbook of Music History*, getting bogged down in the most turgid and long-winded prose in most of the individual contributions, and suddenly encountered a sentence beginning one of the chapters (we translate it exactly): "The homeland of occidental musical instruments is Asia." Period. The author was Karl Geiringer, and we find to our pleasure that thirty-five years later his new book on instruments begins thus: "The function of music in prehistoric times was quite different from what it came to be in later periods. Music was not made to provide pleasure and aesthetic enjoyment. Its purpose was to help man in his struggle against the overwhelming forces of nature."

As a teacher, Dr. Geiringer was as devoted to his students as they were to him. He took a personal interest in them, and was exceptionally generous in furthering their careers. This writer can attest that the first public lectures he ever gave were under Dr. Geiringer's auspices, and so was his first professional post. The history seminars at Boston University (which included among its students H. C. Robbins Landon, who became a noted scholar in his own right), were marked by an attitude of honest inquiry and joint effort. There was an occasion one day when a student presented a paper with some new information, and the renowned teacher said with genuine simplicity, "That's interesting; I didn't know that." The effect was electric, and memorable. On another occasion, Dr. Geiringer noticed that a submitted paper drew rather too heavily and without attribution on some other author's writing; he interrupted the reading as follows: "My young friend, when we copy from one person, we call it stealing; when we copy from many persons, we call it research." This program has been proud to borrow frequently from Karl Geiringer's writing, and has avoided the charge of theft by gratefully acknowledging the source. On the eighty-fifth birthday of this great scholar and fine human being, felicitations and warm appreciation are extended to him.

Reflections on the Water (OCTOBER 1980)

THE CLASSICAL FOUR ELEMENTS are fire, water, air, and earth—not necessarily in that order. Each has a particular attraction for musicians, but not all are equally apt for transmutation into sounding symbols.

There is a piece by Ned Rorem called *Air Music*, and "airy music" can be written by composers who have mastered a light touch, such as Mendelssohn and Berlioz. When air turns to wind, of course, we find it pictured or symbolized in numerous pieces, from a gentle breeze (Vivaldi's *The Seasons*, for instance) to Beethoven's and Berlioz's storm pieces, and Strauss's *An Alpine Symphony*. Earth is conceived of as a "steady state", and its landscapes are grist for a composer's mill, be they forests, meadows, or mountains; yet they are somehow more intractable, for they do not move. As for earth's liquid components, that is the element discussed below. Fire, not really an element but a process, attracts composers for its imagery; Handel's *Royal Fireworks Music* has little to do with the subject as such, but Wagner's *Magic Fire Music* in *Die Walküre* certainly does, to say nothing of Scriabin's *Poem of Fire*. Stravinsky's *Fireworks* duly sparkles and glitters, and his *Firebird* defies descriptive verbiage entirely, so graphic is it.

That brings us to water, and here the musician (whether he can swim or not) is truly in his element. Why? The answer is simple. Water moves and flows, and it does so in a variety of forms much greater than fire and air. The number of compositions which take water as a topic or as a stimulus is immense. Surprisingly, Handel's *Water Music* is not at all a series of images of that element, but simply a set of festive pieces to be performed in the course of royal riverboat parties. But "river music" itself can be counted in the dozens, from the Moldau to the Housatonic, from the Danube to the Volga, from the Mississippi to the Rhine. Lakes and ponds, less "moving" bodies of water, still provide the composer with impressionistic reflection and a great deal of "atmosphere" (although that term more properly belongs with the element of air). Think of Debussy's *The Afternoon of a Faun* and Liszt's *At the Lake of Wallenstadt*, to name but two. Like the Japanese block-print makers, Debussy was fascinated also by another kind of water in motion; his *Gardens in the Rain* attests to that.

Water in its manmade (or, better, man-controlled) form is of course best seen in the myriad shapes and fanciful designs that have been invented for fountains. In Rome alone, there are more than three hundred active fountains, and in the Tivoli Gardens of the Villa d'Este near Rome there is a breathtaking display of many more. In fact, a small river is diverted there during the summer months to provide the water, which flows down a hillside and by natural gravitational pressure activates all the fountains which break into liquid action. Did those miraculous shapes inspire Ravel to write his *Jeux d'Eau*? It was, he said, "the sound of water and the music of fountains, cascade and streams" that he wished to mirror in that extraordinary piece.

What other musical symbols can one find for fountains? Respighi has ingeniously shown us a few. How delightful, for one, is the idea of the call-to-alarm from the brasses in the *Triton Fountain* episode in *Fontane di Roma*, in which the sound from the triton or trumpet shell held by the figure comes vividly to life! And if anyone can escape the almost tangible sensation of the spray that issues from that fountain forthwith, we have not heard of such a person.

Water in its grandest and most varied form is found in the oceans. And there, to be sure, the musical literature bursts its bounds and produces an array of works that can hardly be counted. From Haydn's *The Creation* to Debussy's *La Mer*, from Anton Rubinstein's *Ocean Symphony* to Vaughan Williams's *Sea Symphony*, from Mendelssohn's *The Hebrides* Overture to Rimsky-Korsakov's *Scheherazade*, the great sea roils and rests, frightens and calms, tells of immensities and mysteries and of the infinite rhythm of life itself. For creative musicians, there is hardly any "subject matter" that provides a more attractive model than the sea, in which the wave-forms driven by air, the unfathomable depths below, and the grandeur of it all, evoke those shapes and profundities and subtle fluctuations that are the intrinsic properties of musical art.

"Yes, Virginia, There Is a Fingal's Cave!" (SEPTEMBER 1987)

AMONG THE GREAT COMPOSERS, Mendelssohn was one of the most indefatigable travelers. Whatever he saw, he experienced on many levels: as a tourist of uncommon attentiveness, as a cultured person receptive to all impressions, as a man whose gifts in the visual arts brought forth many a fine sketch, and—most importantly—as a musician whose creativeness was stimulated enormously by the impact of continually new sights and sounds.

Visiting Italy in 1831, the twenty-two-year-old composer was enthralled and invigorated by the festive and lively ambience of the country, and gave us the brilliant *"Italian" Symphony*. His journey to Scotland was made even earlier, in 1829, and bore fruit eventually in the grandiose and moving *"Scottish" Symphony*. On August 7 of that year, the youthful composer visited the Hebrides, and was guided to the Island of Staffa and the famous Fingal's Cave. Writing to his sister, he said, "so that you may understand how extraordinarily the Hebrides affected me, the following came into my mind there," and he noted down the opening measures of what was to become the *Hebrides Overture*, subtitled *Fingal's Cave* (1832). He actually stood in that enormous natural chamber, heard the roaring waves rolling into the cavern, and let the wind and the sea-birds and the powerful landscape become music.

We had often read of his impressions and savored the overture, but had never known what the astonishing place looked like. In the summer of 1987, Harry Herforth, a former long-time trumpet player of The Cleveland Orchestra, had visited there, and when the overture was to be performed that September under Christoph von Dohnányi's direction, he brought us a photograph. It was at that point that we decided we needed to know more about those islands, and did a little searching (let us not, grandiloquently, call it "research"). Here is what we found and added to the program notes on the music:

The Hebrides, also called the Western Isles, are—according to the World Book Encyclopedia—"a group of Scottish Islands off the west coast of Scotland. Tourists have long been interested in their picturesque scenery and in the simple life of the people. The folk songs of the Hebrides are also well known and highly praised by students of music." Frederick G. Marcham, the author of the entry, writes that the group has some five hundred islands, more than three fourths uninhabited. Some forty-eight thousand five hundred persons live on the nearly three thousand square miles. "Many of the people still speak Gaelic. Their way of life has changed little for hundreds of years. The people raise sheep and cattle and weave woolen cloth. The main farm crops include barley, oats and potatoes." Perhaps the best known of the larger islands is the Isle of Skye.

From a brochure published by The National Trust for Scotland (kindly lent by Lydia Herforth, secretary of the Women's Committee of The Cleveland Orchestra), we learn that "the name Staffa is thought to be from the Old Norse word meaning 'pillar island', referring to its basaltic pillar formations." Fingal's cave, its principal feature, "is named after the mythical Irish giant Fin McCoul, also associated with the Giant's Causeway in Northern Ireland. The island was first publicised by Sir Joseph Banks in 1772, resulting in a visit by Dr. Johnson and his biographer Boswell in 1773. Sir Walter Scott describes the island and Fingal's Cave in 'The Lord of the Isles', written following his visits in 1812 and 1814. Regular visits by steamships began in 1828. . . ." Mendelssohn's visit occurred in 1829. "The island has been declared a Site of Special Scientific Interest by the Nature Conservancy Council, and affords magnificent views of the Inner Hebrides."

And now, perhaps, let us hear a performance of Ernst Toch's "Geographical Fugue"!

Phoenix Municipalis (FEBRUARY 1958, REVISED 1965)

*

Watch ye, stand fast in the faith,
quit you like men, be strong.
I Corinthians XVI:13

*

MUSIC HAS ACCOMPANIED the march of history almost as intimately as have the novel, the theater, and the visual arts. How many historical events we can think of that have been observed by the composition of a piece of music! Every war, every coronation, every national or municipal festivity of any scope is likely to bring forth one or more musical commentaries—from a folk song to an oratorio, from a short-lived occasional piece to an inspired masterwork. Battle music, particularly, has been a favorite of composers for centuries—not only because the possibilities for making noise are so immeasurably increased by the background of a good fight, but because the intrinsic elements of conflict in musical structure, the necessary tensions and releases, are so close to the borderline of describing people in action, physical or psychological. There comes to mind Liszt's tone poem, *The Battle of the Huns,* with the inevitable victory of the Christians portrayed by a painfully literal use of a portable field organ. Beethoven's *Battle Symphony* or *Wellington's Victory* (with actual cannons!) is hardly one of his most distinguished compositions, though he bitterly resented a critic's blunt derogation of it. Prokofiev's "Battle on the Ice" (from the cantata *Alexander Nevsky*), on the other hand, belongs to the more successful pieces of wartime depiction in artistic terms.

Geography, too, has had its share of musical map-making; the number of "river pieces", for one, is legion. (To find out who can name the most is a good parlor game for musically erudite persons.) Almost every large city has one or more pieces associated with it, from Delius's *Paris, a Night Picture* to Johann Strauss's *Vienna Blood;* from Kodály's *Psalmus Hungaricus*—celebrating the fiftieth anniversary of the joining of Buda and Pesth—to Respighi's trilogy on the pines, fountains, and festivals of Rome; from Vaughan Williams's *London Symphony* to Rimsky-Korsakov's *Legend of the Invisible City of Kitezh.* Henry Barraud's *"La Symphonie de Numance"*—drawn from his opera *Numance* and performed here in 1958—belongs to a special category: cities-under-siege as dealt with in music. Ancient Numantia, in northern Spain, defied the conquering Romans for a decade after the fall of Carthage, until in 133 B.C. a fifteen-month siege brought it to the point of surrender. The eight thousand inhabitants, preferring death to servitude, committed mass-suicide on an enormous pyre made of all their remaining possessions.

One thinks of whole countries that have risen in rebellion against their oppressors— as Beethoven stirringly interpreted it in his incidental music to Goethe's *Egmont,* or as Sibelius gave his countrymen an artistic weapon in his *Finlandia,* a mighty rallying-point in the fight against tyranny. The courage of towns and cities, fortresses and villages, threatened by the enemy or held under the yoke of the conqueror—and finally liberated by freedom or by death—that is a subject which has called forth many a musico-historical creation. Has there yet been a musical work on the extraordinary event at Masada?

Kodály, who had already produced a memorable work with the *Psalmus Hungaricus* of 1923, brought forth another superb piece with his *Te Deum* of 1936 observing the two hundred and fiftieth anniversary of the liberation of Budapest from the besieging Turkish armies. The *Leningrad Symphony* of Shostakovich, his *Seventh* (1941), symbolized for the Allies of World War II the indomitable spirit of a Russian city under several years of constant bombardment by surrounding troops; from the musical standpoint, the inexorable tramp of the German boots was almost too graphically conveyed. Sixty-one years earlier, Tchaikovsky had exulted in his *Overture, 1812,* over the ignominious withdrawal of Napoleon's French forces from the outskirts of beleaguered Moscow. The *Sixth Symphony* of Vaughan Williams, begun in 1944, seems to mirror in more than one powerful statement the wartime experience of London under the Blitz, and perhaps looks back upon it with somber reflection in the eloquent "Epilogue" to the work. (The same master's *A London Symphony* of 1914 had shown his city in a happier light, though the time was to be no less one of war.)

The gloom and depression of a city occupied by the enemy is powerfully communicated by Arthur Honegger's *Second Symphony* of 1941; the broken spirit of Paris itself speaks through the leaden ostinato of the beginning. The citizens kept their shutters closed, it is reported, while the victorious Germans made what was to have been a triumphal march along the Champs Elysées. And like a challenge, a call of defiance, the solo trumpet which joins the string orchestra at the close proclaims a stirring Bach-like chorale; it reminds one of the true greatness that once came from the hated enemy's people, as it prophesies the city's eventual freedom. (The symphony, by a composer who would not leave Paris in its gravest hour, was not to be performed until 1947!) No hope of liberation, except in a spiritual sense, is implicit in Martinů's *Memorial to Lidice,* an anguished protest against the complete destruction of a Czech village in 1942, as an act of revenge by German soldiers. *The Taking of T'ung Kuan,* by the young Siberian-American composer Jacob Avshalomov, is a striking, short orchestral work (1953) whose subject is a violent battle in eighth-century China, for possession of a mountain pass vital to the defense of the ancient capital, Chang-an. On the operatic stage, we need go no further than "The Fall of Troy", the first part of Berlioz's opera *The Trojans;* and we may remind ourselves that if "The Trojans at Carthage" (the second part) did not actually themselves destroy the city of their hosts (though Aeneas caused the ruin of her queen, Dido), the Romans soon rectified this omission—in preparation for *Numance.*

The list, of course, is by no means complete; we are likely to have missed some apt examples.

Leningrad, London, and Paris—and Hiroshima—remain unalterable facts of geography, with topical works of art providing for them only another dimension of history. But Lidice, Carthage, Troy, and *Numance* are alive for us today largely because of the artistic creations that celebrate their heroism. Who has done more to engrave the name of *Guernica* on our minds than Picasso, by his extraordinary painting? Cities regarded as obliterated, dead, forgotten, rise in youthful triumph from their ashes. Art has this power; in the final accounting, it is all that may survive from an entire civilization—think of ancient Babylonia, Egypt, Etruria, the Aztecs, the Mayans! That which has been embraced or expressed by artists of genuine gifts will endure. By any standard, we call that immortality.

Misia Sert—Catalyst of the Arts (APRIL 1982)

FOR DECADES, the program book has included in the factual data for Ravel's *La Valse* the information that the score was dedicated to Misia Sert. So was that composer's *Introduction and Allegro for Harp, String Quartet, Flute, and Clarinet*. Ravel's *Ma Mère l'Oye* ("Mother Goose") was written for Misia Sert's young niece and nephew, Mimi and Jean Godebski.

Who was that woman, whose admirers, friends, and lovers included the greatest artists of the sixty years between 1890 and 1950? Born in 1872 of half-Polish and half-Belgian parentage, she died at age seventy-eight, the indomitable survivor of two world wars, and the most magnetic patroness and catalyst of the arts in the first half of the twentieth century. Poets, painters, composers, designers were drawn to her as moths to a flame; some were scorched by that consuming fire, but most were illumined and warmed by it. Her life was intertwined with the cultural history of France in a tapestry that has lost little of its vivid glow.

Books and articles in which that astonishing woman plays a role are counted in the dozens. But only now has it all been summed up in a full-length study by the distinguished duo-pianists Arthur Gold and Robert Fizdale: *Misia—The Life of Misia Sert*, first published in 1980 by Alfred A. Knopf. It is, one may be bold to say, the most enthralling book of its kind encountered by this writer and his friends in a decade. "Run—do not walk . . . ."

The book jacket gives us the basic facts, and they are not a "blurb" but a minimal summary: "A charming and magnificent biography of a truly extraordinary woman. . . Misia was a pianist of talent who, as a child, delighted Liszt and, later, her teacher, Fauré. Her greatest talent, however, was the gift of inspiring and bringing together others. She was painted and adored by Renoir, Vuillard, Bonnard, and Toulouse-Lautrec. She was a friend of Mallarmé and Valéry and, later, Cocteau, Colette, and Claudel. It was she who brought Diaghilev and Stravinsky together, inspired two characters in Proust's masterpiece *Remembrance of Things Past* and 'discovered' Coco Chanel."

Reviews everywhere have been appropriately enthusiastic, not least for the admirably graceful writing of the noted duo-pianists (who appeared with The Cleveland Orchestra at Blossom Music Center in 1970 and 1979, in music of Poulenc and Mozart). The authors have not let their exhaustive research, stretching over many years, get in the way of a flowing and absorbing narrative. If one wishes to come closer to understanding the cultural history of more than two generations, one should involve oneself in this utterly fascinating book, which has already been translated into a half-dozen languages. And if this sounds like a rave review, *pourquoi pas?*

*

Misia Sert, from the introduction to the catalogue of the Diaghilev exposition at the Musée des Arts Décoratifs, Paris 1939, as quoted on page 263 of Gold and Fizdale's book:

It is now ten years that you are gone, dear Serge. And we are left without a magician. The last time I saw you, do you remember, it was the eve of your death in Venice. . . .

We have been reliving old memories: you spoke to me then—you who discovered, one by one, all the composers who were to turn the music of our time upside down—of your secret preference for Tchaikovsky's *Pathétique* and for *Tristan and Isolde*. Works of love.

Your whole life was inspired by love. It was in you like a fever that you communicated to artists, artists chosen by your love, which demanded that they give the best of their souls.

For twenty years my eyes watched the prodigies of creation that you provoked in the midst of indescribable storms.

You were right. Works of love never perish. Those that were born of your love had outlived you, prolonging in our hearts the miracle of your existence.

"The Sea Has Been Very Good to Me; She Has Shown Me All Her Moods." (APRIL 1974)

—Claude Debussy (1905)

MOUNTAINS, meadows, forests, and even small ponds or lakes are "steady state". They are *there,* varied only by the seasons and the changing light. To describe them (or, better, to find symbols for them) in music is an act of creative association that is difficult and in need of verbal explanation. This is not so with the ocean, that immense and opulent world of its own. Its constant motion, visible and invisible mystery, and its frightening power are intensely musical in nature. Hardly a composer who has encountered the sea in person could escape its thrall, fail to be stimulated by its grandeur and infinite variety.

While rivers and streams have given rise to an astonishing amount of nationalistic compositions (from the Danube to the Volga, from the Moldau to the Housatonic, from the Thames to the Seine), the sea has tended to inspire composers as a concept, as an idea, as a phenomenon, almost apart from its geographical allusions. Whether the work that takes it as a theme is based on words, like Vaughan Williams's *Sea Symphony,* or on a story, like the "Sinbad" music in Rimsky-Korsakov's *Scheherazade,* or deals "merely" with its rhythmical and tonal suggestions, like Anton Rubinstein's *Ocean Symphony* and Debussy's *La Mer,* there is always the feeling of something above, below and beyond the surface that calls for expression. The odyssey described by Whitman's poem in the *Sea Symphony* is, ultimately, not a journey over the waters, but toward human, superhuman, religious goals. It is the soul that travels, not only the ship and the sailor. In his *Flying Dutchman* overture, Wagner prepares us for the fearful legendary and spiritual struggle that follows; in his *Meeresstille und Glückliche Fahrt* overture (based on poems by Goethe), Mendelssohn pictures a gentler and kinder sea. Of Debussy's *La Mer,* Rachel L. Carson writes, "As the surface of the sea itself is the creation and the expression of the unseen depths beneath it, so underlying the musical re-creation of the coming of dawn to the sea and of the wind-driven procession of waves across the ocean, Debussy has suggested the mysterious and brooding spirit of the deep and hidden waters."

That water itself is a stimulus to musical creation has long been obvious; it moves, it reflects light, it produces sound. But no body composed of that element suggests more powerfully and inescapably than the sea the infinite rhythm of life itself, and occasionally sets in motion musical thinking and feeling that may not be directly related to it. This writer vividly recalls a day in 1942, when he watched the roiling sea on the coast of Massachusetts and heard in his mind's ear a piece then new and freshly exciting to him, Sibelius's *Second Symphony*. It was, surely, not "what the composer had in mind"; but then why not? Let everyone make a private list of "ocean music", so named by the composer or not, and on the next visit to the shore or travel across the waters hear-in as well as look-out, take part in that everlasting musical performance, the gigantic ostinato of the sea.

"The Gilt-Edged Second"
The Acoustical Renovation of Severance Hall
(*Stereo Review*, MARCH 1960)

"We not only want to hear a pin drop, we want to hear it drop longer."
—Walter K. Bailey
Trustee and Hall Committee Chairman, 1958

IF "A MOUNTAIN IS TO CLIMB" makes a good definition, so does "an orchestra is to hear." That, in short, is what an orchestra is for. Yet *hearing* an orchestra is not just in being there when it plays, or in spinning an electronic portrait of it on a hi-fi turntable. The final quality of the music is inescapably governed by its architectural surroundings—the concert hall. It is appalling, then, to note that of all the world's ranking ensembles—there are hundreds of good ones, a dozen or two great ones, and a very few that are tops—only a handful play in halls that do justice to the actual quality of the sound they make as an ensemble.

Now (1) what special qualities make a concert hall good for listening—or, for recording? (2) Are the sonic requirements for listening opposed to those of recording? And (3) Do our ideas about these requirements stay the same from generation to generation, or do they fluctuate? After all, a building is a pretty stable commodity, not an item to turn in for a new model every few years.

Difficult and controversial questions. Let's start with the fundamental one: What makes a good hall?—one that serves the purpose or purposes for which it was built, and brings out as much of the full potential of whatever individual or organization uses it. We like, for one thing, an orchestral sonority that is warm and rich rather than cool and thin. We like our sonorities blended properly, not in clear and isolated strands that refuse to mix. We like to have a sound last long enough so that it makes sense in relation to its context, as music or as speech. We want a volume that won't hurt our ears even in a Berlioz *con tutta forza;* on the other hand, we don't want to have to strain for a Debussy *pianissimo, quasi niente*. We demand balance and blend, and we are convinced that a flat sound is no good: we insist on having color. Color in musical sound means, perhaps, overtones. If you hear an instrument through a partition you can recognize it, but it will be a pointless and sterile sound. If the air, because of the room setup and low humidity, does not carry overtones, the effect will be the same: black-and-white.

That brings us to point two in our quiz. It was thought once that you built one kind of hall for concerts, and yet another, different hall for recording. Perhaps you'd build a third hall to make speeches in, resigning yourself to the use of a mike and an amplification system that would work fine for Row 57, and be useless for Row 59. This kind of thinking led to concert halls in which you couldn't record, to recording studios in which you couldn't perform for a live audience, and to halls where nothing would work but political conventions, boxing matches, and flower shows. Then people thought up the multi-purpose hall, in which all these things were supposed to be done equally well or equally badly, without discrimination, perhaps with opera, ballet and travelogues thrown in for good measure. Now the thinking has changed again. It has been discovered that if a hall is good for live orchestral performances (and assuming that it is not too large, preferably under twenty-seven hundred seats), one could also record in it, and make speeches in it perhaps even without a microphone. A piano recital would work, and so would a chamber music event. If the acoustical conditions are good for one, they should be fine for the other. The multi-purpose hall could, up to a point, be achieved, not by trying to please everybody and thus pleasing nobody, but by first satisfying the primary occupant (like an orchestra) and then finding out that just about everybody else will like it too.

Live performance and recording, therefore, are not at all in opposition. You can't bring a dead hall to life, but you can "calm down" a live one for recording, if you need to. When the Boston Symphony Orchestra, for instance, wanted to record in the empty Symphony Hall, a curtain was drawn across the auditorium (size: twenty-six hundred) about a quarter of the way back. That made the cubic volume smaller, and just right. They still rehearse that way. But at recording sessions, the orchestra is now moved off the stage onto the main floor itself; the reverberation of the auditorium is thus put to work in new and effective ways.* But with a hall in which the sound is stillborn there isn't much to do but record elsewhere or resort to seldom satisfactory artificial reverberation techniques.

But on to our third question. Somehow, "by ear" rather than by slide rule, most of the great halls built toward the close of the nineteenth century were built to be properly reverberant, with a sound-life of about 2.1 seconds when filled to capacity: that includes the Berlin Philharmonie, the Basel Casino, St. Andrew's Hall in Glasgow, the endangered Carnegie Hall, and three widely considered the world's best: the Concertgebouw in Amsterdam, the Grosse Musikvereinssaal in Vienna, and Symphony Hall in Boston. It was Prof. Wallace Sabine who developed a workable formula when the Boston hall was built at the turn of the century. But some of the knowledge was not utilized by succeeding builders, and the pendulum started to swing the other way. Auditoria began to be built for movies as well as music, for live broadcasting, and for recording purposes; resonance to any appreciable degree was considered harmful: a dry, clear sound was the rage. By 1925 or 1930, when a new hall was put up, it was likely to have a reverberation that was so short nobody heard it. This was perhaps the apex of the vogue for tight, non-reverberant sound—the "triple-sec" period. Severance Hall, begun in 1930 and completed a year later, wasn't far behind—but more of that shortly. Another generation has now passed, and we are back to a "sound ideal" that calls for a longer reverberation time—a more echoing quality. Not that we want the sound to hit us from different sides a moment apart, as in some of the "stereo-phony" movie palaces or trick commercials. Nowadays, we want just enough reverberation to produce the richness of sound previously described.

*

---

* 1992: That is what The Cleveland Orchestra now does, on a specially-constructed platform above the main floor seats.—Editor.

The new techniques of recording have put the problem of what makes a good hall into sharp focus. Recording engineers will tell you that in monaural recording you could get away with a lot, though you could surely tell a dry sound from a live one. You could fake and improvise, but stereo has changed all that. An experienced engineer or critic can virtually draw you a sketch plan of a hall a recording was made in, when he hears a stereo disc "anonymously." He can tell you about how large it is, how the ceiling slopes, what kind of furnishings it has. Stereo picks up everything; the room acoustics of this technique are crucial. And since most orchestral recordings are nowadays made in stereo, a good hall means also "a good hall for recording."

Severance Hall is a good example of such an auditorium. But it hasn't always been. Consumers and critics who have bought recent Cleveland Orchestra recordings have pricked up their ears in surprise. "What's this!" they say. "What have you done to the place?" They may not have known that The Cleveland Orchestra had not been recording in Severance Hall for some years before 1958: the ensemble had to go downtown, to the odd-shaped Masonic Auditorium, to record. The sound was good there, though nothing special.

At Severance, as the Orchestra's permanent home is affectionately called for short, you couldn't record at all. In the opinion of some, you couldn't really play there either. What needed to be done? It had been a case, perhaps, of too much luxury and too little concern with the principles of musical sound. When the hall was built, in 1930–31, as a munificent gift of the Cleveland businessman and long-time president of the Orchestra, John Long Severance, as a memorial to his wife, the objective was to make it one of the most aesthetically pleasing structures in the nation. This was achieved. The classic exterior is very impressive. Outstanding Cleveland architects designed a splendid main foyer, with terrazzo floors and multicolored marble pillars. Decoration is highly ornate, but not garish. As one enters the auditorium, one is struck by two things: one, the relative smallness of the hall (it can seat about nineteen hundred people*); two, the sumptuously executed ceiling and wall ornamentation in untarnishable silver leaf. The overall effect is more that of a theater or opera house than a concert hall, with its twenty-five boxes curving about the hall, with the nearness of the first balcony to the stage, two false boxes, and other theatrical features.

The acoustical consultant had been Professor Dayton C. Miller—an expert indeed, thoroughly versed in contemporary standards and techniques. The ceiling was his design, and it remains acoustically superb. But other aspects of the architects' plans as well as the furnishings agreed upon resulted at once in a set of compromises that spelled trouble for the future. One simply can't start to put up a building and then ask the acoustician what he thinks. It may be a bit late. There are some horrifying examples of this in all-too-recent history, with fabulously expensive auditoria both here and abroad having to be done over within a year or two of their festive inauguration.

Since the auditorium volume (five hundred and fifty thousand cubic feet) was small in relation to the audience and surface area, it was found that the reverberation time of a sound was drastically shortened. There were areas to which the sound could come only directly from the stage: it could not be properly reinforced by reflection. For best effect, sound must be both direct and reflected: it is the mixtures of both, in perfect mathematical proportion, which give body to the sonority produced. If one came into the auditorium before the summer of 1958, one would find a rich, blue, custom-loomed carpet on the floors, and heavy draperies of complementing color in the boxes. The seats were heavily upholstered (they still are; for it makes rather little difference to the sound whether one sits in them or not). But all this luxury, so pleasing to the eye and so comfortable physically, turned out to be an acoustical boobytrap. The word "trap" is used advisedly: the

---

* It has since been expanded to over 2000 seats.—Editor.

sound of the orchestra was actually trapped—absorbed—by these furnishings, and died before it could be appreciated.

The stage shared in the acoustical damage. It had been designed to accommodate not only concert but opera. From 1933 on, when Artur Rodzinski had succeeded the first conductor, Nikolai Sokoloff, fully-staged opera was regularly presented. For that reason, the stage ceiling could not be fully closed, and the backdrop could not be a permanent one. Sound would escape upward and backward, into the air and through the very back of the shell, which was then made of scenery-like plywood. A heavy velours contour curtain, which remained visible to the audience during concert performances, absorbed yet more sound, especially the higher frequencies. The stage became, in fact, a stage, instead of a concert platform or orchestra shell. Instead of joining indissolubly with the auditorium, it found itself *behind* the proscenium arch.

All these factors produced a reverberation time that had the unusually low value of 1.45 seconds for the empty hall between the range of sixty-five to five hundred cycles; at two thousand cycles it fell to 0.75 seconds. When the hall was filled, with the audience providing yet more absorption, there was a small but still noticeable further reduction of the reverberance. These things did not escape Mr. Sokoloff, of course, and he voiced complaints. But it was too close to the building's inauguration, and nothing was done. When George Szell succeeded Erich Leinsdorf as musical director and conductor in 1946, he was not long in making known his strong views on the prevailing acoustical conditions, based on vast experience in most of the world's outstanding opera houses and concert halls. To those who knew George Szell, it might have been evident that when he set his mind to do a thing, it would be done, sooner or later, and preferably sooner.

*

It was understandable that Mr. Szell should find much initial opposition to his radical proposals. But he also began to find influential support. Officers of The Musical Arts Association, which operates The Cleveland Orchestra, heard their ensemble in New York's Carnegie Hall. Why, they asked, can't our Orchestra sound like that at home? Why is it that the players so keenly enjoy their annual Carnegie Hall visits? The acoustics of other halls visited by the Orchestra on its tours also supplied food for thought. The conviction that something would have to be done about Severance Hall began to grow during that first decade of Mr. Szell's reign, in which the Orchestra found itself attaining world eminence. The European tour of May-June 1957, in which the Orchestra played twenty-nine concerts in twenty-two cities of ten countries, created the kind of climate which made a reconstruction of its home base imperative. An ensemble called by the critic of *The New York Times* "one of the world's very great orchestras" deserved nothing less than the best for its work in its home city.

As early as 1953, Mr. Szell had invited Dr. Robert S. Shankland, head of the physics department at Cleveland's Case Institute of Technology, to work with him on the highly involved measurements and tests that would have to precede any alterations. Then in 1955, a spectacular job of architectural acoustics at the rebuilt Vienna State Opera aroused worldwide attention. The man responsible was Heinrich Keilholz, then chief recording engineer of the renowned German recording firm, the Deutsche Grammophon-Gesellschaft.

Mr. Keilholz's unique qualifications as a "room acoustician" are due to his vast practical experience with live music and the needs of musicians, to his educated ear, and to his imagination. He has since been appointed acoustical consultant to the Austrian government and has been working on various halls in Germany and Austria; he is at present engaged as chief acoustical counselor to the new Salzburg Festspielhaus. Mr. Szell approached him in 1956 and invited him to inspect and report on Severance Hall.

The engineer subsequently bore out Mr. Szell's views and Dr. Shankland's recommenda- tions. He made sketches for a new stage shell. These sketches were then interpreted architecturally by Edward A. Flynn, and as a sort of an anniversary present for the Orchestra's fortieth year, 1957–1958, it was decided to rebuild the interior of Severance Hall, with the objective of making it into one of the finest concert auditoria in the world. It was a tall order.

*

The actual job began in July 1958. In no time at all, the stage set was demolished, the carpets torn up, the drapes and curtains removed. With a half-dozen local companies supplying their services, things began to take shape again. In place of the carpet, two kinds of blue tile were laid—identical except for the surfaces: a plain, smooth surface below the seats, and a grainy or abrasive surface in the aisles and on the steps to prevent slipping. The floor itself now became a reflecting surface, contributing to the resonance of sound. Instead of draperies, thin-textured fabrics were utilized which would not "drink up" the higher frequencies. So that the orchestra's sonority might pass unimpeded to the listeners, the proscenium arch was raised and more closely integrated with the auditorium: the stage itself became a part of the hall, a properly functioning sound shell. Instead of ornamenta- tion, the arch now contains seventeen recessed lights that particularly help the string players in the front row to see their music better on the stands—an ancient problem solved at last. The heavy curtain went the way of all velours, and a new and light transverse curtain was installed that can be entirely hidden during a performance, but may be drawn easily for commencement exercises or similar functions.

What strikes the eye at once is the totally new appearance of the stage-shell. The old scenery-like backdrop has given way to a permanent stage of finest basswood with a maple veneer on both sides, attached to a rigid steel frame. Mr. Keilholz had come up with two ideas that may represent acoustical "firsts" in this field: one is visible, the other is not. The first idea is a series of convex plywood panels which "mix" the sound of the ensemble directly on the stage. No longer does the sound bounce straight off the back and side walls: it diffuses in certain calculated ways, and the result is that highly desirable quality of blend which had been so long missing. Even a flat lacquer finish contributes to the sound, insuring sufficient reflection of the highest frequencies. The curved panels, more- over, look extremely attractive, combining functional with modern aesthetic values.

The second, invisible factor is this: between the curved wood surface and the back panel attached to the steel frame, there is an air space. That space is filled, up to a height of nine feet, with silica sand. This device has two purposes: it assures that the front panels will function as sound-reflecting surfaces only, preventing them from setting up vibrations of their own. Secondly, it makes it impossible for the bulk of the sound to escape through the shell and be lost backstage. For the stage itself, a new hardwood floor has been provided, as well as a newly designed set of risers for the orchestra and for the participa- tion of The Cleveland Orchestra Chorus under Associate Conductor Robert Shaw.

On the back of the shell may be seen some unusual grilles. These cover two batteries of loudspeakers, which relay the sound of the organ by electronic means from the shut-off organ chamber. The vertical openings serve the lower frequencies. This, too, is a vast improvement, since in the past the fine Skinner organ had never been fully effective. The distance from the console on stage had made it necessary for the sound to travel through openings in the ceiling, and the organist had to be virtually a beat ahead of the conductor. Now, engineering ingenuity has solved this problem too.

*

When the bulk of the Orchestra (actually the seventy-five-man Summer "Pops" Orchestra under Assistant Conductor Louis Lane) tried out the new stage in the late summer of 1958, the result was unexpected: for a half hour, pandemonium reigned. The men simply could not hear what they were doing, and could not hear each other. Slowly it dawned on them that they would have to get used to a new set of conditions, and that their playing style would have to be changed! They no longer needed to force the tone, especially the brass; the sound began to blend, and the musicians discovered that they could actually hear each other much more clearly and meaningfully, once they understood the nature of the changes made. Under those conditions of "getting the feel", the first recording in the greatly modified concert hall was made: *Pop Concert U. S. A.* (Epic BC 1013: mono LC 3539). Martin Bookspan, reviewing this disc in *HiFi Review*, had this to say: "The sound is wonderful and the acoustic enhancement of Severance Hall (which has undergone considerable change to extend the reverberation time) must give all concerned . . . a great deal of satisfaction."

The few weeks before the opening of the season were rather on the tense side. It was a little like taking the bandages off after a corneal transplant: would the patient be able to see, and how well? Everybody stood by: Herr Keilholz was ready with a whole set of minor corrective measures, tools and all. Yet the first test with the full orchestra under Mr. Szell revealed the astonishing fact that nothing, absolutely nothing, needed to be changed on the stage. What had been expected to occur did happen, and all calculations turned out to be correct within the smallest margins.

Opening night was greeted by headlines such as these: "Severance gives Szell New, Rich Sonorities"; "New Severance Sound 'Unchains' Orchestra"; "New Severance Sound Is Rich, Mellow"; etc. "In very simple terms," said Keilholz, "it feels as if after a foggy night the daylight had finally come." Later on in October, The Cleveland Orchestra itself made its first recording under Mr. Szell in the rebuilt hall: Dvořák's Symphony No. 8 in G major (Epic BC 1015; Mono LC 3532). "The new sound comes as a pleasant shock," said Paul Affelder in *High Fidelity*; and Irving Kolodin wrote in *The Saturday Review*, "revision of . . . Severance Hall shows . . . results that appear to be a 're-sounding' success."

As mentioned, many meetings, lectures, commencements, and even religious services take place in Severance Hall: microphones had always been advisable, or speakers had to shout. In a good hall of medium size, like this, there should be no such problem. Perhaps the effect of the reconstruction in this area has been best summarized by the internationally renowned Rabbi Abba Hillel Silver of The Temple in Cleveland: "I have found no auditorium so easy and pleasant to speak in as Severance Hall now is."

*

Two things remained to be done after the summer of 1958, one not connected with acoustics, the other very much so. First, the hall lighting was sharply improved in the summer of 1959, with a new switchboard installed backstage and a good deal of relocation of light sources in the hall. The other, and of extreme importance especially to stereo recording, was the matter of humidity control. A humidity of thirty-five to forty percent is usually enough for patron comfort in the winter. On a cold January day, however, it may drop to twenty-five to twenty-eight percent, and high frequency sound as well as the atmosphere begins to "dry." A wet October or November day may produce from forty to fifty percent or more; but one can't be sure of the exact amount. It was now discovered that the proper humidity in the hall sharply influences the quality of stereo work; a percentage of forty-eight to fifty-four was found ideal for making the hall "live," the sound reverberant enough for the microphones. In order to be able to control this at will, the heating and ventilating systems were completely done over. Whereas, before, air had been warmed by steel coils, now live steam was added to the air: it passes over the coils and through the humidifier, entering the hall evenly at all points with a difference of no more than one degree. Instruments located in the hall automatically call for more or less humidity, depending on the setting; but one can control the "thermostat" manually as well, to obtain the exact extent of humidity desired.

Those who were there will never forget how the first reverberation tests were made the day before the opening of the forty-first season, in October 1958. A student audience was invited for a dress rehearsal, so that the acoustics could be examined with the seats occupied. Herr Keilholz walked about with a pistol, calling "Achtung—Schuss!" in different locations before pulling the trigger. Everyone kept quiet, admonished not to laugh at the spectacle. The reports were recorded, and later tested in the laboratory. The results of these tests show this: Reverberation time in the empty hall has been raised to 2.1 seconds; with a full audience it is from 1.7 to 1.9 in the mid-frequencies, and rises steadily above two seconds in the lower frequencies. This means, in round figures, an increase of reverberation time of almost one second—an extraordinary achievement of engineering. It may not sound like much to anyone who does not know how the quality of sound is altered by such an increase in reverberation; but the fact is that the difference of this one second is the crucial difference between dead sound and live sound.

Severance Hall cost more than three million dollars to erect, almost thirty years ago; the value of the building is now estimated as three times as great, were it to be built today, and this does not take into account all the inflationary factors. The acoustical reconstruction described in these pages cost a good deal of money; but, if anyone had doubted that the job needed to be done, he found himself converted in short order. It has indeed been a "sound" investment.

98

The Gewandhaus Orchestra of Leipzig (JANUARY 1983)

THE CITY OF LEIPZIG, in the German Democratic Republic (East Germany) has had a long and distinguished musical tradition. Its earliest records date back to 1015 A.D., and trade fairs have been held there since the twelfth century. When we think of Leipzig, the name of J. S. Bach comes immediately to mind; he was the cantor (chorus master), organist and music director of the Thomaskirche from 1723 to his death in 1750, and virtually all of his mature compositions were first performed in that city. Today, we think of Leipzig mainly as the home of the great Gewandhaus Orchestra, whose current music director is our guest conductor, Kurt Masur.

The New Grove Dictionary of Music and Musicians, edited by Stanley Sadie (1980), contains a nine-page chapter on Leipzig and its music by Percy M. Young, and includes an extensive bibliography. This brief essay draws upon that article, with appreciation.

The Gewandhaus Orchestra originated in an ensemble called the "Grosses Concert", founded in 1743—seven years before Bach's death. J. A. Hiller, who re-established the concert series in 1763, after the Seven Years' War, conducted the first actual "Gewandhaus Concert" on November 25, 1781, in the newly built Gewandhaus ("Cloth Hall"), the market hall of the linen merchants of the city. Under the direction of Felix Mendelssohn, from 1835 to his death in 1847, the Orchestra became one of the finest in Europe. (It is a sad curiosity of history that when Mendelssohn's music was banned by the Nazis in 1936, his statue was removed from the front of the old Gewandhaus; it has never been found.) Noted conductors followed Mendelssohn as director, among them Julius Rietz, Carl Reinecke, and Arthur Nikisch. In our century, many of the world's great conductors appeared as regular guests; Wilhelm Furtwängler was music director from 1922 to 1929, and Bruno Walter from 1929 to 1933 (when the Nazis forced him out). The series of notable musicians on the podium continued with Hermann Abendroth, Herbert Albert, Franz Konwitschny, Vaclav Neumann—and Kurt Masur (since 1970). For a time, Charles Munch (later conductor of the Boston Symphony Orchestra) was the concertmaster. The Orchestra has always collaborated closely with the Academy of Music in Leipzig (the Hochschule für Musik), an institution founded by Mendelssohn. The many recordings made by the Orchestra, especially of the German symphonic literature, are of notable quality.

Great musical history has been made at concerts of the Gewandhaus Orchestra. Mendelssohn's *Violin Concerto* was premiered there, and many of the works of Schubert, Schumann, and Brahms. The latter, in fact, played his *First Piano Concerto* in its first performance at a Gewandhaus concert, and Clara Schumann was a frequent soloist. Wagner, Tchaikovsky, Grieg, Strauss, Pfitzner, Toscanini, Stokowski, and others appeared on its podium. From the beginning, the Orchestra was involved in the "modern music" of its day, having for example played a cycle of all of Beethoven's symphonies during the composer's lifetime.

While the Orchestra actually had its residence in the old Gewandhaus (which gives an amusing double meaning to the English term, "dress rehearsal"), its splendid new concert hall retained the name when it was inaugurated in 1884. Its structure and acoustics were so fine that they became the model for other auditoria, notably Symphony Hall in Boston (opened in 1900). In 1944, the building was destroyed by aerial bombardment, and it was never reconstructed. From the end of World War II to 1981, the Orchestra played in the Kongresshalle, a structure in the Leipzig Zoo. On October 8, 1981, the new Gewandhaus was inaugurated, an acoustically excellent hall seating one thousand nine hundred and twenty-one, in a complex of buildings also comprising the opera house and the university.

Mr. Masur has told us in conversation that the relationship of the Gewandhaus Orchestra to the citizenry is an especially close one; the ensemble was founded and nurtured "by the people", not by an aristocratic elite. The Orchestra has a season of ten-and-a-half months, and a membership of two hundred; that makes it possible for alternating ensembles to play at the opera house as well as in the concert hall, and to give concerts in St. Thomas Church. Smaller groups are drawn from the membership, including eight (!) string quartets, three chamber orchestras, four wind ensembles, and an early-music group. The Orchestra now tours for eight to ten weeks each year, and is frequently joined on tour by the Thomanerchor (the choir of St. Thomas). It also plays for the touring Leipzig Opera. Its national and international tours, in fact, began as early as 1916.

Historic Preservation 1959

*

The following was written after the editor's return visit to Boston in 1959, and published in The Christian Science Monitor *on October 14, 1959 (the paper for which the author served as a contributing music critic from 1950 to 1958).*

*

The new Opera House is the most perfectly equipped building of its class seen in America. Boston's most beautiful theater stands on what, but a few years ago, was one of her crude outlying sites. . . . It is doubtful whether in the musical history of the world there is to be found a more remarkable instance of unity of purpose than that which has been manifested by the Boston public in its willingness to support this splendid Opera House of its own.—Boston Opera Company, 1909

> Do you remember how, for many a spring,
> We drove to town in flushed anticipation.
> To savor *Carmen, Figaro,* the *Ring,*
> In Metropolitannual re-creation?
>
> Yes, Lohengrin's swan boat would arrive anon;
> We were less sure of our own conveyance.
> Maestro, poise your threatening baton,
> But hold the overture yet in abeyance!
>
> Your ardent fans, your operatic slaves,
> Are circling still your eminent domain;
> How can they join the bravos, cheers, and raves,
> If their attempts to park remain in vain?

The curtain's up; the drama moves *con brio*.
Outside, another tragedy takes place;
And, toward the close of first duet or trio,
Some listeners find a distant parking space.

That vexing problem—could it be abolished?
America's Athens cut the Gordian knot:
The Opera House was finally demolished,
And on its site put up a parking lot!

Grim horsepower engines spark a modern course
Of immolation for Brünnhilde's horse.
We drive past Opera Place, shocked, sad, and thwarted
To find our bodies, not our souls, transported.

Design for a New Concert Hall (DECEMBER 1979)

THE WORK of the German poet Christian Morgenstern (1871–1914) has in recent years become known in the United States through a variety of translations. Long considered "untranslatable" because of the unusual symbolism and individualistic treatment of language, Morgenstern's poetry has now been effectively brought to a wider public. In 1964, the editor's father, Albert Roy (1893–1970), published a volume of selected translations, juxtaposed with the original texts, and wittily illustrated by the German cartoonist Martin Koblo (Oscar Brandstetter-Verlag, Wiesbaden). Imbued with Morgenstern's manner of expression, the translator later tried his hand at a "Morgenstern poem" of his own devising, sensitively imitating the unique style of the poet. His son subsequently attempted an English translation, and since the subject is eminently musical it was thought appropriate to publish it in the program book for the first time.

It remains to be observed that Morgenstern invented a number of characters who became vehicles for his ideas; among these are Palmström and von Korf; like Schumann's Florestan and Eusebius, these became spokesmen for the varying aspects of the artist's own personality.

PALMSTRÖM-HALLE
von Albert Roy
(im Stile Christian Morgensterns)

Palmström denkt sich dieses aus:
ein Konzert- und Vortragshaus,
wo die Leute mit dem Rücken
gegen Pult und Podium blicken.

Umgekehrt sind alle Sitze,
und der Augen eitle Blitze
treffen nicht den Künstler, nein,
nur der Mauern starren Schein.

Ausserdem, wenn's einer wagt,
den die Neugier sticht und plagt,
einmal sich herumzudrehen,
um, was er nur hört, zu sehen—

beispielsweise wenn ein Sänger
einen Ton hält etwas länger,
oder gar beim hohen C,
das so wohl tut und so weh,

oder beim fortissimo
wenn der Generalissimo
beide Arme aufwärts schmeisst
und das Trommelfell zerreisst—

PALMSTRÖM HALL
by Albert Roy
(in the style of Christian Morgenstern)

Palmström makes the following conjecture:
one might build, for music and for lecture,
a performing structure where the clacques
look toward stage or lectern with their backs.

Turned about are all the rows of chairs,
and no arrogant perusal or vain stares
thus may strike the artist; not at all:
they meet nothing but the solid wall.

Furthermore, if anybody twitched—
by sharp curiosity be-itched—
to attempt to turn himself around
for beholding what had been but sound—

For example, if a singer, singing,
beyond measure to a note were clinging,
or indeed to settle on high C,
which gives, equally, both pain and glee—

Or at each fortissimo,
when the generalissimo
launches skyward both his arms,
which the ear drum gravely harms—

dann sofort erlischt das Licht,
und solange jener nicht
wieder sich zurückgewandt,
bleibt der Saal in Nacht gebannt.

Palmström hofft, dass solcherart
man mit Licht und Sehkraft spart,
und erhöht wird andrerseits
der Akustik Kraft und Reiz,

insbesondere da der Menge
Ohren so um Sitzeslänge
näher den Estradeteilen
und dem Schallerreger weilen.

Dies ersinnt sich Palmström und
macht es seinem Freunde kund;
und v. Korf schwelgt hingerissen
schon in Zukunftskunstgenüssen.

Then at once the lights go out;
and until the boorish lout
has again turned 'round withal,
darkness reigns throughout the hall.

Palmström hopes that, in this wise,
one could save both light and eyes,
and, moreover, might enhance
the sublime acoustic trance;

For: the ears of every hearer
find themselves a seat-length nearer
to that part of the estate
whence the sound-waves emanate.

Thus goes Palmström's thoughtful trend,
shared at once with his good friend;
fast a-throb, Korf's heart is captured,
futuristic-art-enraptured.

Sir Thomas Beecham Is Alive and Well, Thank You, at 100
(MAY 1979)

"I SAY," asked Sir Thomas Beecham in a loud stage whisper as he returned to the podium for the last piece of his Severance Hall program in 1956, "what are we playing?" Leaning over, and speaking in an equally conspiratorial tone, Concertmaster Josef Gingold replied: "The Dying Flutchman."

It was one of the few times in Sir Thomas's career when he was on the receiving end of a quip, and the guffaws came from him instead of his audience. One of the wittiest individuals ever to enliven the world of serious music, he was surely the one conductor in history whose remarks received nearly as much attention as his music-making. No one was safe from his acid tongue, but so funny were his comments that even the victims had to join in the laughter—most of the time. One doubts that a certain soprano ever recovered from her rehearsal encounter with Sir Thomas. Engaging the conductor in an argument (an enterprise risky in the extreme) how a certain passage should be sung, she finally exploded: "Sir Thomas, I will have you remember that I am one of the leading singers in the world!" "Don't worry, Madam," the conductor replied in most solicitous manner, "your secret is safe with me."

The Cleveland program of January 19–21, 1956, was a fine example of Beecham's wide-ranging musical interests: *The Corsair* Overture by Berlioz, the *Prague Symphony* by Mozart, and *Tapiola*, the tone poem by Sibelius, in the first half; there followed *Brigg Fair*, the Rhapsody by Delius (a composer rapturously espoused by Beecham), and finally *The Flying Dutchman Overture* by Wagner. For his first appearance at these concerts, April 6–8, 1944, Sir Thomas began with the *Meistersinger Prelude* by Wagner, continued with the *"Amaryllis" Suite* arranged by him from music by Handel, and closed the first half with the *Haffner Symphony* by Mozart; the second half contained a single favorite work, the *Second Symphony* by Sibelius. Beecham conducted what he liked, and only that; his dislikes were as vehemently held as his favorites, and the lists of both are long. His discography was immense; it includes some forty works by Mozart alone, some in multiple recordings made over many decades.

So extensive is Sir Thomas's legacy of recordings, and so vivid is the world's memory of him, that one can take only technical exception to the fanciful title of this essay. Factually speaking, he died on March 8, 1961, having been born nearly eighty-two years before, on April 29, 1879. A Lancashireman, he was the son of a manufacturer and financier, Joseph Beecham, who was created a baronet in 1914. While Thomas succeeded to the title in 1916, he had himself been knighted a year before, for his services to music and especially to opera in England. The family fortune was in pharmaceuticals, and that is why the London Philharmonic Orchestra, founded by him in 1932, was sometimes irreverently referred to as the Pillharmonic. From 1947 on he led another ensemble founded by him, the Royal Philharmonic. Lest it be thought that Sir Thomas despised the "moderns" as much as he adored the "classics", it should be recalled that the contemporary masters of his own early career were Richard Strauss, Frederick Delius, and the young Igor Stravinsky, whose music he supported wholeheartedly.

"Beecham's career," Grove's Dictionary (1954) tells us, "is unique for two reasons: his peculiar service to British music and his interpretative power as viewed internationally and objectively. The second of these is to some extent implied in the first: his combination of supreme talent and will-power has improved vastly the standard of British orchestras, impressed on the public mind numerous operas of all periods, and introduced hitherto little-known music.... Especially during the first world war, his resources kept music alive in even the remotest corners of the country. In addition, as a brilliantly gifted dialectician, he has constituted himself an outspoken critic and adviser-in-chief on the conditions in the musical world, and his good sense is none the less in evidence for being sometimes uttered with a deliberate disregard of tact. . . . He is one of the few executants of his time who have set a standard of performance, forged a new style and contributed something definite and imperishable to musical art and science. For hitherto unsuspected nuances, phrasings, outlines, for sensuous warmth and unerring feeling for drama and climax, the art of Beecham remains one of the most precious discoveries of our time."

Grove's makes a point of particular relevance to this program when it recalls that "to Beecham is due the initiation and maintenance of the Mozart cult in Britain". Indeed, it is important to remember—as critic John Ardoin has done—that "Sir Thomas was born into a world which regarded Mozart as a dainty salon composer, an Eighteenth Century music box. It is difficult for us today, with our constant exposure to all periods of music and with access, on disc, to virtually every note of Mozart, to realize the battle Beecham fought over several decades to 'plug this little fellow'. . . . But it was not so much *what* Beecham did for Mozart as *how* he did it. . . . He humanized Mozart and filled his phrases with full-bodied theater. Not for Beecham a scaled-down, anemic orchestra to play Mozart. He employed instead a complete string choir and frequently doubled winds for stronger sonorities." The composer himself, it should be noted, was always delighted to have as large an orchestra as possible at his disposal. In the Mozart Bicentennial observances in 1956, Sir Thomas delivered at the University of Illinois an extensive lecture (reported to be off-the-cuff) with his customary brilliance, wit, and irascibility. Here are some excerpts from the lecture, with no particular sequence, leaving out some of the conductor's most outrageous historical fibs and gaffes—which were always delivered with the same unshakable conviction as his most remarkable insights.

Mozart is one of the most original geniuses the world has ever seen in the way of spontaneous creation, and, of all the composers who have ever lived, he is the one to whom all succeeding composers are the most indebted. Now, I think it is beginning to dawn upon the larger number of genuinely musical people that this extraordinary person wrote a great portion of the most beautiful tunes in the world. . . . I will champion those tunes as tunes of beauty, of grace, of splendour, of charm, even of humour, against any other tunes written by any other composer since the world began. . . .

Shakespeare had the happy knack of putting thoughts which are in your and my mind and which were in those of the Greeks and Romans into a new language that has come down to us as the most fitting medium for the thought contained. So fitting, that hundreds and hundreds of lines and phrases are part of our current, living consciousness. Now, so far as I'm concerned, so far as all the great musicians of the last fifty or sixty years whom I have known are concerned, this same kind of musical currency by Mozart has passed into our consciousness. . . .

"When I first started giving Mozart in great lumps, the world of London knew three symphonies, two operas, two pianoforte concertos and a miscellaneous porte-manteau of little pieces. I plugged and plugged this fellow. Whenever I played a symphony other than the last three, the press said, 'Oh, an early work.' It is the fashion to talk about 'early works'. There is only one composer in the world the critics will not refer to with disrespect to his early works, and that is Beethoven. They don't even call symphonies one and two early works now; they are afraid. Remember always one thing about people who write about music: Their distinguishing features are conventionality, cowardice and timidity. 'Early works'? Masterpieces! I've plugged and plugged and plugged. I've given over one thousand performances of his operas, translated them into English, and today what are we faced with? A bicentennial. Everyone is playing the man. Of course, they're not doing it with a great deal of sincerity. There's some piety in it, you know, and fashion. In two years he'll be dropped again and carefully put in the dustbin for another twenty years. But that's all right; I've lived through many of those phases. But it's refreshing today to a person like myself to savour this glut, this monstrous festival of Mozart that is taking place all over the world. . . .

Sir Thomas was, happily, mistaken. Mozart, whom he called near the end of his lecture "the central, pivotal point in the music of Europe", is no longer a figure of fashion, who undergoes "phases". The happy glut continues, bicentennial or no. And as we recall Sir Thomas on his centennial, we thank him also for "plugging" Mozart with such vim and vigor, as well as skill and sensitivity in performance. The story is no doubt true that at the party where the seventy-fifth (or was it eightieth?) birthday of the great conductor was being celebrated, he became increasingly glum and annoyed at every telegram, card or other felicitation that arrived. Everyone wondered what the matter was. Finally, Sir Thomas exploded in red-faced rage: *"Nothing from Mozart?"*

It had all been for show. But what a show!*

"Going Home" (APRIL 1964),
by Joseph E. Adams

A YOUNG, broad-shouldered man from far across the sea stood in an organ loft of a small church in an Iowa village with a violin in his hand. He gently raised the instrument to his shoulder and began to play the "Largo" of Dvořák's *Ninth Symphony*, *"From the New World"*. A deep and unique sense of devotion poured forth from the strings.

Who was this young artist? What was his attachment to the village in Iowa? Why did he play with such depth and emotion in an organ loft of an empty church? The story began toward the close of the last century.

In 1893, Antonín Dvořák, weary from responsibilities as director of the National Conservatory of Music in New York, travelled to Spillville, Iowa, with his wife and children. He had heard that the village of three hundred and fifty people was predominantly Czech and that he might be able to speak his native tongue while summering in an atmosphere not unlike that of his beloved homeland. There Dvořák played the pipe organ daily, had an opportunity to spend time with his family, and walked in the woods where he often found inspiration to compose. He would sometimes jot his musical ideas on the starched cuffs of his shirts. The woman who washed his linen passed away in recent years. It is said that she complained it was much too difficult to wash the notes out of his cuffs. These notes have never died—for from them came the *"American" Quartet in F Major*, the *Quintet in E-Flat Major*, and inspiration for later works. The orchestration of the symphony called *"From the New World"* was also completed that same summer.

Dvořák never returned to Spillville, Iowa. He soon went back to his beloved Czechoslovakia where music continued to flow from his pen. Yet the popularity of the works written in Spillville and Dvořák's love for that bit of Czechoslovakia in America soon made the little village far better known in Prague than in the New World—and so it remains today.

Shortly after the Dvořák family returned to Czechoslovakia, his daughter Otilie was

---

*The International Sir Thomas Beecham Society produces and promotes lectures, broadcasts and publications about Sir Thomas and his performances.—Editor.

married to the Czech composer and violinist, Josef Suk, who was one of her father's favorite pupils. The marriage to the already famous artist was cruelly brief, since she died at the early age of twenty-seven; he never remarried, and died in 1935 at the age of sixty-one. The heritage of Dvořák and Suk was to live again when the grandson of Otilie and Josef was born in 1929 and named after his grandfather.

This gentle, talented person grew up in a country and world torn with war, grief, and heartbreak. He was given a conventional education which seemed so practical for the times, but his great inherited gift soon burst from its cocoon. By the time he was in his late teens, after studying at the Prague Conservatory, it was obvious that he had "bettered the instructor" and soon was to become the leading Czech violinist of his generation. Ultimately, he would surely take his place with the great violinists of our time.

In Josef Suk's heart burned the desire to see the country that had so inspired his great-grandfather, and, if possible, that little bit of Czechoslovakia in Iowa called Spillville. When the brilliant young artist came to make his American début with The Cleveland Orchestra in January of 1964, at the invitation of George Szell, he inquired almost immediately: "How can I get to Spillville?" His eagerness to re-establish contact with his heritage was like a powerful lodestone. It became an extraordinary privilege for this writer and for Miss Dorothy Humel to join the artist on this genuine pilgrimage; our sense of anticipation helped us over many a vicissitude in our journey, so severely limited in time: a single day.

Josef Suk seemed in a world apart from us, and we were only observers from the time we arrived in Spillville where we were greeted by Charles Andera, who is curator of the Dvořák museum. Lunch was served in Old World style at the modest home of the Adolph Uhers—almost all conversation was in Czech. Mrs. Uher said that she would never forget the day when Josef Suk played *"Humoresque"* for her. A brief visit to the Dvořák memorial in the park—the old folk of the village coming to talk to him in his native tongue—the warm look in Josef's face as he ran his talented hands over the mementos of his illustrious great-grandfather—all these moments were part of something like a mirage.

Josef was transported to another world spiritually when we visited St. Wenceslas Church where Dvořák played the organ daily. What better way was there for the young artist to show his reverence and respect for the source of his great talent than to play his great-grandfather's music before the organ where it took form and life? The "Largo" from the *"New World" Symphony* which he played in the organ loft at Spillville, Iowa, was a gentle song of devotion, dedication, yearning, and love. When Josef Suk went to Spillville, he was in truth "going home".

War Requiem, Op. 66
By Benjamin Britten (MARCH 1988)

*

This section of the concert program note is included among the essays of this book because it contains commentary on matters of history, politics, and ethics as well as music.

*

BENJAMIN BRITTEN died untimely in his sixty-fourth year, after a long battle with heart disease. In his vast output, music for the voice is prominent, in numerous operas, songs and song cycles, and choral works. "One of my chief aims," he once said, "is to restore to the musical setting of the English language a brilliance, freedom, and vitality that have been curiously absent since the death of Purcell." Surely his most important work combining voices and instruments is his monumental *War Requiem, Op. 66,* of 1961—a composition which one would like to be in the regular repertoire of performing organizations everywhere, for its humanistic message as well as for its magnificent music.

With this music composed and performed as the composer was approaching his fiftieth birthday, Britten appears to have created one of the significant works of art in our century. No other composition within recent memory has caused a "resonance" of such power and duration. This work, he said, had "been boiling inside him for years"; and its shaping into an artwork of perhaps universal validity has only intensified its stature as a personal document. Britten may have felt, with Robert Schumann, that "it is not the praise that uplifts the artist, but the joy in finding that what he had left resounds back harmoniously from the hearts of men."

It is possible that Britten shaped this extraordinary work as a parallel to the juxtaposition of the new and artistically magnificent Coventry Cathedral with the ruins of the old, destroyed in an air raid on November 14, 1940. Just as old and new there stand in a vivid and breath-stopping conjunction, so do the text of the traditional and ancient *Requiem* or Mass for the Dead and the poems of Wilfred Owen, the young Englishman killed at age twenty-five on November 4, 1918, seven days before the Armistice. It is a daring and original concept, and one which brings home the message of both texts in a way that could fail to move only the most insensitive of hearers. This is surely the most dramatic as well as the most deeply-felt setting of the *Requiem* text since the powerful "sacred opera" by Verdi, and one that can be comprehended on many levels.

The intermingling and connection of the old and new texts are self-evident. It remains to be recalled that on the title page of the score is a motto quoted from Owen: "My subject is War, and the pity of War. The poetry is in the pity. All a poet can do today is warn." In addition to its stature as a work of art, the *War Requiem* joins the impressive roster of "protest pieces" in the literature of all the arts, and this anguished outcry brings us face to face with the piteous question when in human history the warning of the artist has ever been heeded. While the survival value of great art is phenomenal, its efficacy in shaping the actions of mankind is minimal. The great cathedrals did not prevent the Inquisition and the religious wars of the past, nor did Schiller's and Beethoven's appeal to human brotherhood affect the relationships of nations. Picasso's *Guernica* did not result in one less bombing of civilians. Perhaps the antiwar sentiments of popular culture (and counterculture) in recent decades have had a somewhat more direct effect on large masses of people.

What would Wilfred Owen have felt had he known that twenty-one years after his needless death in "the war to end wars" a Second World War would break out, killing more than fifty million people; and that a half-century after that several dozen "minor" ones would be raging around the globe, each with its "Mutual Assured Destruction" capability built in? (The acronym for that "policy", of course, is M.A.D.) How would he have responded to the fact that the superpowers are trying to save the world from World War III and nuclear genocide by various "Strategic Arms Limitation Treaties" while busily building brand-new weapons to nullify the effect of those treaties and retain intact the "balance of terror"? Would he have retained a semblance of hope in the sense and sanity of mankind?

Every day of the year, billions are spent by all nations for the weapons, personnel, and supplies of war, on what is euphemistically called "defense". At the same time, billions of people are severely underfed, underhoused, and undereducated, but—or because—they are heavily overarmed.

It is, ultimately, the individual who creates, who listens, and who acts to the best of his or her understanding. But if Voltaire, Swift, Twain, Shaw, and Schweitzer preached in vain, shall Owen and Britten be heard and heeded by those in whom we entrust (or to whom we surrender) the ultimate power over our fragile destinies? We fear the answer. There is (or should be) no way in which the *War Requiem* is heard today "merely" as a work of art whose values must be confined to the concert hall and performance situation. Without question, Britten intended that its "success" or "failure" must ultimately be measured also in the contribution it makes (or fails to make) to mankind's awareness of its vulnerability and to its inescapable duty to pull itself back from the abyss of ultimate—and totally senseless—annihilation. *Nil inultum remanebit.*

*

For the first American performances at Tanglewood, some fourteen months after its world premiere, John N. Burk of the Boston Symphony Orchestra succinctly described the intent and structure of Britten's *War Requiem:*

> The score is divided into three distinct groups. The first is the full chorus and orchestra with soprano solo, who perform the *Missa pro Defunctis.* These performers of the Mass are complemented by the Boys' Choir chanting parts of the service. Their innocent voices sound remote and apart, in complete relief from the turbulence of the larger chorus and the poignant voice of the solo soprano which rises about it. The third group conveys the personal message of the poet, in contrast to the larger group with its formal ritual text. These consist of the solo tenor and baritone, who are accompanied by the small chamber orchestra as they declaim in a free recitative the English verses of Wilfred Owen. The two men are heard separately or together, in close alternation with the sections of the Mass. The poet's tragic contemplation of death, courageous, defiant, protesting, sorrowful, follows quite naturally the dread outcries and anguished prayers of the missal text. The tenor and baritone parts are always accompanied by the lighter chamber orchestra, a device by which the composer has skillfully thrown their words into dramatic prominence and permitted the utmost expressive accentuation. He has thus drawn upon disparate elements, ritual associations and lay dramatic impact, but he has fused them into a unified musical discourse which is peculiarly his own, compiled of a weird orchestral color and harmonic and contrapuntal freedom, with a singleness of mood and style reached above all by the overriding impulsion of his subject.

Writing "The Persistence of Benjamin Britten" in the September 16, 1978, issue of *Saturday Review*, music critic Irving Kolodin comments on the quality of his work, evidenced by numerous continuing performances of a wide repertoire. The *War Requiem*, he observes, exhibits with special power a quality and a preoccupation pervasive in Britten's output: "The quality is the simple, eternal one that ties man to art, and art to man: an overriding sense of compassion for human misery."

"It Must Be Right: I've Done It from My Youth" (MARCH 1983)

—George Crabbe
(1754–1832)

FOR HIS IMAGINATIVE and endlessly inventive "Adventures in Good Music", Karl Haas recently produced an appropriate New Year's program that demonstrated the astonishing precocity of many great composers. He played examples of orchestral works by Mozart written at eight or nine, Mendelssohn and Rossini at twelve, Schubert at sixteen (he wrote *Erlkönig* at seventeen!), Bizet at seventeen. Time permitting, he could have included Brahms, hailed as a genius at twenty by Schumann; Chopin, who wrote both of his concertos before he was twenty; Mahler, who completed *Das Klagende Lied* at twenty; Pergolesi, who died at twenty-six, and many others. But although masterpieces by teen-agers are legion, one should not forget that major works written by composers in their twenties are also by "young people". "Precocity," said Dr. Haas, "cannot be explained; but it holds us in awe."

It leads one to the thought that such creative achievement at a young age is almost entirely a province of music. No other art—virtually no other activity—can match it. There are very few painters whose masterpieces date from their teens, though their gifts were surely evident early. Few poets create mature works at so young an age; only Keats and Rimbaud come instantly to mind, Radiguet and Mailer as novelists. It is almost unheard-of that a businessman is a "success" by his early twenties. Even from "whiz kids" in science and math we do not expect major discoveries and astounding equations. A physician may not begin his practice until his long training period is over. Most professions require long apprenticeships before outstanding and original work becomes possible.

Without attempting to delve deeply into physiology, psychology, genetics, and related subjects, one suspects that the musical gift is one that is there from the beginning, and matures at a rate much faster than virtually any other talent or skill. The prodigy is indeed prodigious, with such endowments as pitch perception, rhythmic sense, and even structural awareness becoming evident when the child is still an infant. Musical children sing before they can talk, and play before they can write. Creativity, and re-creativity, are inborn with them, and their progress is rapid.

Although there is of course an important difference between those gifts, the creative and the re-creative or performing, in most prodigy composers the executant ability is and was exceptionally high. The child that gives its first recital at six, plays with an orchestra at seven, conducts for the first time at eight (as did Lorin Maazel), and composes attractively at nine (as did Prokofiev, not to mention again the masters of the past), is a phenomenon that boggles the mind. So to speak, it is "all there", waiting only for further experience and maturity to reach full capacity. Among prodigious performing children, of course, child actors and actresses stand out; but few if any of them have made their marks as playwrights at so early an age.

George Szell literally wrote some three hundred compositions as a youngster, many of them prominently performed; he appeared as composer-soloist with the Berlin Philharmonic at twelve, and first conducted at sixteen. Arturo Toscanini made his podium debut with *Aïda* at nineteen. At twenty-five Erich Leinsdorf was a conductor in the German wing of the Metropolitan Opera; James Levine, a piano soloist with orchestra at ten and a promising conductor in his early twenties, was appointed principal conductor of the Met at thirty, music director at thirty-two. At thirty-three, James Conlon has been a professional conductor for a decade, and his soloist in a recent concert series here, Michel Beroff, is of the same age with an equally long career already behind him. Riccardo Chailly made his operatic debut at nineteen (shades of Toscanini!) with *Werther,* and is now—at the age of thirty—a podium personality of world renown.

During a "Youth Week" at Severance Hall, Anne-Sophie Mutter, age nineteen, made her spectacular début here; she had been violin soloist with Herbert von Karajan when only fourteen. Christiane Edinger, our violin soloist here last Friday morning, made her orchestral début while still a student, and Dylana Jenson's international career as a violinist also began in her teens. This is quite in the tradition of Yehudi Menuhin, who played the Beethoven Violin Concerto in New York at eleven, and with The Cleveland Orchestra at twelve. In the same week as Miss Mutter, Philippe Bianconi—the Casadesus Competition winner for 1981—appeared with the Orchestra in a Friday morning concert, and gave an extraordinarily mature recital of French piano music at the Cleveland Museum of Art two days later; he is twenty-two. The listing of such young performers of extraordinary gifts and accomplishments is virtually endless. How does it happen?

We do not know. Perhaps the only parallel to such achievement in youth is in athletics, where a phenomenon like Bjorn Borg can be a top-ranking tennis player at seventeen—and "retire" at twenty-six (as a millionaire). Like the natural gift of the exceptional sportsman, it is a central part of the total personality—physical, mental, and emotional—of the genius musician. While there are some "late bloomers" like Beethoven and Wagner and Stravinsky, who were "already" in their mid-twenties when they wrote their first important works, most composing and performing geniuses spring almost full-formed from the head of Jove (like the legendary goddess of wisdom, Minerva). If their physical and emotional development can keep pace with their musical gift, these phenomena of the art become genuine artists, and incomparably enrich our lives.

Martin Luther's 500th Anniversary:
His Musical Contribution (JANUARY 1984)

Indeed I plainly judge and do not hesitate to affirm that except for theology there is no art that could be put on the same level as music, since, except for theology, music alone produces what otherwise only theology can, namely a calm and joyful disposition. My love for music is abundant and overflowing.

—Martin Luther
(in a letter to the composer and court musician Ludwig Senfl,
October 1530)

MARTIN LUTHER was born in Eisleben, now East Germany, on November 10, 1483, and died there on February 18, 1546, at the age of sixty-two. Five hundred years after his birth, he remains a figure of controversy on many levels; yet his contribution to Western civilization, and his role in the history of Christianity, are of profound importance. Pope John Paul II has recently spoken in praise of Luther's position as a sincere reformer of the Church, a step of extraordinary significance in the ecumenical movement; and he has taken a further long step by participating last December in a Protestant church service in Rome. The anniversary has been observed by extensive articles in the *National Geographic*, in *The New York Times Magazine*, *Time* magazine, and many other publications.

Here we are primarily concerned with Luther's work in music and influence upon it. In his notable book of 1935, *A History of Musical Thought*, Donald N. Ferguson wrote that the first Protestant songbook was issued in 1524, just four years after Luther is supposed to have posted his famous Ninety-five Theses on the Wittenberg church portal. In the decades following, states the author, "It was said that these hymns made more converts to Luther's faith than all his speeches and writings, and Heinrich Heine rightly called Luther's hymn, *Ein' feste Burg ist unser Gott*, the 'Marseillaise of the Reformation'."

In his valuable book of 1939, *Music, History and Ideas* (Harvard University Press, Cambridge, Mass.), Hugo Leichtentritt summed up the Great Reformer's musical position:

Martin Luther was not only a great lover of music, a skillful amateur, to some extent even a composer, but he knew perfectly well what powerful aid music could bring to the cause of the new Protestant movement. . . . In his writings many references can be found to music in general and to single composers. . . .

For four centuries Luther's own contributions, his German chorales, have been important for Protestant music. He had a perfectly clear conception of the kind of music he needed for the new Church. He wished to reach the common people, and for that neither the Latin language nor Gregorian chant were of use to him. To achieve his end he introduced German instead of the Latin of the Catholic service, and chose in place of the noble but complex melodic substance of Gregorian chant something much simpler, less pretentious, more akin to German folk song.

One of Luther's immortal accomplishments is the Protestant chorale, the new German spiritual folk song. . . . Even though actual evidence is lacking concerning his activity as composer, he remains the originator of the idea, and he knew how to inspire artists of rank to write in a style adapted to the character of the Protestant creed. And there is no doubt that the words, at least, of some thirty of the finest German chorales were written by Luther. . . .

The most famous chorale attributed to him is 'Ein' feste Burg ist unser Gott'. It was written in 1528, when pestilence, at that time a frequent and dreadful guest in Europe, was approaching once more, and to a certain extent it is a poetic paraphrase of the Forty-sixth Psalm. But what a power of language, what a strong manly soul in these verses, what consoling confidence in the help of God, what a courageous, militant spirit against the evil in the world!

Most of Luther's chorales were written in the years 1523 and 1524. The melodies were new only in part; a number of them were taken over from the Ambrosian hymns of the Catholic Church, from medieval sequences, from Gregorian chant, and from German popular songs. Luther did not simply copy these old melodies, he changed them and adapted them to their new purposes with eminent insight and skill.... Through four centuries these Protestant chorale tunes have been the most precious material of German church music. Innumerable compositions have been written on them. One cannot imagine Bach's art without the cantus firmus of those glorious spiritual folk songs. No cantata, no Passion music, no Bach motet, no organ chorale prelude exists without these tunes. They are the center of all Bach's church music, its deepest and most solid foundation....

Martin Luther sang tenor, played the lute, made music at home, composed and edited. Had he not had another mission, he could have been a professional musician.

Beethoven's Second Symphony and "Escapism" (JANUARY 1983)

WHAT IS OUR CONCEPTION of an "escapist"? Perhaps this: one who refuses to face the facts, covering his awareness of them with a veneer of merrymaking or of neurosis. Rare, however, is the man who has in himself the creative genius to transform his "escape" into a masterwork. It is an odd fact, but a fact nevertheless, that virtually every great composer leads a double-life, one which involves continual and repeated withdrawal from the realities of his daily existence. To be sure, he carries with him into that other world the sharpened perceptions gained during his personal maturing, and they profoundly influence his creative act; but he does not—even if his name is Tchaikovsky—mirror his day-to-day experiences in his musical production. What he writes may offer hardly any clue to the way he feels on that day, in that week, or even that year. He demonstrates his command of the musical art; he creates, with utter sincerity, those sound-combinations which will call forth specific emotional and intellectual reactions in his listeners. He searches, as Susanne Langer has put it, for "significant form". He "com-poses" in the sense of building, or, as Beethoven himself explained, he "thinks in sounds"; yet what he offers are hardly ever his personal feelings of the moment, but their images, known and remembered by him, and, he trusts, by his future listener. As Debussy said, the composer picks from memory the emotions he needs. "But those who write masterpieces in floods of tears," he continues, "are barefaced liars."

These things are true, as any real composer knows. And they explain, perhaps, why Beethoven was—and needed to be—the greatest escapist of them all. We cannot listen to the *Second Symphony* without a keen sense of joyfulness, of an out-going, affirmative cast. This music says "yes", with hardly a shadow of darkness. Beethoven the man said "no", with hardly a ray of light, at exactly the same time. The year was 1802, Beethoven was thirty-one, and spending the months from May to October at his favorite summer place, in Heiligenstadt near Vienna. It was there that the impact of the physical disaster which had struck him became almost too much to bear: his deafness was getting worse. He could not then know that it was just the effect of that most horrible affliction for a musician which would make his work the unique expression we know as the later Beethoven style; he knew at that time only that he had but one means of escape from suicide or madness: and that was his art. When he wrote his will, the so-called "Heiligenstadt Testament", in October of 1802, taking a symbolic (and highly "literary") leave of his brothers, of all joy, and of life itself, his *Second Symphony* was almost finished before him. "O you my fellow-men," the document begins, "who take me or denounce me as morose, crabbed, or misanthropic, how you do me wrong! You know not the secret cause of what seems thus to you." And those were the days of this most joyous, powerful, and compelling music of his young manhood, the *D major Symphony*. He had not only escaped, but—for the first time of many—he had conquered.

"Esprit de Choeur"
The Inspiring True Story of
The Cleveland Orchestra Chorus's European Tour
(MARCH 1986),
by Judith M. Weiss

WHILE THE CLEVELAND ORCHESTRA made its triumphal march across Europe last month, The Cleveland Orchestra Chorus made history in its own way with its two-week performing tour to England and Belgium. This was the first time an American symphony chorus had appeared with its parent orchestra outside the United States. How appropriate for a group which was once dubbed "the first chorus in the land"! Throughout its thirty-year history, the one-hundred-and-eighty-member, all-volunteer chorus has worked hard to maintain a professional standard worthy of our great Cleveland Orchestra. Now, in order to take our place with the Orchestra on tour, we rose to a new level of commitment and accomplishment in the process of planning and fund-raising.

The chorus managed to raise two hundred and eighty thousand dollars during the course of the year, through our personal pledges, the Chorus Operating Fund (a permanent Musical Arts Association fund established by the chorus with fees earned for recordings and television appearances), sales of a Cleveland Orchestra recording underwritten by the J. M. Smucker Co., numerous donations from individuals, groups and foundations, and tour concert fees. The generous outlay of time and energy by members of the staff and administration of the Musical Arts Association in helping to prepare and organize the trip was greatly appreciated. Through the courtesy of the performing artists, Severance Hall, and the Church of the Covenant, two benefit concerts were given: a recital by soprano Susan Cady assisted by members of the Orchestra, and a chamber music marathon arranged by cellist Harvey Wolfe. Support came from other members of the Orchestra family as well; both the Junior Committee and Women's Committee made substantial gifts. For us, the greatest—and unsolicited—tribute came from the Orchestra members themselves, who took up a collection in our behalf.

*

By the time our planes left the ground, every chorus member had a tremendous personal stake in the tour, so we were determined to make it artistically rewarding. And our indefatigable director Robert Page was there to demand our utmost musical effort.

High points of the tour were two performances of Beethoven's *Ninth* with The Cleveland Orchestra under Christoph von Dohnányi. It's always a privilege to perform with them, no matter how often we do it at home in Severance Hall—but to share the stage of London's Royal Festival Hall and Brussels' Palais des Beaux-Arts for the roof-raising "Ode to Joy" was a thrill that made the whole trip worthwhile. In Brussels, there was a man in the balcony who jumped to his feet, clapping resonantly and rhythmically, keeping it up until the rest of the audience, around the fifth or sixth curtain call, joined in. I would have liked to pack up that gentleman and bring him back to Cleveland!

Two performances of Brahms's *Requiem,* with the Oxford Pro Musica conducted by Philip Simms and with the Belgian National Opera Chorus and Orchestra conducted by Günther Wagner, gave us an insight into the workings of European ensembles that made us appreciate our own all the more. Two *a cappella* concerts of twentieth century American music conducted by Mr. Page rounded out the series. The first provided us with a delightful, though freezing, day at Radley College, a traditional English public school. The second offered us the merest glimpse of the charming city of Bruges.

Our schedule was crowded with rehearsals, performances and bus transfers, leaving little time for the usual tourist pursuits. Shopping, however, was one diversion that everyone found time for. The colorful wool scarves we bought in England soon became a chorus emblem, as we kept our throats wrapped against the chill indoors and out.

While we quickly learned to adapt to unheated buildings, our European hosts seemed unable to cope with extreme weather conditions. The day we arrived in Oxford, a "blizzard" had closed down a conference at our hotel, preventing the delegates from vacating our rooms. What blizzard, we wondered, seeing only what Clevelanders call a dusting of snow. At our concert that evening, one of the locals apologized for the half-filled hall. "People just don't go out in this weather," he explained. Likewise in Brussels, an attempt to reach the program editor for the Belgian National Opera at his office proved futile. The reason? "It's cold outside, and he lives in the suburbs."

As they say, you've got to be tough. . . . If the cold couldn't stop us, neither could the flu, though it spread like a plague through our ranks. Three chorus members, doctors Michael Powell, Dean Wochner, and Robert Weiss, found themselves with an *ad hoc* group practice. Not being licensed to prescribe drugs on foreign soil, the best they could offer was advice: try to rest, take aspirin, drink fluids. By the end of the tour, we were all carrying our personal bottles of mineral water. Meanwhile, the two chorus clerics, Rev. William Lucht and Fr. Robert Sanson, looked after our spiritual health. Father Bob celebrated Mass for about thirty-five of the faithful on Sunday morning in Oxford, praying for our continued safe journey across the Channel. Physical safety had been a concern since the day of our arrival in London, when an I.R.A. bomb threat forced a hasty though temporary evacuation of our hotel.

*

A few other tour members deserve honorable mention for making things go smoothly for everyone: Chorus coordinator Nancy Gage and librarian Eleanor Kushnick worked out the logistics of every bus transfer, rehearsal room and stage entrance. Michael Evans and Nicholas Corbould, couriers from Specialised Travel, Ltd., helped us find our way around, arranged sightseeing tours, recommended restaurants and faithfully attended every rehearsal. Chorus Operating Committee chairman G. Michael Skerritt's enthusiasm inspired us throughout the long planning period as well as the tour itself. The skills of assistant director Michael Seredick and accompanist Betty Meyers could always be depended on. Fine solo work was delivered by Joanne Daykin, Sherri Weiler and Susan Cady. Our unofficial chorus jester was Stephen Di Lauro, whose well-timed wit kept us all in stitches. And twenty-two loving family members, who paid their own way to accompany us, put up with our demanding schedule, listened to our gripes and cheered us at every concert.

Gluttons for punishment—or triumph—we began laying plans on the return flight home for the Second International Cleveland Orchestra Chorus Tour!*

A Letter to the Chorus (DECEMBER 1963), by Robert Shaw

*

When Beethoven's Missa Solemnis *was performed at these concerts in 1963 under Robert Shaw's direction, the program contained a letter from Mr. Shaw to The Cleveland Orchestra Chorus, discussing some spiritual as well as technical issues posed by this work. Excerpts from this letter are here reprinted by kind permission.*

*

I WONDER if there is anything in the choral-symphonic repertoire which can prepare the singer for the ordeal of the *Missa Solemnis.* Certainly it must be true that those who have endured for some weeks the physical and intellectual agony of "getting it into the voice" are uniquely prepared for its deeper understandings.

The *Missa Solemnis* is symphonic in scope and detail. Instrumentalists are not only more familiar with its style and technical demands; their instruments also render them more capable of coping with them. For the singer, however, the work is a frightening and frustrating experience. He is asked to perform feats absolutely unequalled in vocal literature—still unique after almost a century and a half . . . . (A number of these technical problems, in range, dynamic alternation, rhythm and tempo, were then illustrated in the letter.)

The point of course is *not* that Beethoven did not know how to write for the voice. He knew precisely what he wanted to say. He exhausted, exploited and ennobled the voice. He gave it things to say which never had been imagined. In this sense the *Missa Solemnis* is a terrifyingly *avant-garde* piece of music.

Finally, of course, what all the agony stems from and comes to is the explosion which he has proposed to the aesthetic, emotional and religious nature. None of the religious—or anti-religious—traditions of Western civilization can prepare us for this.

---

* Judith M. Weiss has been a member of The Cleveland Orchestra Chorus for seven years, and so has her husband, a pediatrician. She formerly served as Director of Communications and Development at The Cleveland Music School Settlement, and she has recently published articles in *Northern Ohio Live* and *New Cleveland Woman.*—Editor.

We may not be able to verbalize this experience. ("Music exists to convey that which cannot be otherwise conveyed.") But those of us who have bet our voices against his notes, who have suffered through the long hours of rehearsal and performance, may have a closer sense of what Beethoven may have suffered in the writing.

The Cleveland Arts Prize

From the time of the first Cleveland Arts Prize Awards in 1961, the Cleveland Orchestra program book each year included an article of this nature which named the current honorees. Among the recipients of special citations have been Cleveland Orchestra conductors George Szell, Louis Lane, Lorin Maazel and Christoph von Dohnányi.

THE CLEVELAND ARTS PRIZE is an institution unique to Cleveland, exemplifying this community's eagerness to say "thank you" to this area's artists who have enriched and enhanced our lives. Established in 1961 by the Women's City Club of Cleveland, with the cooperation of the mayor of the City, the project was designed "to symbolize a perceptive community's respect and need for its creative artists, and to encourage the free pursuit of excellence." It was hoped, in addition, that the Prize would stimulate the growth of enlightened patronage and help to foster a special relationship between the community and its artists. In 1992, The Cleveland Arts Prize observed its thirty-second anniversary.

From the outset, the project coordinator has been Martha J. Joseph; after thirty years of imaginative and dedicated service in that post, she has now passed the functions of chairperson to Mary Louise Hahn. Nominating and selection committees of highly qualified individuals assist in the choice of winners, based on specific and demanding criteria. Several foundations have generously supported the Prize over the years, and the project is now pleased to be endowed in perpetuity.

Since the first awards were made in 1961, over one hundred artists of this area or with significant Cleveland roots have been honored in an annual ceremony, in the fields of music, literature, visual arts, architecture, and dance. It was recognized from the beginning that the creative arts do not exist or flourish in a vacuum, and require not only an aware and interested public but a large number of participants among the area's performers, patrons, educators, and cultural catalysts. Thus there have been more than fifty individuals or organizations that have received Special Citations for their noteworthy contributions to the health and progress of the arts in the Greater Cleveland area.

The motto of The Cleveland Arts Prize is a statement by the poet J. W. von Goethe: "The recognition of excellence is the mark of the educated person."

It was announced in September 1993 that the Special Citation of the annual Cleveland Arts Prize would be awarded to the men and women of The Cleveland Orchestra on December 10, 1993, as part of the Orchestra's Seventy-Fifth Anniversary celebrations.

Between 1970 and 1988, twenty distinguished Cleveland artists contributed existing art works for reproduction on more than thirty Cleveland Orchestra program covers. Their names are listed on page 211. Three examples that could be printed adequately in black-and-white are shown here.

CLOCKWISE FROM UPPER RIGHT: "Byzantine Madonna" by Roger Coast; an abstract lithograph by Julie Bubalo; and "Wreathed Knight with Kettledrums" by Margaret K. Duff.

Severance Hall was originally built for use as both a concert hall and for staged dramatic productions. For orchestra concerts, a number of different stage sets were used between 1931 and 1958. TOP TO BOTTOM: an early photograph taken soon after the inauguration of the hall in February 1931; The Cleveland Orchestra's first official photograph in Severance Hall, with Nikolai Sokoloff, the Orchestra's first music director, 1931; the Orchestra and its second music director, Artur Rodzinski, on stage in 1938 *(Photograph by Geoffrey Landesman)*; the Orchestra and George Szell on the Severance Hall stage in 1957 *(Landesman)*.

LEFT: The acoustical renovation of the Severance Hall stage in progress during the summer of 1958, as described in the article beginning on page 91.

BELOW: George Szell and The Cleveland Orchestra on the renovated stage. *(Photograph by Peter Hastings)*

OPPOSITE: George Szell, music director of The Cleveland Orchestra from 1946 to 1970, with principal guest conductor Pierre Boulez in front of Severance Hall in 1969. *(Photograph by Don Hunstein)*

TOP: Associate conductor Robert Shaw, music director George Szell, and assistant conductor Louis Lane, circa 1958. LOWER LEFT: Szell acknowledges the cheers of the audience in Tokyo, May 1970. The two Japanese girls had just presented him with flowers. Also visible are concertmaster Daniel Majeske and violists Frederick Funkhouser and Abraham Skernick. *(Peter Hastings)* LOWER RIGHT: Posthumous bust of George Szell by Cleveland sculptor Norman Poirier; the bronze, a gift to the Orchestra from the Kulas Foundation, was placed in the Severance Hall Green Room in 1973. *(Ralph Marshall)*

TOP: Music director George Szell, associate conductor Louis Lane, general manager A. Beverly Barksdale, and Musical Arts Association president Frank E. Joseph examining a document in the Severance Hall Green Room, circa 1965. Mr. Joseph, president from 1957 to 1968, played a leading role in the creation of Blossom Music Center.

MIDDLE: A. Beverly Barksdale preparing to appear as narrator in a performance of Tchaikovsky's complete *Nutcracker* ballet music with The Cleveland Orchestra at Severance Hall, December 1958.

BOTTOM: Erich Leinsdorf, music director of The Cleveland Orchestra 1943-46, conducting the Orchestra at Severance Hall in 1943 *(Photograph by Geoffrey Landesman)*, in a 1943 portrait *(Landesman)*, and a later portrait, circa 1975 *(Christian Steiner)*. Although his tenure as music director was brief, he returned to Cleveland regularly as a guest conductor in later years. He died in Zurich in September 1993 at the age of 81.

A number of guest artists have established long-standing relationships with The Cleveland Orchestra. Among pianists appearing with regularity were Rudolf Serkin, Robert Casadesus, Rudolf Firkusny, Gary Graffman, Leon Fleisher, and Artur Rubinstein. A tribute to Rubinstein begins on page 186. AT LEFT: Rubinstein performing with The Cleveland Orchestra in 1937, with Artur Rodzinski on the podium. *(Photograph by Geoffrey Landesman)* CLOCKWISE FROM MIDDLE LEFT: Rubinstein in the conductor's studio with George Szell, 1964; in rehearsal with Lorin Maazel in Paris, 1975; and in performance in Paris, 1975. *(Peter Hastings, from his book MUSICAL IMAGES)*

ABOVE: Lorin Maazel, music
director of The Cleveland
Orchestra from 1972 to 1982,
leads the Orchestra and The
Cleveland Orchestra Chorus
in Berlioz's Requiem
Mass during a recording
session in August 1978 at
Cleveland's Masonic
Auditorium. *(Photograph
by Peter Hastings)*

MIDDLE: Robert Page in
Blossom Music Center's
Pavilion, designed by Peter
van Dijk. Page served as
director of choruses for The
Cleveland Orchestra from
1971 to 1989. Among his
notable predecessors in that
post were Arthur Shepherd,
Boris Goldovsky, Robert
Shaw, and Margaret Hillis.
An article beginning on page
113 describes The Cleveland
Orchestra Chorus's first
European concert tour in
1986. *(Michael Edwards)*

BOTTOM: The Cleveland
Orchestra and Chorus on
stage at the Palais des Beaux
Arts in Brussels, 1986.
(Peter Hastings)

Christoph von Dohnányi was appointed Lorin Maazel's successor as music director of The Cleveland Orchestra in 1982; his tenure began with the 1984-85 season. TOP: Dohnányi conducting the Orchestra at Severance Hall *(Photograph by Jack van Antwerp)*; MIDDLE: Dohnányi with his wife, internationally renowned soprano Anja Silja, and Alfred M. Rankin in the Severance Hall Green Room in February 1983. Mr. Rankin served as Musical Arts Association president 1968-83, and has been chairman of the board since 1983. Visible in the background is a portrait of Adella Prentiss Hughes, founding manager of The Cleveland Orchestra *(Peter Hastings)*; BOTTOM: Dohnányi with conductors Robert Shaw and Pierre Boulez backstage after a concert at Paris's Théâtre des Champs Élysées in 1990. *(Jack van Antwerp)*

Soon after assuming the post of music director in 1972, Lorin Maazel inaugurated the "Composers of Our Time" series, in which outstanding composers appear annually at Severance Hall for a weekend of concerts. TOP: In October 1977, the guest was British composer Sir Michael Tippett, shown here with the Prince of Wales, an ardent music lover, who attended the opening night concert, and Lorin Maazel in the Severance Hall Board Room. *(Photograph by Peter Hastings)*; MIDDLE AND BOTTOM: Hans Werner Henze was the honored guest composer-conductor in 1985 *(Peter Hastings)*, Witold Lutoslawski in 1988 *(Peter Hastings)*. Visible with Lutoslawski are cello soloist Roman Jablonski and Orchestra cellists Richard Weiss and Stephen Geber.

Aaron Copland was the first to be
chosen to appear in The Cleveland
Orchestra's "Composers of Our
Time" series in 1974. TOP: Copland
conducts the Orchestra at Blossom
Music Center in 1968; BELOW:
Copland in the Severance Hall Board
Room in 1974, before an old Italian
sculpture of music-making children.
*(Photographs by Peter Hastings,
from his book* MUSICAL IMAGES)

TOP: A portrait of Sir Thomas Beecham taken in Cleveland in 1944 by
Cleveland Orchestra photographer Geoffrey Landesman. Beecham appeared
as guest conductor of the Orchestra in 1944 and 1956.

LOWER LEFT: A rare portrait etching of Gustav Mahler, circa 1907,
by Viennese artist Arthur Paunzen; from the legacy of Albert and Mary Roy.

LOWER RIGHT: Pianist, teacher, and author Arthur Loesser, who served as program
annotator for The Cleveland Orchestra 1936-1941. Loesser's essay "The Challenge
of Public Performance" appears in this book, beginning on page 21.

ABOVE: Three Cleveland portraits of Béla Bartók on display in the Severance Hall Green Room. The photographs were taken by Geoffrey Landesman at Severance Hall in December 1940, when the composer-pianist appeared as soloist with The Cleveland Orchestra in his Second Piano Concerto with conductor Artur Rodzinski. This display case was used each week between 1958 and 1988 for materials relating to the week's concert program.

TOP: One in a series of wartime paintings, circa 1941, by Daniel C. Brown (1912-1989), a poet, art teacher, urban environmentalist, and enthusiast for The Cleveland Orchestra. This painting was published twice in the Orchestra's program book for performances of Benjamin Britten's *War Requiem*.

MIDDLE LEFT TO RIGHT: The great musicologist Karl Geiringer (1899-1989) during a visit to Cleveland in 1983. An article about Dr. Geiringer begins on page 83 *(Photograph by Gene J. Roy)*; composers Karl Weigl and Ernst Lévy, who are the subject of an article beginning on page 74.

BOTTOM: Cleveland composer, violist, conductor, and teacher Marcel Dick (1898-1991) in a photograph from the 1960s *(Fred Gerard)*. See articles beginning on pages 179 and 181.

TOP: The Island of Staffa in Scotland's Hebrides Islands, showing the legendary Fingal's Cave as photographed by Harry Herforth, former Cleveland Orchestra trumpeter 1951-58. See article beginning on page 86.

LOWER: Czech violinist Josef Suk in St. Wenceslas Church in Spillville, Iowa, in 1964, See article beginning on page 105. Suk's great-grandfather, Antonin Dvořák, resided in Spillville in the summer of 1893 and wrote his "American" String Quartet and finished orchestrating his "New World" Symphony.
This photograph was taken by Joseph E. Adams, who was a Cleveland Orchestra trustee. A Dvořák Centennial was held in Spillville during the summer of 1993.

UPPER LEFT: Composer Paul Hindemith in 1953 with Richard Wagner's grandson Wieland, director of the Bayreuth Festival, and conducting Beethoven's Ninth Symphony at Bayreuth. *(Photographs from ZEUGNIS IN BILDERN, a pictorial biography of Hindemith; Schott & Co. Ltd., Mainz, 1955).*

UPPER RIGHT: The Wagner statue in Cleveland's Edgewater Park, sculpted by Herman Matzen in 1911. When the composer's son Siegfried (father of Wieland) was in town in 1924 to conduct The Cleveland Orchestra, he laid a wreath at the statue and planted an oak tree nearby. *(Robert Walther)*

LOWER LEFT: A pencil sketch of Igor Stravinsky drawn in the Severance Hall Green Room in 1964 by Laszlo Krausz, Cleveland Orchestra violist 1947-69 and accomplished visual artist.

LOWER RIGHT: Composer Dmitri Shostakovich with his disciple Solomon Volkov in Moscow in 1974. Volkov, a Soviet musicologist now living in New York, edited the composer's memoirs, which Harper & Row published in 1979 under the title *Testimony*. The photograph is from the personal collection of Solomon Volkov, and is republished with his permission.

IV. POINTS OF VIEW, SPECULATIONS, AND FURTHER SECOND THOUGHTS

Certain things are extremely difficult to discern by dint of their being excessively obvious.

L. E. Dupin
(*ca.* 1700)

The vindication of the obvious is sometimes more important than the clarification of the obscure.

Oliver Wendell Holmes, Jr.

Among mortals, second thoughts are wisest.

Euripides

"Anniversary Music" (MARCH 1982),
A Poem by Leonard Trawick

*

Because this program includes pieces by two current anniversarians, Haydn (1732) and Stravinsky (1882), it seemed particularly appropriate to publish for the first time a poem by Leonard Trawick, with his kind permission. Dr. Trawick is a native of Alabama, professor of English at Cleveland State University, and widely published poet. He is the founder and editor of The Gamut, *the attractive and stimulating new journal sponsored by Cleveland State University, written by Northern Ohio professionals and designed for readers of wide-ranging interests from the arts to medicine, from athletics to engineering, from the physical sciences to linguistics, from politics to sociology—in short, the gamut.*

*

1.
Riding our bicycles through the Haydn sonata
Down avenues of flowering trees
We stop to skip stones on the lake
And fill our pockets full of cherries.

2.
Mushing through Tschaikowsky's concerto
We sink over our ankles in snow;
It's pink and warm, the taste is birthday cake,
With a linger of wormwood and headache.

3.
Rowing the Brahms quintet all night
Under low red clouds
We stroke deep into velvet
Dark as plum sauce, sweet as shrapnel.

4.
Climbing Mahler's symphony, past the bells,
Past the small blue flowers, the last shrine,
We keep looking up; the vacant sky
Grows larger and larger.

5.
Picking Schoenberg's crabapples into a tin pail
Is a pain, but they make good pickles.
Cheer up—over there is a big Stravinsky,
Some nice Ives, and all the Poulenc you can carry.

Leonard Trawick wrote the texts for Klaus George Roy's opera "The Enchanted Garden" or "Zoopera" (1983) and Bain Murray's "Mary Stuart: A Queen Betrayed" (1991).—Editor.

"On Second Hearing" (MARCH 1985)

Music without ideas is unthinkable. . . . Every true work of art to be under-stood has to be thought about; otherwise it has no inherent life.

—Arnold Schoenberg

*

ONE IS TEMPTED to assume that so clear, direct, and communicative a work as Men-delssohn's *Fifth Symphony*, the "Reformation", would be hardly in need of being "thought about" for complete enjoyment. After all, the music itself conveys its message in satisfying sounding forms, and the "program" of the conflict between the "old" and "new" faiths (Catholicism and Protestantism) with its ecumenical resolution is simple and easy enough to follow. Moreover, in so vibrant and committed a performance as that given by The Cleveland Orchestra under the direction of Christoph Eschenbach, the symphony belies the old canard that it is a weak or even second-rate composition. For all too many years, the *"Reformation" Symphony* has received what in contemporary parlance is called a "bum rap" for its alleged weaknesses; Mendelssohn himself looked back on it as a "thor-oughly youthful work" and wondered why in later years he never improved it. In hind-sight, one might say that even if the symphony is not quite on the level of the *Scottish* and *Italian* symphonies, there was nothing to improve; the very element of youthfulness is a part of its charm, and one should recall that at the age of twenty, when the composer wrote it, he could already point to thirteen delightful symphonies for strings and such a masterpiece as the *Midsummer Night's Dream* Overture of his eighteenth year.

We know that the symphony was by no means his fifth, a numbering assigned to it when it was published more than twenty years after Mendelssohn's death. Completed in 1830, it preceded the *Third* of 1842, and the *Fourth* of 1833. The opus number 107 is equally nonsensical in that context and has only added to the confusion. Yet there are aspects of this work that are indeed worth thinking about, and that may contribute to our understanding and continuing enjoyment of it.

First of all, how deeply indebted to the music of his time was the twenty-year-old composer! Haydn, Mozart, Beethoven, and Weber were in his bloodstream, and his devotion to Bach bore fruit in the year of the symphony's composition, 1829, through his epochal performance of the *St. Matthew Passion* in Berlin—thus sparking the renaissance of Bach's long-neglected lifework.

The *"Reformation" Symphony* begins with a motto symbolizing the ancient tradition of the Catholic liturgy, a "psalmodic incipit" of four notes which we know also from its frequent use by Haydn and Mozart, especially in the finale of the *"Jupiter" Symphony*, Mozart's *No. 41*:

Soon comes a phrase which reminds us of one in the opening movement of Haydn's *Symphony No. 104*, the *"London"*:

And that this is not accidental is proved by the beginning of the *Allegro con fuoco*, which is a clear echo of Haydn's stentorian opening theme:

Mendelssohn could hardly have expected his audiences at the first performance in November of 1832 *not* to recognize the distinguished model. The elements of turbulence in the fast body of the first movement (*Allegro con fuoco*, "with fire"!) apparently implied the growing conflict between the old and the new faiths, the first of which had just been symbolized by the ethereal use of the "Dresden Amen" which Wagner was to use again— almost fifty years later—in his *Parsifal*:

Toward the close of the first movement, in D minor, Mendelssohn acknowledges his admiration of a work then only five years old, and in the same key, namely Beethoven's *Ninth Symphony*. A musical example would hardly do justice to that relationship, which is not so much thematic as it is textural and dramatic. No young musician of consequence could escape the powerful influence of Beethoven's work. (It was the teen-age Mendelssohn who introduced his aged friend Goethe to Beethoven's symphonies, by playing them for him on the piano!) In the second movement there are reminders of two other symphonies of Beethoven: the *Eroica*, in a scurrying string figure leading back to the main theme, and the *Pastoral*, in a staccato cadence figure near the close—in the same key, B flat major, as the slow movement in Beethoven's work which is "quoted" there.

It is evident how much Schumann, Mendelssohn's slightly younger colleague and friend, learned from this music, not only in the Scherzo but even the very beginning of the symphony, the tone and technique of which he adopted—very appropriately—for the "Cathedral Scene" in his "*Rhenish*" *Symphony* nearly twenty years later. And if we are concerned with the "point in time" of the "*Reformation*" *Symphony*, we may be astonished to discover that it is identical with that of Berlioz's *Symphonie Fantastique*, completed in 1830 when that adventurous and vastly different composer was only twenty-seven.

Music lovers acquainted with the nineteenth-century repertoire will recognize a romantic phrase later adopted by both Schumann and Grieg:

In the *Andante* (which can be seen as a third movement proper or as the introduction to the finale), there is a violin figure associated with the operatic recitative. What does it symbolize here?

Yet the most unusual and striking instance of interrelation in this Symphony occurs in the finale, after the "A Mighty Fortress" theme of Luther and Bach has been stated and symphonically developed. Suddenly, there is heard a fugal theme, polyphonically worked out in "severe" contrapuntal style:

If this sounds strangely familiar, it is. We find it again, nearly *verbatim*, in the central fugue of No. 22, "Be not afraid", in Mendelssohn's oratorio, *Elijah:*

Now this is indeed remarkable, for several reasons. The words sung at that point are: "Though thousands languish and fall beside thee, and tens of thousands around thee perish, yet still it shall not come nigh thee." This text, from Psalm 91, would be entirely consistent with the poetic idea of the finale; in fact, the fugue theme is combined later in the movement with the "Ein' Feste Burg" theme—providing, so to speak, the answer to the Psalmist's plaint and the confirmation of his faith.

Yes, but the symphony was completed in 1830 (perhaps revised for the première in 1832), and *Elijah* was not finished until 1846, though conceived in 1838! How did Mendelssohn make the connection between his youthful symphony and the late oratorio, with so "prophetic" a quote? Could it be that the Chorus No. 22 already existed by 1830 and was later incorporated into *Elijah*? And furthermore, is it not remarkable that the fugal theme appears to be based on a cantorial fragment from the synagogue service? In writing a "Reformation" symphony, Mendelssohn—a convert to Christianity from Judaism—may well have wished to add an element of a still older faith than both Catholicism and Lutheranism.

"Knowing What Composers Wanted" (APRIL 1983)

TO AN EXTENT much greater than we tend to believe, our expectation how a familiar piece should sound in performance is based on our mental image of it, derived from previous performances and especially from the recordings we prize. "So-and-so did it this way, and therefore it must be right", becomes for many of us an article of faith. Since there is usually no way for most listeners to consult the composer's own score, and neither time nor interest permit an intensive study of what those scores actually say, demand, or suggest, we rely on our actual experience of the music as conveyed to us through the minds and hearts and hands of leading conductors.

George Szell used to say, with his customary emphasis, "Never mind so-and-so's recording! Only go by the score." For most of us, that is easier said than done. There will always remain arguments what *adagio* or *vivace non troppo* mean, in exact measurements of tempo, and even when the composer has provided metronome markings (like sixty quarter-notes per minute, or one quarter-note per second), that is only a guidepost to a general time-pulse. How much slowing-down is meant by *ritardando,* or *un poco tenuto*? Such things cannot be delineated with mathematical exactitude; they depend on the style of the piece, the executant's conception of what the composer meant; they become a part of what is summed up under the catchall title of "interpretation".

But there is much that a conductor or performer *can* discover in the score, and if he wishes to ignore or contradict it he must at least know why. In his remarkable book, *The Composer's Advocate—A Radical Orthodoxy for Musicians* (1981), Erich Leinsdorf has provided us with material of exceptional value, and above all with a set of attitudes toward music that demand not only feeling but knowledge. His chapters are called "Knowing the Score", "Knowing the Composer", "Knowing What Composers Wanted", "Knowing Musical Tradition", "Knowing the Right Tempo", and "Knowing the Conductor's Role". At hand of more than sixty musical examples, Mr. Leinsdorf gives musicians and concerned music lovers a rationale for dealing sensitively and knowingly with musical scores, and to learn to make decisions based on a more solid foundation than "I like it that way".

All this as preface to the warning that in the present performances of Beethoven's *Ninth Symphony* there are likely to be some surprising moments, especially in the areas of tempo and tempo relationships. Audiences should know that those "surprises" represent not arbitrary departures from a so-called norm, but are based on a fresh and thorough study of the original score. Mention may be made of only one such example. In his book, Mr. Leinsdorf discusses the memorable *maestoso* section just before the closing *prestissimo*, so often taken at a tempo largely unrelated to its context. He shows us, in a whole series of incontrovertible equations, what Beethoven wanted, and what the "right" tempo must be. Here then is "interpretation" based on as much fact as is available, and those listeners who may find their customary expectations upset should at least know who in this encounter has made an arguable decision—they or the conductor.

Music and the Machine (JANUARY 1986)

WHEN WE EVALUATE performances, the terms "machinelike" or "mechanical" have negative connotations. To playing of that kind, we ascribe a regularity too scientific, an absence of expressive phrasing and "breathing". Although, after all, the musical instrument is itself a machine, we demand that it be operated in a flexible manner and with human variability. Yet the boundary lines between these approaches are extremely subtle, and often quite narrow; on the one hand, we ask for rhythmic precision and accuracy, and on the other we look for a natural inflection. In musical compositions also, we tend to become impatient with a work that moves metronomically for too long a time-span, or with one in which rhythmic or tempo changes are pervasive and unpredictable.

Yet the very concept of the machine (according to Webster's New World Dictionary "a structure consisting of a framework and various fixed and moving parts") has always attracted composers, and especially in the century-and-a-half during which the Industrial Revolution has gone—so to speak—into high gear. One of the reasons for the current popularity of baroque music lies in its sense of the motoric; some of Bach's work has been waggishly called a product of the "inspired sewing machine". In nineteenth-century music, such a piece as Saint-Saëns' *Omphale's Spinning Wheel* comes at once to mind, in a long tradition of other revolving musical wheels from sleigh rides to spinning-songs by Schubert and Wagner. Mechanical devices to "tell time", such as clocks, are very ancient indeed, and watches were finely developed hundreds of years ago. What has been especially appealing to composers in the action of a machine is exactly its metrical regularity, its "automatic" forward motion, the controllability of its speed and its "inhuman" power to get the job done.

In the first two decades of this century, when technology had reached a new plateau of sophistication and efficiency, the machine became a legitimate musical subject, not only to be imitated but celebrated. The movement called Futurism proposed the artistic use of new machines; many works (but by no means all) by Stravinsky, Bartók, Prokofiev, and Hindemith used mechanistic, motoric devices. Hindemith's *Kammermusik No. 1* of 1922 employed a siren for its raucous close. Honegger's *Pacific 231* of 1923 glorified the brute power of a locomotive. The *Toonerville Trolley,* and its German equivalent, the *Bahnfahrt,* sent audiences into hysterics of laughter. The merry chugging of Villa-Lobos's *The Little Train of the Caipira* (from his *Bachianas Brasileiras No. 2,* orchestrated in 1938) has amused audiences of all ages. Yet the infatuation with transportational devices is much older; Christopher Rouse has drawn our attention to a choral-orchestral piece by Berlioz, written in 1846, called *Le chant des chemins de fer* ("The Song of the Railroads")! In 1928, Alexander Mossolov composed his *Iron Foundry,* subtitled "Machine Music"; we heard it at these concerts in 1984, nearly fifty-four years after it first clanged in Cleveland. Edgard Varèse and several of his colleagues initiated music made by electronic means, opening a vast new area of sound sources and possibilities; more or less conventional materials co-existed, such as the thirty-seven percussion instruments in Varèse's *Ionisation* of 1931, under the hands of thirteen players. The first really great piece electronically produced was also to come from Varèse, in his *Poème électronique* of 1958, composed for the Brussels World's Fair.

Of course, all sound-producing and reproducing structures are machines, from Edison's wax cylinder to digital recording, from magnetic tape to the synthesizer. Every record player, of whatever vintage (including the ubiquitous jukebox) is a machine, to be used for good or ill. The computer now stands as the ultimate (if not ultimately desirable) music machine. But it is as Varèse warned: "A machine can only give back what is put into it. It does not create. . . . A bad musician with instruments will be a bad musician with electronics."

Christopher Rouse's *The Infernal Machine,* with its classical allusion to the grinding mechanism of fate, is a youthful member of a distinguished family. Among its forebears is Gunther Schuller's witty and charming *The Twittering Machine,* from his *Seven Studies on Themes of Paul Klee* (1959), in which the painter's whimsical birds are literally cranked up to "do their thing".

Stravinsky once said that it was the primary function of music to organize time; if that is so, then composers of our era will most naturally look to the machine for inspiration or guidance. But let them—and all of humanity—remember Goethe's admonition: "In the end, we still depend on creatures which we ourselves have made." How that dependence may be overcome is most beautifully shown us by poets and composers. Perhaps the finest metaphor of that never-ending conflict between the inert and the living machine (such as the body) was created by Hans Christian Andersen, whose real nightingale—though not as virtuosic and glittering—still could do what the mechanical nightingale could not. Stravinsky's opera and suite, *Le Rossignol,* transform the story enchantingly into music.

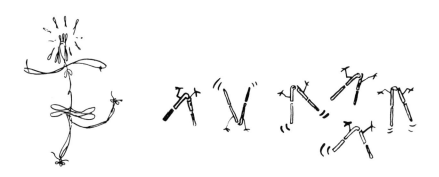

Mozart's Clarinet Concerto (FEBRUARY 1987)

*

The real "story" of the 1987 performances of the Mozart clarinet concerto is the use of the solo instrument for which Mozart apparently wrote the concerto, namely the basset clarinet. Following the customary annotation, the revival of that legendary instrument is discussed, and some of the musical results of this venture are pursued.

*

THE INSTRUMENT played by Franklin Cohen in these performances is a clarinet, but a "clarinet with a difference". The difference is an extension or elongation of the bell by four semitones, which for an instrument pitched in A provides the actual sounds of C, B natural, B flat, and A below the usual bottom limit of C sharp. The instrument is called a basset clarinet, and is not a modern invention. It has been ascertained that Mozart wrote his clarinet concerto for it, to be performed by his friend and fellow Freemason, Anton Stadler. This older of the two clarinet-playing Stadler brothers (the other's name was Johann) was also a noted virtuoso on the basset horn, an alto clarinet pitched in G or F, and a descendant of the "bass chalumeau". Mozart wrote several works including one or more basset horns, notably in his music for masonic occasions, the *Serenade, K. 361*, and the *Requiem, K. 626*. The basset horn in the eighteenth century was a peculiarly shaped instrument, with curves and angles; its form was simplified in the nineteenth, and the instrument appears in music by Beethoven and Mendelssohn, and even by Richard Strauss. The so-called basset clarinet, it must be emphasized, is not the same instrument at all, but a close relative. As Nicholas Shackleton remarks in *The New Grove Dictionary of Music and Musicians* of 1980, "clarinets have probably been made in a wider range of sizes and pitches than any other instrument." On one page of his long article he gives pictures of eight clarinet family members, from the sopranino to the contrabass clarinet.

It appears that Mozart sketched the first movement of a concerto for basset horn and orchestra in 1789, in the key of G, but broke off part of the way through. When in 1791 Anton Stadler showed the composer an improved version of an elongated clarinet in A designed by Theodor Lotz of Vienna, Mozart took up his sketch and completed the concerto in the key of A, and in its present three-movement form. The autograph has unfortunately been lost; only the earlier sketches for the basset horn concerto are extant, and provide important clues.

In the 1940s, various scholars—particularly in England—began to draw attention to a possible "original version" of the concerto. In 1951, an instrument built to accommodate those specifications was used in a performance of the work in Prague; in 1957, a Czech scholar by the name of Jiři Kratochvil made an extensive study of the matter, suggesting the term "basset clarinet"; and in 1967, the German scholar Ernst Hess reported his discovery of a review dated March 1802 (only ten years after Mozart's death!) of one of the newly published versions of the *Clarinet Concerto*, in the *Leipzig Allgemeine Musikalische Zeitung*. In that review, the critic stated unequivocally that Mozart wrote the concerto not for the usual A clarinet as published but for an instrument encompassing "low C" (sounding low A). The reviewer continued with musical examples, showing what the publisher had done to make the music accessible to players of the "conventional" clarinet in A, and pointing out that even in 1802 an extended instrument was already a rarity: "Thanks are due the editors for these transpositions and alterations, although they have not improved the concerto. Perhaps it would have been just as well to have published it in the original version and to have inserted these transpositions and alterations in smaller notes."

In an extremely detailed and valuable article in the April 1969 issue of *The Musical Times*, London, Alan Hacker has discussed the issue, and has provided a list of "proposed amendments toward a restoration of Mozart's original text". There are twenty of these for the first movement, seven for the second, and sixteen for the third! It is evident that if all these are adopted, the actual sound of the concerto will be noticeably different.

It was Mr. Hacker who gave the first London performance of the *Clarinet Concerto* in its original version for the basset clarinet, in a concert on April 11, 1969, at the Queen Elizabeth Hall, in a program of old and new music by the Orchestra Nova of London conducted by Peter Maxwell Davies.

In 1977 the *Neue Mozart-Augabe* (New Mozart Edition of the Complete Works) by the Bärenreiter Verlag of Kassel issued an extraordinary volume (edited by Franz Giegling, Basel) in which *both* versions appear in full score: the one with which we are familiar, and a reconstructed version of what Mozart wrote, based on his own original sketch for the basset horn in G, and on the practical evidence of the music itself, which is clearly intended for an instrument of extended range. That this is not imaginary or arbitrary is clear from many instances in which the published version forces the clarinet to leap to the higher octave instead of completing its phrase naturally; furthermore, only the "basset clarinet" gives the player access to the low A which in a piece in that key serves as the logical tonic or foundation. Here is just one of many examples:

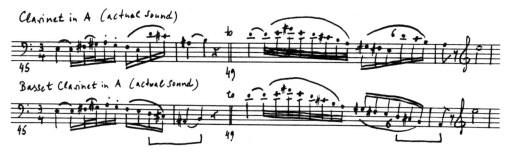

Now, is the basset clarinet itself a figment of the imagination? Mr. Shackleton writes that it is not known "how common 'basset' clarinets were; the fact that no eighteenth-century examples are at present known may be due only to the fact that they have been overlooked. The discovery of a nineteenth-century example, now in the Bate Collection (Oxford), was something of a surprise."

A word on the designation *basset clarinet*. Evidently, it cannot be "bass clarinet", for that is an instrument pitched an octave lower than the regular B-flat clarinet. *Basset* is a diminutive of *bass*, i.e. a size smaller than bass. The same is true of the *cello*, whose full name is *violoncello*, i.e. a low-pitched instrument smaller than the *violone* or string bass. The spelling of *cello* has become so accepted in the public's mind that the version with the apostrophe, *'cello*, once considered *de rigueur*, has been almost everywhere abandoned. "Cello" simply means small; if one encounters the misspelling "violincello" one would have to assume it to be a small violin, like a *violino piccolo*. (The wind instrument called *piccolo* for short is really a *flauto piccolo*, or small flute.) The suffix *et, ette, etta* and *etto* seem always to refer to a smaller version of something; thus *opera—operetta, clarino—clarinetto* (clarinets once reminded listeners of small trumpets or clarinos), *basin—basinette, corno* (horn)—*cornetto* (a type of trumpet). Surprisingly, the terms *bassetto, bassett*, even the slang diminutive *bassetl*, stood in the eighteenth century for the cello; if a wind instrument was meant, the term *corno* had to precede it, as in *corno di bassetto*, the basset horn. It is amusing to recall that when George Bernard Shaw worked as a music critic in London, late in the nineteenth century, he used *Corno di Bassetto* as his pseudonym.

The trend in musical performance today is toward original versions and period instruments, toward authenticity, toward "what the composer really wanted". The rehabilitation of the basset clarinet is in that context a worthy and exciting enterprise.—Editor.

In his article, Alan Hacker writes that "it should be noted that the extra length of the basset clarinet gives the whole compass of the instrument a darker tone quality than the normal length A clarinet; and this aspect alters the character of the concerto as much as the restoration of the basset notes." In the last decades, numerous new basset clarinets have been constructed; Mr. Hacker's own instrument is credited to the clarinetist and maker Edward Planas, and Mr. Hacker describes the method used in elongating "a Boehm system A clarinet of late nineteenth-century design made by Albert".

Mr. Cohen's instrument was made by Mr. William McColl of the University of Washington faculty, and a member of the Soni Ventorum Woodwind Quintet in residence there. Mr. McColl built the extension, some eight inches long, as a new bottom section of a regular clarinet in A. All four additional notes are played with the right thumb on keys on the back of the instrument. To play them, the thumb must leave the security of the thumb rest, and reliance on a neck strap becomes necessary.

A surprising number of leading clarinetists have turned of late to the "original" version of the concerto, and have recorded it in that form. Among them are David Shifrin (former principal clarinetist of this Orchestra), playing with the Mostly Mozart Orchestra under Gerard Schwarz, on the Delos label; Thea King, with the English Chamber Orchestra under Jeffrey Tate, on Hyperion; Antony Pay with the Academy of Ancient Music under Christopher Hogwood, on Oiseau-Lyre; and an outstandingly good recording, by Hans Deinzer as soloist with the Collegium Aureum on Harmonia Mundi-Teldec-EMI.

Introductory Comments to an
Annotation for Beethoven's Symphony No. 5
in C minor, Op. 67 (MAY 1980)

"OH NO, NOT THE *Fifth* again!"

It is astonishing how often one hears such a remark when Beethoven's Op. 67 is scheduled for performance. The very popularity of the work, its nearly indecent over-exposure (more than two hundred commercial recordings have been made!), and the feeling that "we know it all too well"—all this and more have contributed to a kind of automatic resistance and reluctance on the part of many listeners.

But surely the majority respond differently: "Oh *yes*, indeed, let's welcome it, and eagerly!" For once a masterpiece, always a masterpiece.

Indeed, if sufficient time-space has been allowed between hearings, the work comes to us fresh. We may still resent the use of the main theme for television and radio commercials—"there should be a law" against that sort of thing! But a live performance of the entire symphony by a great ensemble and conductor is sure to tell us and show us things that are new and revealing. (In fact, it is the very difference between performances, between the approaches and concepts of different conductors, that keeps all of the works in the standard repertoire alive and absorbing.) Nor should one forget that there are patrons who have heard the symphony on recordings and broadcasts, but who have never attended a live performance of it!

The claim by some that they know the piece too well is not likely to stand up, were they to be questioned on this detail or that. And all too often that "too well" is based on a single and classic recorded performance—yes, a good classic recording can be great, but beyond that there is a vast range of possibilities open to every distinguished interpreter. Not even the first few measures are the same under the hands of two different conductors, and Beethoven's exact intentions in that famous beginning still cause arguments between listeners and performers alike.

That we have had, over the years, the opportunity to build up what is for us an "ideal image" of Beethoven's *Fifth* is all to the good; but we must be ready for ideas that differ from it and are still faithful to Beethoven's blueprint. Just as we would never expect two productions of a Shakespeare play to be identical in concept and execution—nor wish them to be so—we should fervently hope that our reaction to a musical work is extended, expanded, and deepened by successive exposures. While the overall effect of the composition will be very similar if not exactly the same, it is in the details and in the variances that we gain new insights, relive the music in a way never before experienced. "Masterpieces," said American music critic Lawrence Gilman (1878–1939), "are capable of infinite self-renewal," and with them, so are good listeners.

*

Beethoven's *Fifth Symphony* is the most powerful work of musical rhetoric in orchestral literature. It does not beg you, the listener, to agree with its message; it does not cajole or attempt to persuade; it demands imperiously that you accept it. Few are skeptical enough to resist; most are convinced immediately that the composer means what he says, and submit to a will stronger than theirs.

What is the "message" of the *Fifth Symphony*? It is the intrinsic quality of music, its central fact, that it cannot be explained in words. The poet Heinrich Heine said that music begins where words stop. Yet it will call forth verbal associations, paint pictures for one hearer, build philosophical structures for another. As French pianist Elie Robert Schmitz (1889–1940) once wrote, "music should not be accounted for solely in terms of tonal structure." That is certainly true even of "absolute" music. If pressed for the meaning of the *Fifth Symphony* in human terms, one might conceive it as an almost pagan challenge: "I am the master of my fate." The musical language itself, through its melodies and rhythms, stirs up feelings in us that we know from interior and personal experience: those of conquest, of overcoming, of triumph. But if we were to try to make a piece of literal program music out of the symphony, we should fail miserably in comprehending the overwhelming artistic structure of the work, and would merely succeed in diminishing the scope of its human drama. . . .

After hearing Beethoven's *Fifth Symphony*, the noted French composer Lesueur is reported to have said to his former pupil Berlioz: "It moved and excited me so much that my head was reeling. One should not be permitted to write such music." "Calm yourself," replied the composer of the *Symphonie Fantastique*; "it will not be done often."

Brahms's Symphony No. 4 in E Minor, Op. 98 (MAY 1987)

WE FIND in Brahms's *Fourth Symphony* little to commend to the attention of a music-loving public. The orchestration is, like most of Brahms, of a certain sameness, rather thick and of India-rubber-like stickiness. Brahms evidently lacks the breadth and power of invention eminently necessary for the production of a truly great symphonic work.

The reader may have been forced by the paragraph above to execute the proverbial double take. It should, of course, have been placed between quotation marks.* Yet when it first appeared, it was not a quote, but an opinion widely shared and generally seconded. We find it in the *Musical Courier* of January 19, 1887, reporting one of the early performances in this country. Europe, too, had not taken kindly to the *Fourth Symphony*, having perhaps forgotten how long and arduous a road had been traveled before the first three could be accepted as masterpieces. The new work was met with respect, perhaps largely because the composer was by then a figure to be respected; but of warmth it elicited little. The less respectful commented that Brahms seemed once again to have set his beard to music, to have delivered a grimly serious dissertation on classical form, instead of giving the public a work which it could, by its own lights, enjoy.

Apart from the difficulties which new works of substance have traditionally presented to audiences, why did particularly the *Fourth Symphony* of Brahms fall upon reluctant ears?. . . .

At the time of this symphony's composition, Brahms had been reading the Greek tragedians, particularly Sophocles. He may well have wished to convey in the *Andante moderato* something of the legendary and timeless quality of classic literature. The tonality of the piece is not E major or E minor, but E in the Phrygian mode. (With E as the first and last note of the scale, playing only the white keys of the piano will produce the Phrygian mode.)

A surprising sidelight on this "legendary" character of the music came into view on a visit to Switzerland by the editor and his wife during the 1975 WCLV Music Festival Tour. As we passed Schaffhausen on the way to the Rhine Fall, our guide on the bus offered to sing for us an old and plaintive folk song of the town, about an abandoned lover and the bells in the church tower sending greetings to his love. To our amazement, at least three motives in the melody bore a strong resemblance to this movement in Brahms's *Fourth Symphony*, especially the striking (and indeed, melodically unique) beginning. Since we knew that Brahms had often visited Switzerland, and had utilized an actual Alphorn tune in the finale of his *First Symphony*, the possibility of a connection here too was not far-fetched.

The prospect of having made a musicological discovery was an exciting one. However, the editor's long-time friend and former teacher (as well as abiding influence), Dr. Karl Geiringer, advised caution and further research. Correspondence with the public library in Schaffhausen resulted in puncture and deflation of the high-flying balloon. It turned out that the situation was backwards: a minor Swiss composer had, around 1920, utilized Brahms's melody as a basis for his new "Schaffhausen Lied"! As *The New Yorker*

---

*On file in Severance Hall is a letter, from a listener who heard The Cleveland Orchestra's performance of this work in New York in February 1963, rebuking the editor for an act of inexcusable insolence toward a masterpiece. It appears that the correspondent had become so incensed by this opening paragraph that he read no further in the notes. Brahms appears to have been just as successful as his arch-rival Wagner in stimulating (one recoils from using the term inspiring) in many of his hearers emotions not only of derision and dislike but of actual hatred.—Editor.

might have put it, "back to the old drawing-board." Yet the possibility remains open that both Brahms and the Swiss composer may have drawn on a common local or national source from a much earlier time. Further research might produce some interesting results; musicology students are urged to try their hand at such a pursuit!

Editorial Reflections on Musical Background and Dramatic Foreground (APRIL 1977)

AS WE LISTEN to Bach's *Mass in B minor* or his monumental *Passion According to St. Matthew*, some of us may recall a feeling of growing unease with the musical background to the recent television film, *Jesus of Nazareth*.

Perhaps it is an indication how little importance we tend to attach to the incidental music for films and television that we have thus far heard not one comment about the one in question, nor have seen a critical comment in response to it in a review. As the six-hour TV production proceeded, at least this viewer found himself increasingly disturbed and ultimately exasperated by the musical score accompanying the action. It accompanied—in the sense of moving-along-with—almost entirely without dramatic motivation or correlation. The only really effective sections, it seemed to this listener, were the occasional songs performed at festivities, probably based on ancient tunes. The rest of the score, if memory serves, ambled along in a kind of "pseudo-Parsifal" manner, without notable invention, originality, or memorability.

Worst of all, the use of the music consistently jarred and distracted the viewer who was trying to concentrate on what the characters were saying, and the sudden diminishing of the volume during speech only pointed up the servile role of the music. Why, for instance, could the great encounter scene between Jesus and Pilate not have been left as dialogue, instead of being larded over with irrelevant sound? The more musical a viewer, the more disturbing was that "wallpaper music", which did not even succeed in setting an atmosphere, conveying a feeling. Was it really the assumption of Franco Zeffirelli (who has so widely directed opera) that people so accustomed to background music as our generation are not really expected to listen?

Credited as composer-conductor was Maurice Jarre, a 1924 native of Lyon, who has some reputation in France as a serious creative musician. His previous screen assignments include *The Last Tycoon* and *Dr. Zhivago*. What his technical instructions and practical limitations were, we do not know; certainly it was an exceptional challenge to produce four to five hours of music. In any case, we can only assume that this particular score does not represent him at his best. When one thinks of the distinguished incidental music for films created by major composers, one's disappointment increases. Think of Prokofiev's *Alexander Nevsky* and *Ivan the Terrible*; recall Honegger's *Pygmalion*, Walton's *Major Barbara* and *Henry V*, even Nino Rota's delightful score to Zeffirelli's own *Romeo and Juliet*!

If the subject matter of *Jesus of Nazareth* is indeed "the greatest story ever told", then was it not incumbent on the director to insist that his producer commission the best music that could be found and then to use it as sensitively as he did his camera?

Musical Detective Work in Schubert and Liszt (MAY 1977)

SCHUBERT'S SIXTH SYMPHONY has long been a prime example of that composer's "inspired indebtedness" to the masters whose works he knew and loved, especially Mozart, Haydn, Rossini, and Beethoven. Mention of some of those relationships was made in the program, while stressing that Schubert's own and inimitable style is ever present, his profound originality and musical personality never in question. To the editor's delight, he just found an essay in the 1974 Eulenburg miniature score of the work which discusses the "sources" of the symphony in some detail. The author, Roger Fiske, gives more than a dozen examples, though he—surprisingly—omits the obvious relationships of the scherzo to that of Beethoven's *Seventh Symphony*. Incipient writers of theses and dissertations might well take Schubert's frank and honest avowal of his "roots" as a starting point for their research.

*

Hearing Liszt's *Malediction* live for the first time last week set off a flood of ideas and speculations which had not found their way into the annotation itself. First of all, how astonishingly "avant-garde" is that music, a thrust into virtually uncharted seas of harmony! The "extreme modernism" of that early composition (begun in the year of Beethoven's death, and a year before Schubert's) may well have been one reason why it was apparently not played by other pianists during Liszt's lifetime, and was eventually lost until its rediscovery in 1916. The Weimar manuscript is not in Liszt's hand; that may explain the curious last page, which—after the nearly Scriabinesque chromaticism of most of the work—is ludicrously conventional and "square". It may well have been a case of "mistaken identity", a copyist's or editor's well-meaning addition. As a perceptive listener observed, Liszt liked endings too much to commit such a one.

Humphrey Searle, the Liszt biographer, says that "the concerto is a succession of mood pictures, poetical, romantic and emotional...." One would go further than that: it may well be a tone-poem for piano and strings, with a "story-line" we may never know. Liszt, who more than anyone was the creator of the symphonic poem symbolizing poetic images, legendary happenings, and actual events, must here have had a specific idea in mind, without divulging it. Instead of a cadenza, we hear a brief *recitativo*, which is marked *patetico*, and contains markings such as *disperato* and *andante lacrimoso*. Yet more fascinating is Mr. Searle's reference to Liszt's plan of "introducing a transcription of Schubert's song 'Du bist die Ruh' at one point, but afterwards, wisely thinking better of it." But did he? There is indeed a reference to a Schubert song, a relationship Mr. Searle seems to have "miszt". The songlike phrase that first appears clearly on page nine of the Breitkopf (or Kalmus) score is a direct quote of the melody from the last song of Schubert's *Die Schöne Müllerin*, titled "Des Baches Wiegenlied" ("The Brook's Cradle Song")! The text invokes "good repose" and consoling peace just as does the song Liszt did *not* use. In the concerto, moreover, the passage is marked *soave lusingando*, which means "sweetly caressing!" The final guidepost to the tone-poem theory is the discovery that the figure drawn from Schubert's song occurs not only in that obvious quote, but pervades the entire work in various transformations, appearing as early as the second measure, in the so-called "malediction" theme! Might not, ultimately, a "benediction" have been intended after all?

Sherlock Holmes, where were you when we needed you?

Mahler and Bach—A Conjectural Reflection (FEBRUARY 1970)

THERE ARE DANGERS, to be sure, in the musician's sport of reminiscence-hunting. Many apparent relationships between different works are simply a matter of merging styles, or symptomatic of the fact that there are only twelve tones in the chromatic scale, the patterns of which may quite naturally resemble each other when similar expressive purposes are aimed for. Striking similarities are often unconscious, or subconscious. We are not talking, of course, of "Augenmusik" (passages that look alike but do not really sound that way), of actual quotes or acts of homage (like the bow to Schumann's *Third Symphony* in Brahms's *Third*), and certainly not of outright plagiarism. The issues are subtle and complex, and there is much illumination to be gained from such a study as Irving Kolodin's recent book *The Continuity of Music* (Alfred A. Knopf, New York 1969), in which he also discusses Mahler's *Das Lied von der Erde* along this and other lines.

All that as introduction to a "discovery" which may already have been made by someone else but has in that case not been encountered by the writer. It may be suggested that a musician or music student interested in such matters might take a closer look at it and examine its possible merits; one would be delighted to hear from such a person.

The final song of *Das Lied* is in two parts, divided by an orchestral interlude in the form of a funeral march or dirge. It is acknowledged as one of Mahler's greatest utterances, both as orchestral writing and as artistic expression. The question posed is the following: could Mahler, consciously or subconsciously, have related this piece to the closing chorus of J. S. Bach's *The Passion According to St. Matthew*? The points of contact that strike the ear and mind are these: Both are in the key of C minor, with its own and unique tone color. The closing phrase of Bach's chorus, with its expressive leading-tone to tonic resolution, appears also in Mahler's work, emphasized and repeated. The rhythmic pattern so memorably stressed and echoed in the interlude finds its parallel in the antiphonal "rest thou softly, softly rest" of the voices. The name of the last song is "Der Abschied" ("The Farewell"), in which "the world goes to sleep", and in which the singer says "I seek but rest for my lonely heart—I journey to my homeland, to my haven . . . ." Bach's piece is of course a "farewell chorus", a large-scale lullaby. The words say, "Here bide we still with tears and weeping . . . For the anxious, the despairing, Heaven's pillow, comfort bearing, and the soul's sweet resting place . . . ." And just as Bach's chorus ends with a sense of hope along with all the poignancy and resignation, so does Mahler's song.

There are other thoughts to consider here, such as Mahler's lifelong and often anguished quest for a viable faith, and his penchant for subtle allusions; further, what can be found in the records about his having known and conducted the *St. Matthew Passion*? The forum is open.

An Addendum on Indebtedness (1977)

WE ARE FAIRLY FAMILIAR with the debt Mozart owed—especially in the music of his boyhood and early teens—to the music of Johann Christian Bach, the "London Bach". Apart from Haydn, it was certainly the youngest son of Johann Sebastian who influenced him most strongly, both in design and expression. But it is likely that as Mozart matured, he came to know and learn also from the music of Sebastian's eldest son, Carl Philipp Emanuel, the "Berlin" or "Hamburg Bach".

Catharina Meints, a member of The Cleveland Orchestra's cello section and also a noted performer on the viola da gamba, drew the editor's attention to that particular influence in a recent conversation. In her work with the Oberlin Baroque Ensemble, she had become acquainted with some of Carl Philipp Emanuel's music, and she pointed out that some of that master's boldness and burgeoning romanticism had surely left its traces on such a work as Mozart's *D minor Piano Concerto*. It is possible, of course, that this influence came more directly by way of Haydn, who was profoundly indebted to that outstanding member of the astonishing Bach family. John N. Burk has observed that the *D minor Piano Concerto* does not "in the least" resemble C. P. E. Bach's concertos in the minor mode, but remarks elsewhere that Mozart probably knew the older composer's works in that medium and was impressed by such devices as the expressive instrumental recitative. Some of the techniques and expressive patterns found in later works, however, have their sources in Mozart's earliest music, whatever its "models" may have been; thus we find, to our surprise, that the stormy and virtuosic G minor episode in the *D minor Piano Concerto*'s slow movement is clearly foreshadowed in a little piece in the same key, Koechel-number 15p (or Appendix 109b), written in London in 1764, when the boy was not yet nine years old!

It is always a fascinating pursuit to speculate where a style or even a certain composition had its origins, or—better—what tributaries aided in the formation of the great river which is the comprehensive output of a leading composer. Important music never comes about in a vacuum, as a totally new thing; its growth is organic and indebted to the past as it flows forward toward and beyond previously established frontiers.

What Is a Sinfonia Concertante? (DECEMBER 1977)

NOBODY TODAY, one may assume, would consider this work a "symphony in E flat"— although the thematic index in *Koechel* lists it among the symphonies. There are, after all, two solo instruments, in the limelight most of the time. But then, why not call it a "concerto for violin and viola with orchestra"? Mozart did designate his E-flat composition now known as K. 365 (but written several months earlier than 364) as a "concerto for two pianos", the presence of the orchestra understood. It is not easy to disentangle the conflicting terminologies—particularly when, in our own century, Stravinsky invents a concerto for two pianos *without* orchestra, and is followed therein by David Diamond and others! And there is further fuzzing of the issue when Prokofiev writes a major cello concerto entitled *Sinfonia Concertante,* and Britten composes a *Symphony for Cello and Orchestra.*

We might look at it this way. A *symphony* is a large-scale orchestral work in several movements, without specified soloists (though some may come to the fore during the course of the music). A *concerto* displays one or more solo performers, well in front of the accompanying body. A *sinfonia concertante* blends the idea of symphonic scope and development of material less with the idea of soloistic exhibition than with the time-tested methods of the baroque *concerto grosso* (Corelli, Vivaldi, Handel, Bach). There, the complete performing body (the *grosso* or *ripieno*) had shared the labor and the honor with a smaller group of players (never merely one!) called the *concertino* or "little concert". These soloists are integrated with the parent ensemble, and are, in fact, a physical part of it in location. Surprising proof of this concept may still be had from the score of Mozart's work here offered. In all the *tutti* passages by the orchestra, the soloists are meant to play right along with their respective sections; they detach themselves only for their individual musical tasks, and then return to the fold. In modern practice, this is rarely if ever done, so that we get more of a solo concerto than originally intended.

The *sinfonia concertante* form largely disappeared during the nineteenth century, if we except such similar attempts as Beethoven's *Triple Concerto* and Brahms's *Double Concerto*. Only in our century, within the strong neoclassical movement, have there been serious efforts to revive it. Mozart himself really applied himself to it only during the short span of about a year (not counting the *Concertone for Two Violins* of 1773). He had come into contact with practitioners of the form on his journey to Paris, particularly on his way through the highly musical city of Mannheim. On his trip to and from France in 1778, he experimented with this blending of symphonic and soloistic elements, beginning a number of pieces he did not complete, and carrying out several finished masterpieces like the *Sinfonia Concertante* for woodwind quartet and orchestra, K-Anhang 9, the *Concerto for Flute and Harp*, K. 299, and the present work. It seemed necessary for him to grapple with the twin problems of symphony and concerto within the confines of one structure, to enlarge and extend the scope of both, until he could lay aside the hybrid medium and devote himself to each separately for the rest of his life—with the results we know. But for a fruitful time, the idea of combining display with development, sharpest textural contrasts with the sonata-allegro form, of shaping a concerto-like symphony before perfecting the symphonic concerto—all this appealed greatly to the young master then on the threshold of richest musical maturity. That he should have given us so superb a work as this, and never again attempted to write something to match it, is yet another indication of his breathtaking fertility and range.

On the One Hundred and Fiftieth Anniversary of Schumann's Birth (OCTOBER 1960), by George Szell

*

This article was written for The New York Times, *and was published in the issue of March 13, 1960; it first appeared in the programs of The Cleveland Orchestra on October 6–8, 1960, the opening concert of the 1960–61 season. In 1980, when we commemorate not only the one hundred and seventieth anniversary of Schumann's birth but also the tenth anniversary of George Szell's death, it seems appropriate to reprint the article in a program containing a Schumann symphony conducted by one of Mr. Szell's outstanding disciples, Louis Lane.*

Since the George Szell Memorial Library was established at Severance Hall, musicians from all over the world have come to study here. The books and scores bequeathed to The Cleveland Orchestra by Mr. Szell continue to be invaluable source material for interpreters; it is especially his markings on the scores of Schumann symphonies that have attracted conductors of all ages and degrees of experience, who are permitted—indeed encouraged—to transfer the great conductor's subtle but important "orchestral retouches" to their own scores. In this way, George Szell's solutions to many of the technical problems in performing Schumann's symphonies have become part of a living tradition, and perpetuate his memory in a vital and significant manner.

*

ROBERT SCHUMANN has not been faring too well at his recent anniversaries. In 1956 the centenary of his death was overshadowed by the bicentenary of Mozart's birth. This year he has to share his one hundred and fiftieth birthday with Chopin, who, as the only great composer of his nation, has a whole country and its government behind him.

Schumann deserves better. For me he is the greatest purely romantic composer and his music the exponent of the more affecting traits of German character, nobly representative of a people of "Dichter und Denker", before their fatal unification and their ominous entry into the arena of world politics. The originality of his musical thought and design, his imagination and his warmth, his tenderness and his fire, his solemnity, and also his frolicsome boisterousness, the infinite variety of characters populating his musical stage, have secured Schumann a place in the heart of every sensitive musician and music lover.

But it might be appropriate to ask today the question: What does Schumann mean to us and what is his significance in the history of music? While his position as a composer of piano music, of songs and also of chamber music seems established beyond doubt, I find Schumann's merits and his influence as symphonic composer sadly underrated. I see in him the originator of the Romantic symphony, the inventor not just of lovely tunes, but of interesting, novel designs of harmony and formal structure which have influenced and stimulated great composers after him.

Berlioz's device, prompted by a poetical idea, to link the various movements of a symphony by the red thread of a "leitmotiv" was taken over by Schumann, transformed and enriched and given purely musical motivation. In this, as in certain turns of phrase, Schumann's influence on Brahms is too obvious to need further elaboration.

Less obvious, but equally provable, is Schumann's influence on Tchaikovsky—for better or worse. I could never help feeling that the device of sequential repetition, and the trend to rhythmical stereotype in some of Tchaikovsky's development sections, are due to the influence of Schumann, who for this mannerism has come in for severe strictures from pundits and pedants for more than a hundred years.

But Schumann's influence on Tchaikovsky goes even deeper and can be shown in a striking similarity between the middle sections of two symphonic movements. The middle section of the second movement of Schumann's *Third Symphony ("Rhenish")*, with its throbbing tympani-pedal built on the third of the relative minor chord, and its harmonization which oscillates between this chord and its neighboring diminished seventh, has indubitably inspired the corresponding middle section of the *Allegretto con grazia* movement of Tchaikovsky's *Pathétique*. The similarity of mood and of harmonic device are far too striking to be pure coincidence.

It would be easy to furnish proof for the deep influence Schumann exercised on many composers of his time and after him, both in Germany and in France. In France, incidentally, Schumann has remained to this day probably the most beloved German composer. But as I have started to talk about that throbbing tympani-pedal, I want to say a few more words about the most misunderstood and misrepresented Schumann—the Schumann of the four symphonies.

These four symphonies, full of the most glorious music, have occupied and should again occupy a permanent place in the ever-shrinking repertory of unhackneyed symphonies. They undergo eclipses not because of their intrinsic weaknesses, which are negligible, but because of the fallacy that Schumann did not know how to write for the instruments of the orchestra, that his scoring is "muddy", and that it is "inflated pianoforte music with mainly routine orchestration", as the contributor to the last edition of Grove's dictionary puts it.

This opinion is too fatuous to merit refutation. Schumann's symphonies are orchestrally conceived, if not altogether expertly realized, and the inspiring image of orchestral sound can be found often enough even in his piano works.

To be sure, a Schumann score is not foolproof, as "self-rising", as a score of Wagner or Tchaikovsky or Richard Strauss, nor has the musical substance of a Schumann symphony the kind of inexorable propulsion of some Beethoven symphonies, which will survive even a shabby performance relatively unharmed. But is it really Schumann's fault that it takes a little trouble on the part of conductor and orchestra to make his symphonies come off? I know from experience, both as a performer and as a listener (remembering unforgettable performances under Weingartner, Furtwaengler and Bruno Walter), that each one of the Schumann symphonies can be a thrilling experience to both performers and audiences if Schumann's case is stated clearly and convincingly through the proper style of interpretation.

*

That Schumann didn't know how to write for the instruments of the orchestra is simply not true. His imagination of characteristic phrases or passages for the individual instrument is vivid and accurate. Let us only remember the oboe melody in the *Adagio* of his *Second Symphony*, the clarinet tune in the third movement of the "Rhenish", the innumerable bravura passages for horns in all the symphonies, the use of the brass choir in the fourth movement of the "Rhenish", the horn and flute cadenza in the *First*, the dazzling, moto-perpetuo-like strings in the scherzo of the *Second*—to mention only a few examples.

Schumann's shortcoming as orchestrator—apart from minor lapses due to inexperience—is his inability to establish proper balances. This can and must be helped with all means known to any professional conductor who professes to be a cultured and style-conscious musician. Much soul-searching and discrimination in the choice of the remedies has to be applied. They cover the whole range from subtle adjustment of dynamic marks to the radical surgery of reorchestrating whole stretches. The wholesale reorchestration of the Schumann symphonies by Gustav Mahler, however, I must consider a most unfortunate mistake on the part of a great conductor. Mahler adulterates the character of these works by wrapping them in a meretricious garb of sound completely alien to their nature and in some instances even goes so far as to change the music itself.

The delicate question how far to go in orchestral retouches must be settled by each conductor in accordance with his own conscience and taste. At this anniversary and in conclusion, may I make this plea to my younger colleagues: Take a loving interest in Schumann's four masterpieces! You will be richly rewarded not only with deep musical satisfaction, but, if you do your job well, with just as much applause as after a Tchaikovsky symphony.*

_____

* George Szell's recordings of the Schumann symphonies have been reissued and are still available. In the 1980s Christoph von Dohnányi and The Cleveland Orchestra made new recordings of the four Schumann symphonies, received with enthusiasm. Mr. Dohnányi provides his own and quite individual solutions to the technical problems mentioned in this article.—Editor.

The Creative Artist and Success:
An Anthological Survey (JANUARY 1963)

I have never thought of composing for fame and honor. What is in my heart must come out, and that is why I compose.

—Ludwig van Beethoven

It is indeed dreadful to have to tell oneself with pitiless certainty: what I find beautiful is beautiful for me; but it may not be so for my best friends.

—Hector Berlioz

It is the fate of great geniuses to be misunderstood by their contemporaries. . . . Take the most intelligent audience and play the greatest pages which our art possesses for them— the *Choral Symphony*. They will understand nothing, absolutely nothing. We have had this experience; we repeat it every year with the same result. It is only that Beethoven is fifty years dead and it is the fashion to find his music beautiful. . . . Auber, who had so much talent and few ideas, was almost always understood, while Berlioz, who had genius but no talent at all, was almost never understood.

—Georges Bizet
(whose opera, *Carmen*, was very coolly
received at its première in 1875,
three months before his death)

Difficulty in being quickly understood by the public is a cross all must bear who would speak a new language.

—Sergei Prokofiev

At a first hearing I am used to having my compositions—especially the better and deeper ones—not understood by the greatest part of the public.

—Robert Schumann

My prince was satisfied with all my works, I was praised, as head of an orchestra I could experiment, observe what heightened the effect and what weakened it, and so I could improve, expand, eliminate, take risks; I was cut off from the world, there was no one near me to torment me or make me doubt myself, and so I was forced to become original.

—Joseph Haydn

The symphonies of Mr. Haydn have been performed on all the concerts (last year). Everyday one becomes more aware and consequently admires increasingly the productions of this all-encompassing genius, who in each of his works knows so well, with unique subject matter, how to construct a development in a rich and varied manner; quite different from those unimaginative composers who go continuously from one idea to another, without knowing how to present one differently from the other and mechanically put one effect after another without regard for context or good taste.

(From a review in the *Mercure de France*, Paris, April 8, 1788.)

My *First Piano Concerto* was a brilliant and decisive—failure. . . . At the close, three pairs of hands attempted slowly to strike against one another, whereupon a perfectly unequivocal hissing from all sides forbade such demonstrations. . . . I believe this is the best thing that could happen to one; it forces one to pull one's thoughts together and stimulates one's courage. After all, I am only experimenting and feeling my way as yet. But the hissing was too much, wasn't it?

—Johannes Brahms

How people hissed us thirty years ago! In the life of a significant composer there are, after all, only three stages: first one calls him an impudent youngster, then a hope of modern music, and finally an old fool.

—Arthur Honegger

My time will yet come.

—Gustav Mahler

Too much for what I do; too little for what I could do!

—W. A. Mozart
(about his income as Imperial Court Composer
between 1787 and 1791, an honorary stipend
considerably smaller than that of his predecessor, Gluck)

We have the pleasure of painting pictures. If, in addition, we were smothered in gold, life would be too perfect! . . . The only reward one should offer an artist is to buy his work.

—Auguste Renoir

. . . And now the bad news. Our situation is getting daily worse and worse. All I can say is that never in my life since I earned my livelihood (that is from my 20th year) have I been in such a dreadful situation as I will be probably very soon. To say dreadful is probably exaggerated, but not too much. Mrs. Bartók bears this very valiantly: the worse the happenings the more energetic, confident and optimistic she is. She tries to do some work, teaching for instance. But how to get pupils or a job. . . I am rather pessimistic. I lost all my confidence in people, in countries, in everything" . . . (Letter, March 1, 1942) . . . At Columbia I am "dismissed" from Jan. 1 on. They seem to have no more money for me . . . but from Febr. on, I am invited to Harvard University to give there a certain number of conferences and lectures. . . This gives us a respite until next fall. . . My career as a composer is as much as finished; the quasi boycott of my works by the leading orchestras continues; no performances of old works or new ones. It is a shame—not for me of course. (Letter, Dec. 31, 1942)

—Béla Bartók
(As in the case of Mozart just before his death, there came then a final
upward trend in Bartók's fortunes: as Mozart had his *Magic Flute*,
Bartók could still enjoy the triumph of his *Concerto for Orchestra*.)

The tragedy of life is what makes it worthwhile. Any life which merits living lies in the effort to realize some dream, and the higher that dream is, the harder it is to realize. The only success is in failure. Any man who has a big enough dream must be a failure, and must accept this as one of the conditions of being alive. If he ever thinks for a moment that he is a success, then he is finished.

—Eugene O'Neill

If a man does not keep pace with his companions, perhaps it is because he hears a different drummer. Let him step to the music which he hears, however measured or far away.

—Henry David Thoreau

By nature the arts must always be venturesome, or even outrageous. The worst thing that can be said about an artist is that he lacks talent. But it is almost as bad to say that he takes no chances. Don't give that poet a home: give him a limb to crawl out on and to saw off behind him. His business is not to win honor and status. His duty is to fail. It is his duty because he must want so much and must reach so far for it that he cannot hope to succeed. As such, his failure is a better success than all the killings on Wall Street and all the posies of the public wreaths. The artist has no right to trust government. All he can trust is in himself and in the demands of his form. He has no way of knowing where those demands will lead him, but he is on his way with no other road to travel. In glad selfishness he has a right to grab any handout that will keep him functioning. But the instant he begins to tailor his way of doing things in the hope of making himself more available to the handout, official or unofficial, then he has begun to destroy himself.

—John Ciardi
(Poetry Editor, *Saturday Review*, 11/3/62)

Art has much to do with the drive or fanaticism of the person who has made his choice and will eschew anything else—money, the elite identification of a degree, even health—to develop the talent he has. It comes also from the pride of doing for oneself, of making ends meet, of giving society what it will pay for even if what it pays is inadequate to sustain a normal life, of working in the midst of a fraternity that will show the same fanaticisms and abnegations. It comes from the endless time, time spent on doing one thing, only one thing, and then starting all over again. . . .

—W. McNeil Lowry
(Program Director, The Ford Foundation, 1962)

It is a remarkable thing that often in the lives of the great men, just at the moment when all seems lost, or things are at their lowest ebb, they are nearest to the fulfilment of their destiny. [In 1741] Handel seemed vanquished. Just at that very hour he wrote a work which was destined to establish permanently his immortality. . . . On April 12, 1742, the first hearing of the *Messiah* took place in Dublin. The proceeds of the concert were devoted to charitable objects, and the success was very considerable. But not in London, where Handel gave the *Messiah* only three times in 1743, twice in 1745, and not again until 1749. The cabals of the pious tried to stifle it. He was not allowed to put the title of the oratorio on the bills. It was called A Sacred Oratorio. It was only at the close of 1750 that the victory of the *Messiah* was complete. . . .

1744 was one of Handel's most glorious years from the creative point of view, but one of the most miserable in outward success. . . . Never was the hostility of the English public more roused against him. The same hateful cabal which had already twice threatened to bring about his downfall again rose against him. . . . Handel, whose force of energy and genius had weakened since his first failure in 1735, was involved afresh in bankruptcy at the beginning of 1745. His griefs and troubles, and the prodigious expenditure of force which he made, seemed again on the point of turning his brain. . . . But in 1746, the two great patriotic works, the *Occasional Oratorio* and *Judas Maccabaeus*, . . . brought more fortune to Handel than all the rest of his works together. After thirty-five years of continuous struggle, plot and counterplot, he had at last obtained a decisive victory. He became by the force of events the "national musician of England"!

—Romain Rolland

The characterizing trait of all authentic masterworks is their capacity for infinite self-renewal. . . . The great artists, wrought upon by the wonder and the mystery of human life, its transient vanishing loveliness, have known how to outwit dissolution. . . . The

truths that were true for such artists need not be our truths. Often they are not. The point is the degree to which the depths were stirred, the intensity with which the spirit flamed. Dante survives his cosmos, and Bach his faith, and Beethoven his pantheism, and Blake his sublime insanities, and Wagner his ideology. But they survive these things, not merely because they are great artists, masters of pattern and of style, but because their art bears the irremovable impress of their intensity as mystics and visionaries and fanatics. . . .
—Lawrence Gilman

It hurts me to see people, like Picasso at the end of his life, who take themselves seriously. The artist is a fellow who doesn't stay put, who falls, gets up and then keeps on going. The man who makes mistakes should be venerated. You must accept being a fool. But people don't, and so they are fools.
—Robert Tatin
(French sculptor and architect of "fantastic" art;
quoted in an article about his work in
Smithsonian magazine, February 1979.)

The only way to escape the personal corruption of praise is to go on working. One is tempted to stop and listen to it. The only thing is to turn away and go on working. Work. There is nothing else.
—Albert Einstein

Now for our Salzburg story. You, most beloved friend, are well aware how I detest Salzburg—and not only on account of the injustices which my dear father and I have endured there, which in themselves would be enough to make us wish to forget such a place and blot it out of our memory forever. But let us set that aside, if only we can arrange things as to be able to live there respectably. To live respectably and to live happily are two very different things, and the latter I could not do without having recourse to witchcraft . . . . Salzburg is no place for my talent. In the first place, professional musicians there are not held in much consideration; and, secondly, one hears nothing, there is no theater, no opera; and even if they really wanted one, who is there to sing? For the last five or six years the Salzburg orchestra has always been rich in what is useless and superfluous, but very poor in what is necessary, and absolutely destitute of what is indispensable . . . .
—W. A. Mozart
(Letter to Abbé Bullinger, Aug. 7, 1778)

Mozart could obtain his due position only in the role of creator: as "Court Composer"; as a musician receiving commissions to compose specific works—operas, symphonies, quartets—and having the leisure to do so. Nevertheless both father and son always exerted themselves to obtain a position, the more strongly when their relations with Archbishop Hieronymus Colloredo . . . made their work more and more unpleasant, and made them look upon it as drudgery . . . .
    The Empress Maria Theresa of Austria to her son, Archduke Ferdinand, Governor of Lombardy, December 12, 1771: "You ask me about taking into your services the young Salzburg musician. I do not know in what capacity, believing that you have no need for a composer or for useless people. If, however, it would give you pleasure, I do not wish to prevent you. What I say is intended only to urge you not to burden yourself with useless people, and not to give such people permission to represent themselves as belonging in your service. It gives one's service a bad name when such people run about like beggars; he has, besides, a large family."
    The docile archduke naturally thought no more of engaging Mozart, and did not

confer any title upon him. If Leopold had any idea what Maria Theresa, the kindly Queen who had once presented his children with the cast-off clothing of her royal children, really thought about him and Wolfgang . . . his loyalty would have suffered a bit.

—Alfred Einstein
(From *Mozart—His Character, His Work*)

Erich Leinsdorf Goes to Bat for the Composer (OCTOBER 1982)

WITHOUT the slightest intent of commercial promotion, it may be claimed that Erich Leinsdorf's book, *The Composer's Advocate—A Radical Orthodoxy for Musicians* (Yale University Press, New Haven and London, 1981) is the single book on the art itself published during the last decade that is absolutely indispensable for professionals. It is the work of a conductor who has thought with enormous care, and for more than half a century, about the nature of music and the responsibilities of the performer, and is eager to share his discoveries with his colleagues as well as his students. It is so "loaded" with insight (as well as "loaded with opinion") that no serious musician should do himself or herself the disservice of not reading it, and not marking it up in the margins of pages.

Its chapter titles tell some of the story: Preface, 1. Knowing the Score, 2. Knowing the Composer, 3. Knowing What Composers Wanted, 4. Knowing Musical Tradition, 5. Knowing the Right Tempo: I, 6. Knowing the Right Tempo: II, 7. Knowing the Conductor's Role, Finale, Index.

It is an argumentative book, even at moments a somewhat belligerent one. But this is understandable; the author is impatient with sloth (the Austrian "Schlamperei"), mindless repetition of what is considered "traditional", imitation of others' methods to avoid original thinking, and so on. And although the book is in part highly technical, with many music examples and detailed analytical points, it contains many pages of interest to non-professional music lovers (as the chapter headings demonstrate). Here are some examples of both kinds of approach, the technical and the general:

From the chapter "Knowing Musical Tradition":

It is most important for conductors to study the music of periods when the traditions were taken for granted, immersing themselves in it until the meaning and the rightness of the conventions become self-evident . . . . Before beginning Bach's Third Suite (example 20), the conductor cannot simply announce that all dotted quarter notes should be double-dotted. In each part he must have the double-dotting and the extra sixteenth flag marked, as if each occurrence were a new event. In bar 9 the oboes and the first violins must be so corrected; similar corrections must be marked in bar 10 for the second violins and violas and in bars 11 and 12 for all high instruments; and so on, throughout the piece. . . .

One reason why otherwise expert orchestral players adhere so rigidly to printed orthodoxy became clearer to me recently when I heard a fine orchestra of one of the great American conservatories perform the entire introduction of this piece as if it were marked *grave*—as indeed a misguided German editor specified in one edition. The orchestra played the section in a heavy "eight beats to the bar," hammering out each note as if it had been written by Bruckner. Any musician who directs youngsters in such an outdated, discredited style commits a musical crime and should be given assignments of a less sensitive nature. Such a disregard for tradition makes it difficult for students to learn a crucial stylistic distinction and the proper way to realize it in performance.

An excerpt from "Knowing the Composer":

... The implication that great composers must show contrapuntal mastery is disturbing. Schubert was not a master contrapuntist, yet his music has a uniquely transcendent quality. His chamber music, piano sonatas, lieder, and several symphonies will live with the music of Mozart and Beethoven; he wrote a few wondrously beautiful masses in which only the fugues are inferior. Schubert, to whom Mahler owed a great debt, showed how absurd it is to consider contrapuntal expertise an indispensable element in the creation of great music. One might perhaps identify two types of intellect in music. One produces enormous technical proficiency, but of a sort that is often wanting in profound emotional qualities. The other, which manifests itself through the emotional responses it evokes, is less easily measured and is consequently not well appreciated, though it is a bosom companion of invention, inspiration, and indeed genius.

From "Knowing the Conductor's Role":

When I assumed the post of music director for the Boston Symphony, I was asked by journalists if the orchestra would now have a "German sound", assuming that during the years of Charles Munch's incumbency they had played with a "French sound". All this is nonsense. These terms are made up by slogan breeders who understand music simply in terms of clichés that, when scrutinized, prove to have no meaning at all. There is no German sound and there is no French sound. There is a right sound and a wrong sound for every work performed. If this is understood, sound takes an important role in interpreting music. A violinist, playing a very craggy work, was quite rightly offended when a leading critic found her tone lacking in sensuous beauty. The work would have taken on different significance altogether if its deeply introverted slow movement had been performed with a lush tone. If the violinist had been concerned with displaying a gorgeous tone she would have selected the Tchaikovsky concerto. A record producer expressed his disappointment to me, when he was assigned to tape a cycle of Beethoven's works, because "his orchestration is not good for recording."

*

If there is a "problem" with this book, it lies in the assumption that there may after all be only one way to conduct or perform a piece of music, so that it must sound according to "the most exact and explicit directions" that composers have placed in their scores. Thus it stands to reason that many a reading based on musical intuition beyond the evident instructions would have to be regarded as "wrong"; but where does that leave differences of approach between such master conductors as Toscanini, Furtwängler, and Mr. Leinsdorf himself? Nor is it really possible at all times for audiences "to hear the music performed the way the composer conceived it" (page 62, slightly paraphrased); modern instruments, halls five times as large, and conductors on the podium instead of composers directing from the harpsichord—these are just a few of the unavoidable differences. Yet there can be little argument with the crucial statement below (also reproduced on the back jacket cover).

*

From "Knowing What Composers Wanted":

Today special courage and energy may be required to sweep away the detritus of misinterpretation and reveal a composer's work as he first constructed it. Ironically, faithful interpretation of a great master's wishes often seems not conservative but radical. But to discover the composer's grand design for each work is both the conductor's mission and his reward.

"Music, of All the Arts,
Best Ministers to Human Welfare" (APRIL 1980)

—Herbert Spencer
(English Philosopher, 1820–1903)

*

The Cleveland Music School Settlement has adopted this saying by Spencer as a motto for its services. In April 1988, HARVEY WOLFE—with The Cleveland Orchestra cello section since 1967—paid tribute to the School on its 75th anniversary. His essay for the program book closed with the following paragraph.

*

I was lucky to grow up in a great American city with fine institutions like the school system, a great library, free museums of the first rank, and a socially conscious institution like the Cleveland Music School Settlement, now in its 75th year. Democracy at its best was demonstrated in those years when the public school had the power and determination to give any student full chance to develop his talent. Education was the highest priority of our society, academic achievement the highest goal, liberal arts highly respected. It is not wise to generalize about such things, but there is some sense that values have changed. It is said that society is becoming more polarized between rich and poor, that the arts are more and more a symbol of the 'upscale' with Mozart used to sell BMWs and Vivaldi to advertise expensive frozen dinners; music lessons are the birthright of the affluent along with orthodontia and summer camp. I have always believed that great music and art belong to everyone—to all who want them, and that it is the responsibility of the institutions who make and house these works to make them available to all who have the capacity to love them. In its 75th anniversary year the Cleveland Music School Settlement still serves this function, and I, for one, say "Thank you."

V. MODERN? NEW? CONTEMPORARY?

They are so enamored of themselves as to think it within their powers to corrupt, spoil, and ruin the good old rules handed down in former times by so many theorists and most excellent musicians, the very men from whom these moderns have learned to string together a few notes with little grace. For them it is enough to create a tumult of sounds, confusion of absurdities, an assemblage of imperfections. (1600)

> Giovanni Maria Artusi
> leading Italian theorist, attacking
> the greatest composer of Venice,
> Claudio Monteverdi

All impartial connoisseurs are fully agreed that never has anything been written so incoherent, so disagreeable, so revolting to the ear. The most grotesque modulations, in truly ghastly cacophony, follow one another throughout the piece.... (1805)

> August von Kotzebue, noted critic,
> on the first performance of
> Beethoven's *Leonore Overture No. 2*

The old order is always afraid of the new. The new need never be afraid of the old. The law of change is the law of growth. Too many in authority fear change. Too many lack the necessary perspective, vision, and courage to face the law of change. Principle is the only safe tradition.

> Frank Lloyd Wright

But I already know that song! Why don't you sing me one that I don't know yet?

> Silas K. Burdick
> age three-and-a-half
> to his grandmother, 1986

Composers Who Deviate from the Right Path (MAY 1978)

THAT MOST NEW WORKS by composers of all periods have met with something less than enthusiasm from the critics (as well as audiences) is a fact well enough known and amply documented. We have often had occasion to quote, for example, from Nicolas Slonimsky's endlessly entertaining *Lexicon of Musical Invective—Critical Assaults on Composers Since Beethoven's Time* (Coleman-Ross Company, 1953). The critics, after all, have it as their purpose in life to criticize—if one takes the word in its considerably altered meaning, which is "to find fault", rather than "to evaluate".

But from encyclopedists, from scholars who write or compile dictionaries of music and musicians, we expect judgments that are entirely "objective", whatever that word may mean in the highly opinionated arts. We assume that they will be as irreproachable in fairness as they are invulnerable in facts. Perhaps there are some contemporary writers of whom this is true, but one tends to be skeptical. For encyclopedists are forced to become practicing critics in the very moment when they move from dates and data to the sphere of evaluation. There are delightful surprises for us in the study of some of those earlier dictionaries; must it not have been reassuring to be informed, around 1825, that "in melody, Mozart is inferior to Sarti"?

*

Recently, a book published in 1854 came to hand, a production which not only provides amusement but also an intrinsic warning to our generation to be a little less sure of its judgment, a little less categorical in its sense of what is "the right path" for music to follow, and perhaps to learn from hindsight some foresight. We refer to the *Musical Hand-Book for Musicians and Amateurs, a Miniature Encyclopedia containing Explanations of all the Technical Terms Used in Music, together with Biographical and Critical Notices of Composers, Singers, Executive Artists etc. Edited by* Julius Schuberth. *Fourth Edition, Schuberth & Comp. Hamburgh, Leipsic & New York. London, J.J. Ewer & Co.—Entered according to Act of Congress A. D. 1854 by Schuberth & Co. in the clerks office of the District Court of the southern District of New-York.* (The name of the translator into English is not given.)

Julius Schuberth (born in Magdeburg in 1804, died in Leipzig in 1875) describes himself in his *Hand-Book* as "head of the well-known firm of Schuberth and Co. in Hamburgh, Leipsic, and New-York [*sic*]; he is a thorough musician and violinist, an enterprizing publisher, and founded the North-german musical Association. He was for some years editor of the Hamburgh mus. Journal, and has received the order 'pour le mérite' from the king of Wurtemberg."

In his preface (dated January 1854), the author writes that he was greatly assisted in writing the book by his "personal acquaintance with almost every living musician of eminence". One can understand the absence from the book of Bruckner, then only thirty; but one is struck by the fact that Verdi (born in 1813), who by 1854 had composed nearly twenty operas including *Rigoletto, Il Trovatore,* and *La Traviata,* is not listed either in the body of the book or in the brief appendix of sixteen names. Mr. Schuberth writes: "I have endeavoured to be as correct as possible in my researches, and to give much information in a small space, *multum in parvo.* That there are still considerable deficiencies in the work I am well aware, but my utmost efforts could not succeed in making it more perfect . . . . I have had the strictest regard to truth in my criticisms and remarks, and hope therefore to give no offence where certainly none has been intended. In all cases where my personal knowledge did not suffice, I have had recourse to standard authorities, and biographical or other omissions will be rectified in the next edition . . . ."

*

Mr. Slonimsky is surely right that one of the major stumbling-blocks in the issue of "modern music" of every era is the natural attitude he classifies as "Non-Acceptance of the Unfamiliar". One would therefore expect that virtually all the great music of the past (his past) would appeal to Mr. Schuberth, and indeed he is very kindly disposed toward Palestrina, Purcell, Haydn, and Mozart. But as we shall see from his discussion of Bach, his love of the past was hardly more automatic than his knowledge was complete. At a time when a Beethoven program is the apex of audience popularity, it is fitting to begin these excerpts from the *Hand-Book* with a part of the entry on that master, deceased only twenty-seven years before:

> To discuss minutely all the numerous works of Beethoven would be beyond our limits; we will therefore briefly touch upon the more conspicuous among them. First and foremost stand 3 of his grand symphonies, viz. that in C-minor, the "pastorale" and the "eroica"; these are undoubtedly his greatest and most successful works, nor can we agree with some critics (ger. and engl.) who incline to place the 9th., or choral symphony, on an equality with them. We rather hold with the author of the "musikalische Briefe" that the 9th. is a decidedly retrograde movement, and proved that B's creative power was seriously diminished, as also that he had deviated from the right path and had entered the region of conjecture and incertitude;—"thus far shalt thou go, and no farther" stood inscribed on the portals, but B. ventured to pass them and found himself wrapt in clouds and darkness. Nothing was gained by the colossal dimensions of the 9th. symphony, or by the introduction of the chorus which is both superfluous and ineffective. Throughout the work there is a palpable effort, a straining after something unaccomplished; it is full of fits and starts and is quite wanting in that delightful unfettered flow of thought which all his other symphonies present. Still it is evidently the work of a great mind, and with all its faults is superior to any other symphony—formed upon the same model—as yet produced. But the model itself was defective; B. erred in not adhering to the faultless mould in which he cast the "eroica" and its two illustrious fellows:—even the symphonies in D [No. 2] and A [No. 7] are superior . . . .

How fascinating that the *Eroica*—which had broken virtually every "faultless mould" of symphonic structure at the beginning of the nineteenth century—"a new path", as the composer himself proclaimed it—was by now considered a "standard work", while the *Ninth* was destined to remain a mystery for a good while longer. One recalls that as late as 1875 (the year of Mr. Schuberth's death) Georges Bizet remarked about the reception of Beethoven's *Ninth* in Paris: "It is the fate of great geniuses to be misunderstood by their contemporaries . . . . Take the most intelligent audience and play the greatest pages which our art possesses for them—the 'Choral Symphony'. They will understand nothing, absolutely nothing. We have had this experience; we repeat it every year with the same result. It is only that Beethoven is fifty years dead and it is the fashion to find his music beautiful . . . ."

Mr. Schuberth's Beethoven chapter continues with an observation about the *Missa Solemnis* which may have kept him from going to—or remaining in—heaven:

> B.'s Masses are important works, but can scarcely be called successful; that in C is the best, being clear and largely designed; the one in D must, to a certain extent, be classed along with the 9th. symphony—it is vague, unvocal, and does not achieve its purpose; its vast but somewhat rude proportions do not endow it with sublimity.
>
> Berlioz: a remarkable but very eccentric composer . . . [His composi-

tions, listed] are all more or less distinguished by poetic intention, novel and brilliant but often noisy instrumentation, and a kind of glaring originality which sometimes assumes a grotesque and almost monstrous form. These works display abundance of imagination, but it resembles "the frenzied visions of a feverish dream" and can never please a pure and refined taste.

As an orchestral conductor B. is almost unrivalled, and his treatise on instrumentation is comprehensive and valuable. His music is seldom or never performed except under his personal superintendence, and has not yet obtained, after the lapse of 20 years, (and in spite of great exertions on his own part and that of his friends) any firm hold upon the favour of the public either in France, Germany, or England.

Again one thinks of Bizet, who continued in the same statement quoted earlier: "Auber, who had so much talent and few ideas, was almost always understood, while Berlioz, who had genius but no talent at all, was almost never understood." Berlioz himself penned, in his *Memoirs*, the perfect answer to the encyclopedist's complaints: "Generally speaking, my style is very bold, but it has not the slightest tendency to subvert any of the constituent elements of art. On the contrary, it is my endeavor to add to their number . . ."

Bach: . . . a celebrated and most original composer, the greatest master of counterpoint that ever existed . . . . His works are still considered standard in the contrapuntal style, but are more to be admired as elaborate combinations and triumphs of art than as effusions of genius; his vocal music is so deficient in melody and grace that very little of it is now performed.

Händel: Palestrina, Leo, and Clari have more strictly ecclesiastical solemnity in their music, but they do not equal Händel in sublimity. Händel was an admirable and ready fugue-writer, but not such an adept in counterpoint as Seb. Bach. though infinitely superior in talent to that pedantic composer.

The most popular, effective, and celebrated chorus in the whole oratorio, the "Hallelujah", is constructed entirely upon points of imitation, and bears no resemblance to a regular fugue. All the learned combinations of Bach are but as "dry bones" when compared with that vivid and inspiring effusion, or with the fluent and melodious "lift up your heads."

It is an example of how much "behind the times" Mr. Schuberth found himself that he could ignore the extraordinary Bach renaissance then well under way, a movement that had begun dramatically with Mendelssohn's performance of the long-forgotten *St. Matthew Passion* in 1829, and resulted in the publication—over many decades—of the master's collected works by the *Bach-Gesellschaft*, founded in 1850.

Liszt: His own compositions are strange vagaries, in the confused fantastical manner of the so-called new-romantic school, of which Chopin was the best interpreter. He is now operatic conductor at Weimar, and plays no more in public; the influence (happily not great) which he has exercised upon the music of the present day is decidedly of an injurious tendency.

Schubert: A celebrated composer; he wrote more than 200 songs [actually, more than 600] of which about 30 are extremely fine and about 30 more very interesting; the rest are not likely to survive. He also cd. operas, symphonies, P. F., trios, etc., the former are indifferent, and are not published; his symphony in C is very ingenious, but noisily instrumentated and in no respect firstrate; his Trios are well-written and imaginative.

In these, as in many of the others, there is great originality of conception, poetic feeling, and not a little dramatic expression; his melodies are sufficiently vocal and often captivating, but they were not very abundant and he often spoils them by overloading the accompaniment, by a slightly pedantic adherence to one figure or form, and, not seldom, by surcharged and complex harmony, which is out of place except in works of greater extent and a higher class.

Schumann: He is a learned musician, ingenious in the art of combination, gifted with very considerable poetic feeling (though of a morbid species) but, like Berlioz, Wagner, and Halévy, deficient in the divine gift of melody, and tries hard to supply its place (a Sisyphean attempt) by artificial means, complicated harmony, and a perpetual straining after an originality which is denied him.

*

Still, time marches on. In the 1870s, among the more than six thousand titles published by Schuberth's firm were numerous works by Schumann and Liszt, as well as by Mendelssohn and Chopin!

Wagner: His operas "Tannhäuser" and "Lohengrin" were the first pressed upon the public notice by F. Liszt at Weimar, who wrote pamphlets about them, endeavouring to prove that they contained the germs of important innovation in dramatic music. The fact is, however, that Wagner has given nothing new to the world except a portentous amount of bombast and chaotic ideas. His "Rienzi" is a musical monstrosity, "full of sound and fury, signifying nothing." W. has, indeed, no style at all, unless confusion and an absence of any distinct form can be termed a style. He is not without dramatic conceptions, and would fain achieve something great; but he resembles Icarus, who assayed to fly with waxen wings and fell into the sea. Some consideration is due to a praiseworthy ambition, and it is perhaps better to strive after something unattainable than to be content with what may appear imperfect; but desire and fruition are very different things.

W. is not a musical genius, and can scarcely be termed a musical talent, for he is strangely devoid of melodic invention, and his harmonies are crude and ineffective, often harsh and betraying imperfect command of the science; he is one of the many musical poetasters who essentially belong to the Decline of the Art, and who assist in hastening its fall in Germany:—that country which brought forth such numerous and great composers is now reduced to praise incompetence and mediocrity, unless it adopt foreign genius and renounce the once justifiable price of possessing it indigenous.

*

The appendix of the *Hand-Book* contains sixteen names of which only about three are known to us today. One of these is Johannes Brahms, then twenty-one years old and already hailed by Schumann as the true contender for Beethoven's mantle. Mr. Schuberth treats him concisely thus:

Brahms, Johannes, born 1833 in Holstein, pupil of Ed. Marxsen, a composer of much Talent and very considerable acquirements. An attempt has lately been made by a musical clique, which is labouring to establish a new School based upon false principles, to foist the productions of this young musician upon the world as masterpieces.

Some Fallacious Assumptions in Music
or
"All Generalizations Are False, Including This One"
(JANUARY 1980)

All great masterpieces were failures at their first performances.

Haydn's symphonies, particularly the late ones written for London, were enormously successful there, and so were his last two oratorios produced in Vienna, *The Creation* and *The Seasons*. Mozart's *The Marriage of Figaro* and *Don Giovanni* were hits in Prague, and *The Magic Flute* in Vienna. Verdi's *Aïda, Otello, Falstaff* and *Requiem Mass* were overwhelming successes from the first. Britten's *Peter Grimes* and *War Requiem* were recognized as masterworks from the outset. Stravinsky's *The Rite of Spring*, though greeted by a riot at its premiere (for reasons largely unconnected with the music itself) quickly won over its audiences as a concert work. Bartók's *Concerto for Orchestra* was regarded as outstanding immediately.

Works now accepted as masterpieces were always immediately recognized as such.

Beethoven's *Third Symphony*, the "Eroica", was severely criticized by almost everyone, for its length, its instrumental difficulties, and its new musical language. His *Ninth Symphony* was greeted warmly, but primarily in deference to the aging and deaf composer who stood on the podium. Bach's *St. Matthew Passion* was regarded as an aberration both musically and theologically, and was relegated to the shelf for nearly one hundred years. In the same city, Leipzig, Brahms's *First Piano Concerto* was a disaster with audiences as well as with critics. Schubert's last symphony was regarded by a London orchestra as unplayable, even ridiculous. Bruckner's *Third Symphony* was virtually booed off the stage (while the *Seventh* and *Eighth* captivated audiences and critics). Mozart's last three symphonies were not even considered worthy of performance during his lifetime. Most of Berlioz's larger compositions reaped extraordinary abuse from all sides, and so did Wagner's music dramas. Debussy's *La Mer* was perceived widely as *Mal de Mer*. As to the music of the twentieth century, a considerable proportion of those works now in the regular repertoire were regarded at first as unsuccessful.

Conclusion, to both assumptions? The conditions of performance, the nature of the audience, the location and occasion of the premiere, have much more to do with initial success or failure than the intrinsic quality of the works. While it is of course expected that an audience will react to a new work, positively, negatively, lukewarm, or "undecided", these reactions tend to be misleading as to the actual future of the music; in fact, many pieces now forgotten had a much greater initial success than works which had much tougher sledding. Posterity, ultimately, makes the lasting judgment.

There is only one way that composers belonging to any particular age should write.

It is true that Bach and Handel, while masters of very different occupations and preoccupations (Handel: fifty operas; Bach: none), spoke essentially the same musical language, a "common discourse" that could be understood and followed by musically educated listeners. The same can be said of Haydn, Mozart, Johann Christian Bach, and Boccherini. Yet Weber did not always follow Beethoven on his explorations, and the great master from Bonn wrote music vastly different from his great contemporaries, Rossini and Cherubini. While Schumann and Mendelssohn were again quite close in their musical idiom, individuals though they remained, Wagner and Brahms were considered in their own day as totally antithetical. "Romanticists" both, they became the willing or unwitting leaders of "camps", surrounded by all the venom of which dedicated camp followers are capable. Wagner was the avant-gardist, the "music of the future", and his partisans depreciated the "conservatism" or even "reaction" of the Brahms camp. To us today, who admire both masters, this may seem ridiculous; but in the nineteenth century this difference was vivid and crucial enough for bitter attacks and recriminations. In Vienna of about 1890, you could not be a Bruckner fan and a Brahms fan at the same time; you had to choose. Only a few, like the great conductor Hans Richter, had a keener insight, a wider scope, a more solid historical viewpoint.

And in our century, we have seen the sharp divisions of the Schoenberg-Berg-Webern camp on one side, and the Stravinsky-Hindemith-Bartók camp on the other. It makes no more sense than did the Wagner-Bruckner-Brahms controversy. Even closer to our own day, we witness battles between the avant-gardists and the moderates, the experimentalists and the neo-this and neo-that, as if each side, and each individual composer, had the total answer to the riddle of creation. It occurs to few of them that musical history has always moved not in a single direction, but in circles, eddies, by-ways, even reversals, re-discoveries, re-interpretations of past styles (did Brahms in the nineteenth century find anything peculiar about writing passacaglias and chaconnes based on eighteenth century models? And did not Berg organize his opera, *Wozzeck*, into sonatas and rondos?). The current brouhaha between the followers of Elliott Carter, Pierre Boulez, Donald Erb, Witold Lutoslawski and those of Benjamin Britten, Gian Carlo Menotti, of Samuel Barber, Ned Rorem, and Elie Siegmeister is largely based on a misapprehension: that one side is right, and the other wrong. Both are right; neither is wrong. It may be that the avant-gardists will "advance" the art of music by doing some things that have not been done before; but they have forgotten that it was Stravinsky who said, "in music, that lasts longest which is oldest and most tried." The neo-classicists, the eclectics, attempt with more or less success to establish or re-establish a more or less "common language", one that will communicate with musical symbols already known and understood; if they are gifted, they contribute to the total literature. It is not necessary to be "up-to-date" in your musical speech, according to the latest score received from the Warsaw Autumn or the IRCAM in Paris; some individualists, as for instance George Crumb, are reaching audiences without any regard for what is "current" and "approved". By the same token, there is little point in merely echoing (though the result is often pleasant enough), to do over what Bartók and Prokofiev did to perfection; there must be individuality, personality, a point-of-view, regardless of the musical language spoken.

But the "right" path, with all the others deprecated and depreciated (the opposite of appreciated)? Nonsense. There are many paths, some parallel, some diverging, some converging. It is our task as listeners to recognize them, to see and hear with the eyes and ears of the artists as far as possible, to accept and reject on the basis of what our education and experience enable us to do. It is not for us to be caught up in the acrimonious and often unethical backbiting of creative artists, who claim to have the law from Olympus. Their job is to produce, according to the best of their abilities, to leave the judgment of what they have done to audiences, hopefully perceptive and sympathetic ones, and to realize with some humility that there are "many mansions in my Father's house", many roads to salvation, many different artistic slots yet to be filled with work of integrity, talent, and vision.

New Music at the Symphony:
An Approach in Three Movements
(1961)

I. Principles and Attitudes

Just as little as one can understand the New and the Young without being at home in tradition, just as non-genuine and sterile must the love toward the Old remain if one closes one's mind to the New which came forth from it with historical necessity.

—Thomas Mann (1948)

1. Unless Western civilization is at an end, music (and all art) is not at an end. As long as life is worth living, new music will be created, taking its historical place with that of the past. Walking along the banks of the Danube one day, Brahms and Mahler spoke of the future of music. The older man glumly pondered its imminent demise. "See," said Mahler, pointing to the river, "here comes the last wave!"

2. Musical revolutions, which seem to occur at regular intervals of one hundred and fifty years, soon prove to have been evolutions: necessary, inevitable, fruitful. "Thirty years ago," said Richard Strauss as an old man, "I was regarded as a rebel. I have lived long enough to find myself a classic." Great works of art remain eternally fresh; modernism changes into timelessness; the merely fashionable and the meretricious disappear, while the truly pathbreaking and original establish a new classicism.

3. The art of music can progress only in a technical sense; but it must change. Change is the law of life. No great composer is "better" than one before him; he is different. Respect before the older master, and a realization that what has been perfected cannot be duplicated or imitated, force the young composer of talent to find his own way. It would be a confession of artistic bankruptcy to try to do over again what the masters brought to completion. "Children," Wagner said to his disciples, "make new things!"

4. Resistance to change is a fact of history. It is a fact in art as in science, in music as in medicine, in politics and international relations. The stronger and more original an idea or discovery, the fiercer and more outraged the opposition. Schoenberg and Stravinsky (and Beethoven) found this so; but so did Galileo in astronomy, Pasteur in medicine, Voltaire in literature, Cézanne in painting, Wilson in statesmanship. History has been a pitifully ineffective teacher, or man an unteachable pupil. Humanity persists—in most areas—in making exactly the same mistakes again and again.

5. Music can no more stand still than can science, transportation, communication, medicine. If audiences wish to stand still, they will be left behind. The traditional "fifty-year lag" in the appreciation of new art (and new ideas in general) always has one major cause: public inertia and indolence. Conservatism has its values; sheer reaction has none. Listeners too may "proceed with all deliberate speed"; but they must proceed. To try to hold back the inexorable motion of historical change is a waste of effort and energy.

6. The familiar is well regarded with affection. But this affection need not be exclusive, or limited in scope. The dimensions of the human mind are vast; it can without conflict accommodate the most diverse ideas and styles. The fact that Mozart may be our favorite composer need not prevent us from deeply enjoying Hindemith. Let not "I know what I like" be a cover-up for "I like what I know".

7. Goethe warns us in his *Faust:* "So narrow-minded, scared of each new word—wilt only hear what hast already heard!" To meet the new and challenging, the listener must know that he has a responsibility toward the artwork as well as to the performer. Genuine listening is an activity, not a "passivity". There is no purpose to making music in public

unless an audience is willing and ready to participate in the musical experience. There is a modicum of effort involved. It is a worthwhile effort.

8. The first requisite of an intelligent listener is this: two open ears. The next: an open mind. All art, as one philosopher said, is modern art. All art of value first attacks our stereotypes, jeopardizes our cherished beliefs; soon we learn that it has replaced nothing: it has only added something new. Either we respond to the challenge which new art provides, or we escape from it. A noted art critic, James Thrall Soby, wrote recently that "a basic standard of enduring art is to extend and deepen our awareness, not merely to confirm or illustrate what we already know by heart."

9. The act of music-making is not one whose first and only purpose is to please or to entertain. It goes deeper than that. The aim of art is not beauty, but experience; there may be beauty, in the areas of sensuous pleasure, but this is a byproduct. Musical experience may at times be un-beautiful; but it must have meaning.

10. The meaning of music is a symbolic one. We "understand" Beethoven only because we have learned—over the years—his language. A language of music which is largely new to us has little meaning; it is our task to learn it, and it can be done. The principles of art—as they concern such concepts as contrast and repetition, freshness and staleness, setting a mood, sustaining the motion—are immutable. We must learn to recognize their application in new art as we have learned it in the old; and we do this as we become familiar with the idioms and the styles of our century.

II. Idioms and Techniques

Contrary to general belief, an artist is never ahead of his time, but most people are far behind theirs. —Edgar Varèse (1961)

11. The languages of music today are varied, perhaps more so than those of earlier times. But they are learned by repeated exposure, by some awareness of techniques and stylistic avenues, and by accepting a composer's message as he offers it, rather than demanding of him that he speak in terms that we already know from past ages. Any musical phrase by a gifted composer, however new, will begin to make "sense" when repeated a few times, and as our familiarity with the idiom grows it will make sense even the first time. Again, Goethe: "And he who understands me not might well improve his reading!"

12. *Dissonance* is not the same as discord. Discord is noise; dissonance has a function: contrast with consonance. All music of value has both. There is, functionally, no more dissonant a music than that of Bach. As history moves on, most "dissonances" become recognized as what they really are: elements of tension. Some music today seems highly dissonant; that simply means the tension-content is high. No attempt is made in such music to be purposefully ugly or cacophonous. In all worthwhile music, there are high points, and plateaus of tension ("dissonance"); we must hear them for their dramatic and musical purposes, not as combinations of noises. We have done that much for the *Eroica*.

13. The accusation of "ugliness" (largely caused by a misunderstanding of "dissonance") is age-old. Debussy's *Faun* was called, only sixty years ago, "a strong example of modern ugliness". Strauss's *Till Eulenspiegel* was "a blood-curdling nightmare", the work of "a deadly and determined decadent". The music of Wagner and Brahms was derided with the same epithets; even Mozart's string quartets were once regarded as "much too highly spiced to be palatable for any length of time". We find the same terms leveled against Monteverdi in 1600 A.D. as against Mahler in 1900; against Berlioz in 1850 as against Bartók in 1950. The issue is always the same: the language had not been learned; people thought they knew exactly what beauty was, and what its limits were. Beauty, we

now know, is in the eye of the beholder, or the ear of the listener. This concept too is eternally in flux.

14. A *melody* is any succession of notes with a recognizable direction and rhythmic pattern. Melodies can be short and scrappy, long and lyrical. Some are singable, some are not. Some are vocal, some are instrumental. It is not necessary to be able to whistle it after one hearing to have a melody. Too many people equate melody with a romantic tune in the manner of Tchaikovsky; there are others.

15. *Rhythm* is not the same thing as "beat". Rhythm goes against beat and meter, using them as foils for stimulating excursions. Let us not expect to be able to tap our feet to all rhythms; some are challenging and complex, as is the pulse of our lives. Order it must have, but regularity in the accepted sense it need not.

16. *Harmony* must change as all music changes. There are tonal ("key-centered") harmonies, and atonal ("key-less") harmonies. There is no sense in trying to "figure out" an unfamiliar harmony on the spot; it can't be done. Let the listener hear it as sound—interesting or not, unusual or not, harsh or mild, sour or sweet. And let him ask, as he actively listens, "Where does it go? What is it like in relation to the next harmony? What can I remember—what can I anticipate?"

17. *Form* in music is not the same as forms of music. "Form" has to do not with sonatas and rondos, but with design, with structure, with logical progression, with "the balance between tension and relaxation" (Ernst Toch's fine phrase). Whatever "system" a piece follows or utilizes proves nothing about its value as art. But if we know something about how a piece is made, we shall come closer to its essential meaning as communication. The more we can know, the keener will our ultimate experience become, and the more solidly founded our evaluation.

III. Feelings and Discoveries

As life is action and passion, it is required of a man that he should share the passion and action of his time, at the peril of being judged not to have lived.

—Oliver Wendell Holmes, Jr. (1884)

18. Against much widely held opinion, the modernists are no more "cerebral" than composers ever were. Their feelings are just as impassioned as those of earlier creative musicians. Let us not demand of them a way of expression which duplicates that of an earlier day, that uses the same musical symbols to express or reflect emotions. Composers today are using a wider field of expressivity than ever, with a myriad of subtle psychological fluctuations. Art has ideas as well as feelings, and an idea passionately held is worth more in art than an emotion badly expressed. The finest art today, as we find it in the work of dozens of composers, is as expressive as one could wish—once one has learned the musical symbolism employed. If a listener tells us that Bartók's *Violin Concerto* "leaves him cold", that he finds nothing "spiritual" in Hindemith's *Mathis der Maler*, and that Copland's *Appalachian Spring* is "largely technique", all one can say is "how sad for him!" How much he is missing!

19. The nature of our musical responses is very complex, and very individual. It matters greatly how musical we are, and what we expect from a concert. Should it provide us with rest and relaxation, or should it do more than that? Should it only entertain, or should it be full of profound revelations? How many of us frankly feel that life is quite tough enough, and when we go to hear music we would just as soon that the tensions of the day were not reflected in the music offered? Justified or not, this view of art is limited, and lowers music to a level of "wasn't it nice?". Even a tense and astringent work can be therapeutic, if rightly heard; if it is good, it will transcend—in a spiritual sense—the grim realities it means to reflect. But the fact is that most new music does not search for

ultimates any more than does the music of the past; much of it is quite pleasing, even jolly, and there is no point in fighting with it over "dissonances".

20. When we say "new music", we do not mean "novelty" for its own sake, or "shock value", fads or cults. Deliberate hoaxes are extremely rare. By "new" we mean music that says new things in old ways, old things in new ways, and—occasionally—new things in new ways while retaining a demonstrable bridge to tradition, to our musical heritage. Virtually nothing is totally new, and the new is not ipso facto good. But enough of the new is always "good enough" so that all of it should be considered with genuine and ever-hopeful interest.

21. Some new music is far ahead of general comprehension. We may regard it as useless for that reason. This is often quite unfair; for the work may be truly pathbreaking, rather than abstruse. The problem of recognition and evaluation is ours, not the composer's. He is under no obligation to make things easy for us; but we have the obligation to meet him at least halfway. Let us beware of stating with emphasis, "the music had nothing to say", when we really mean "the music had nothing to say *to me*", or even more truthfully, "I didn't understand what it said". Nothing pleases a serious composer more than the approval of an educated and demanding audience. It is simply not true that composers do not care about their listeners; but their first responsibility is to their own principles. Nobody demands of us that we "like" everything; there is, in every period, a good deal to criticize. But we should know why, with criteria that are sound and solid. Our contribution to the inevitable decisions of "posterity" is an evaluation as just and well-informed as we can make it. Whether ours is a "golden age" or only one of brass and alloys, we cannot tell with certainty from this vantage point. But since the spirit of man is indivisible, one may assume that an era great in science is also likely to see a flourishing of the arts; history shows us that.

22. We have all heard this conversation: "Do you know Mr. . . . . .?" "Well, I wouldn't say I know him: I've met him." Why is this honest admission so rare in a musical situation? After one hearing of a work, we have only "met" it; if it is music of value, with substance as well as surface, we do not yet "know" it. Historically, all important new art surrenders its secrets slowly; it may make a pleasing or even overwhelming first impression, but to be really understood it must be "lived with". We can read a novel with care, and look back to refresh our memory; we can look at a painting as long as we wish. But music, like drama, moves in time-space. We cannot check back; we must remember and we must anticipate. Much is expected of us. Only "repeated exposure"—so hard to obtain under current cultural conditions—can do real justice to an ambitious new work. For many persons, however musical, the first hearing of Beethoven's Ninth Symphony is plain "too much"; the second makes things clearer; by the third, we are familiar enough to be "with it" some of the time. After a lifetime of listening, there is yet more to be discovered here. Now, with a musical idiom still unfamiliar to most, can a complex new work expect to be absorbed any faster? It cannot, and it does not. It wishes, at first, to make a general but distinct impression, in the hope that we the listeners may say, "I'd like to meet that one again."

23. Why new music at the symphony concerts? An orchestra is not a museum for accepted masterpieces. It is historically a battlefield, a source of stimulation and education, a try-out place for the burgeoning creativity of an era. Great conductors choose wisely from the vast material of new music available; but all of them feel that it must be heard, in proper proportion to the existing orchestral literature of three centuries. They believe that sophisticated listeners really demand to know "what's going on" in music today. No new masterpieces can be discovered if the audience is not given a chance to hear and judge and choose. Nor can a young talent blossom to maturity if it is silenced to death. The percentage of what survives is always small. In every age, there are hundreds of talented, competent, and valuable composers who help provide a healthy "climate" for

the few geniuses; is it not always through the pleasurable foothills that one approaches the majestic mountains? Many "modern classics" already exist; we hear them with regularity. The idea, sometimes advanced, of "segregating" the moderns in special programs only, is fallacious, and would ultimately fail. Under those conditions, art withers and dies. It is for us to come to terms with the art of our own time. Serge Koussevitzky once reminded us that we can best pay our debts to the creators of the past by giving our support to those of the present. And unless we do so in ever-increasing measure, a true American culture— first regional, then national—will never come to flower.

24. Many factors militate against our enjoyment of new music. They have to do with our insufficient musical education, our sense of haste, the deluge of distraction and low-value entertainment. Older people understandably find it hard to adapt themselves for a second or third time to change in musical styles, having outlived the modernists of their youth, Debussy and Ravel and Strauss and Sibelius. But if we can recapture the sense of adventure and excitement that we had as young people and that young people have (or should have) today, we shall see the gap between us and the creative artists closing at a rapid pace. For what any genuine creator tries to do is to show us what he has found, to take us with him on his exploration of music. In that he needs our interest, our response, and our wide-awake concern. As the Mexican composer Carlos Chavez put it so beautifully, the basic intent of all real creative artists is simple: "We are not trying to break anything; we are trying to make what does not yet exist."*

Recommended readings:

Aaron Copland: "The New Music—1900–1960". Revised and enlarged edition. W. W. Norton & Co., Inc., New York, 1968.

Eric Salzman: "Twentieth Century Music—An Introduction". Prentice-Hall Inc., Englewood Cliffs, N. J., 1967.

Nicolas Slonimsky: "Lexicon of Musical Invective—Critical Assaults on Composers since Beethoven's Time". Coleman-Ross Co., 1953.

This listing of books in 1960–62 is valid, but now outdated; many more sources now exist. Furthermore, new styles and devices have sprung up since this essay appeared in 1961, such as the "minimalist", the "third stream" (blending of jazz and "classical" elements), combinations of electronic instruments with conventional ones, etc. All of these are at best hinted at in an essay of more than thirty years ago. Stravinsky's comment of 1960 remains valid and apt: *"When I compose something I cannot conceive that it should fail to be recognized for what it is, and understood. I use the language of music, and my grammar will be clear to the musician who has followed music up to where my contemporaries and I have brought it."*

---

* This article was first published in longer form in *Fine Arts*, Cleveland, February 12 and 19, 1961, and in its present version appeared several times in the Orchestra program book.—Editor.

Fine Arts, Cleveland, June 14, 1964—
Severance Hall Replies to "A Rearguard Action?"

*

Raymond Wilding-White, an accomplished and original young composer resident in Cleve-land during the 1960s, had written an extensive article for the June 7, 1964, issue of Fine Arts *magazine. His argument, wittily and lucidly presented, took issue with the program-ming policy of The Cleveland Orchestra at Severance Hall. He questioned whether music by Hanson, Honegger, Hindemith, and others from the decades of 1920 to 1950 should be considered as "contemporary", and deplored the relative absence of more genuinely "contemporaneous" music, which would include the "avant-garde". He compared the apparently conservative programming of this Orchestra with that of the Boston Symphony under Koussevitzky in the 1930s and 1940s. He questioned the commitment to new music even of the local festivals, and claimed that Cleveland had lost the "space-race" not only to Boston but to enterprising music departments of universities in New York and Michi-gan.*

The present response from Severance Hall was followed by three further ones in a succeeding issue of Fine Arts *from composers Jane Corner and Frederick Koch, and from Cleveland Orchestra Chorus member Richard J. DeGray. Nothing, surely, was settled for all time; but the controversy aroused much interest and may ultimately have shed more light than heat.*

*

DR. RAYMOND WILDING-WHITE has raised some valid questions in his article of last week, and has made a valuable contribution by tackling a complex subject. His comments are entertaining as well as provocative, and deserve to be thought about—by those who offer concerts as well as those who listen to them.

But even though any reply from Severance Hall would have to be taken as an "official" one, it can be proved that the situation is not as shocking as the author has painted it. He has unfortunately weakened many of his critical points by a whole series of factual errors and dubious historical judgments, and he has failed to put the programming policy of The Cleveland Orchestra into proper perspective.

How Is a Season's Repertoire Determined?

Dr. Wilding-White projects his own vast professional knowledge of the literature as if it were shared by the public at large. This is a serious error; for what may be old-hat to him may be new or unfamiliar to thousands. Subscription concerts are not given to stimulate avant-garde musicians; they must be planned to embrace as wide a spectrum of the music-loving public as possible, and must be balanced so as to interest the largest possible number. This results inevitably in a repertoire in which the existing literature is "covered," with the masterpieces from all periods as the mainstay.

The writer forgets that the "classics," while giving new pleasure and insight to the connoisseurs, reach hundreds of new listeners each time they are revived; this constantly changing audience must also be served, and served with all the freshness of a world premiere.

It remains quite arguable whether the "contemporaneous" is truly "contemporary," whether what is most "modern" is most worthwhile, and whether style should be considered more crucial than content. It is no more absurd today to regard Stravinsky's *Rite of Spring* as "modern" than it was for Parisian audiences of 1875 to so regard Beethoven's *Ninth*. They had not heard it often enough to know it; we have Bizet's word for that. If the author will look about him at concerts in Severance Hall, he will note that even Stravinsky's *Symphony in Three Movements* of 1945, and Bartók's *Music for Strings, Percussion and Celesta* of 1936 or *First Piano Concerto* of 1926, remain uncomfortably new for most hearers. If a work is a masterpiece, it will not date; but it will require many hearings to become a "classic" in the ears and minds and hearts of the concertgoing multitude.

The *Six Pieces, Op. 6* by Webern were indeed new and unusual to all but a few, and to repeat them in the same program was imaginative and wise. It must also be said that this music of 1909 remains viable in a large concert hall, while most of Webern's later works do not. Let the author also be given the surprising news that Cleveland heard the work for the first time in 1959, from George Szell, while Boston was not offered it until 1962, by a guest conductor. Was not Stravinsky right when he wrote, just last year, "What is most new in new music dies quickest, and that which makes it live is all that is oldest and most tried. To contrast the new and old is a '*reductio ad absurdum*,' and sectarian 'new music' is the blight of contemporaneity. . . ."?

The Public and the Latest Trends

The point is that while a great symphony orchestra is surely not a museum for the display of established masterworks, it need not regard itself as a tryout place for every new departure, every latest fad or fashion. The experience of the New York Philharmonic last season would prove this strikingly. There is a solid foundation for the view that the public of a large city should be made aware of the latest trends in musical development; but this is largely what festivals and special concerts try to accomplish. And even though the splendid local contemporary festival charges no admission, it expects and gets only the most minimal of audiences, from three hundred to six hundred. This is a discouraging but not surprising symptom.

In their regular series, great orchestras wish first of all to present good programs; and while these should more often than not include a recent work, it should be chosen for its value rather than for its shock effect, its substance rather than its degrees of newness. The fact that Stravinsky has "kept up with the times," as the author says, no more invalidates his earlier production than Beethoven's *Seventh* invalidated his *Third*. Certainly there is room for improvement at Severance Hall as elsewhere; there is much music we have not yet heard, and should hear; but the best of it will get here sooner or later, of that we can be sure. It took a century to discover Bach; there is no rush.

The Statistics and the Facts

Dr. Wilding-White's statistics are misleading, and even mathematically shaky. He quite ignores the fact that George Szell has conducted, in his eighteen seasons here, no fewer than twenty-nine world premieres, as well as numerous first performances in America. It was here that George Rochberg's extremely advanced and demanding *Second Symphony* had its premiere, and was—against considerable opposition—repeated the following season. It was here that Easley Blackwood's *Second* was premiered, commissioned for this orchestra after the success of the *First*; and this composer had been studiously ignored by his resident city, Chicago. It was for this ensemble and conductor that Peter Mennin wrote his *Seventh Symphony*. Twice, Dr. Szell has invited Marcel Dick to conduct his works in first performances. The ten commissions for the fortieth anniversary season should not be forgotten, out of which three works have survived: historically a high percentage. If one can dispose of the "contemporary" bugbear raised by the author, and does not limit the label to that which even professional musicians would consider "advanced," the statistics begin to look very different indeed.

In one recent year, for instance, out of forty-six composers represented, nineteen (or almost forty percent) were living or twentieth-century masters, and of these eight were Americans. Out of eighty-five works presented, twenty-five percent were from this century. The usual percentage of works from the last sixty years runs from one quarter to one third of the total, which is quite reasonable in the light of the three centuries from which the orchestral repertoire is drawn. Most orchestras show very similar figures.

Accounting for the Music of Our Time

But the most misleading aspect of Dr. Wilding-White's article lies in the limiting of his statistics only to Dr. Szell's own programs. That does not represent the Orchestra's total repertoire. The conductor's own repertoire is vast, but he does not feel—as many do—that every new large work by a leading composer must instantly be programmed here. Very few conductors share the missionary zeal of Koussevitzky and Mitropoulos and Stokowski. But the planning of the season's repertoire, which Dr. Szell guides and approves, takes this clearly into consideration. Therefore, the associate conductors, Robert Shaw and Louis Lane, are urged to seek out and present those twentieth-century works which Dr. Szell does not do. Thus Mr. Lane has recently given us works by Gunther Schuller and Leon Kirchner, as well as the piano concerto of Arnold Schoenberg; Mr. Shaw has offered symphonies by Lukas Foss and William Schuman and Roy Harris and Walter Piston and Wallingford Riegger. Furthermore, guest conductors are asked—at the time of invitation—to bring new pieces they may espouse; Sixten Ehrling, for instance, was specifically requested to present Karl-Birger Blomdahl's *Third Symphony*. Stanislaw Skrowaczewski has brought two works by the leading Polish composer Witold Lutoslawski, as well as his own *Symphony for Strings*. Pierre Boulez, when he comes next season, is sure to lead one of his own works.

The Crucial Second Hearing

The problem the author ignores, and it is a more crucial one, is that of second performances. It is true that Dr. Szell has championed certain "modern classics" by Hindemith and Bartók; but it is unfortunate that most new works are simply not played often enough for the public to get to know them intimately—even if they prove successful at the first hearing. There have been exceptions, with pieces by Walton and others; but it is here that proposals for new approaches and solutions would be welcomed.

Conservatism and the Facts of Life

There is no doubt that Cleveland's musical public is conservative; but the writer has not convinced us that the situation here is worse than in other large cities. The general lack of curiosity on the part of the public is a fact of life everywhere, and in all the arts. This must be counteracted, but one must also be realistic enough to know that a subscription audience can be pushed and pulled only so far. Last century, Margaret Fuller said, "I accept the universe." Told of this, Emerson exclaimed, "Gad, she'd better!" The Cleveland Orchestra has long accepted the twentieth century. Its record over almost fifty years shows that it has done more: it has led that part of the public which has wished to be led, and has insisted on guiding the rest toward an awareness of value in the music from all periods and styles. The Orchestra is eager to improve its service, and welcomes sound criticism; but it believes that little is gained from misrepresenting its stand in this complex matter, and from misunderstanding the reasons that move a public to come to concerts.

New Sounds and New Ears (MAY 1988)

Difficulty in being quickly understood by the public is a cross all must bear who would speak a new language . . . It is time that listeners put away stereotyped verdicts and arbitrary classifications and try, with new eyes, to consider what the composer himself has seen.

> —Sergei Prokofiev (*Europe*, an American magazine, Paris 1936)

There is no such distinction as old and modern music, but only music good and bad. All music, in so far as it is the product of a truly creative mind, is new. Bach is just as new today as he ever was—a continual revelation.

> —Arnold Schoenberg

And so, Franck had to make his way here, as in Paris, misunderstood, abused, regarded by some as an anarchist, by some as a bore. This, men and brethren, should make us all tolerant, even cautious, in passing judgment on contemporary composers whose idiom is as yet strange to us. Cocksure opinions are valuable chiefly to the one who expresses them. Let us hear what is going on in the musical world, even if it is going on noisily and queerly in our ears. . . . Music is not necessarily bad because it is of a strange and irregular nature. For audiences to have no curiosity about new works, no spur to hot discussion concerning them, is a sign of stagnation in art. Thus César Franck, a great teacher, teaches us all indirectly a lesson.

> —Philip Hale
> (c. 1900, about the *D minor Symphony*)

For a very long time everyone refuses and then almost without a pause almost everyone accepts . . . When a first-rate work of art becomes a classic, the only thing that is important from then on to the most intelligent majority of the acceptors is that it is so wonderfully beautiful . . . Of course it is beautiful, but first all beauty is denied and then all the beauty of it is accepted. If everyone were not so indolent, they would realize that beauty is beauty even when it is irritating and stimulating: not only when it is accepted and classic.

> —Gertrude Stein, 1926

Most listeners criticize a work uncharitably or harshly merely because they do not measure it by the standards according to which it was written, or they do not view it from the standpoint from which the composer can see it by virtue of his talent, culture and the conviction and purpose stemming from them . . . Criticism is desirable and truly helpful, when, looking through the composer's eyes, it directs him and unravels his secret, thereby revealing him to himself, since in every human being there exists a pardonable natural bias in favor of his own horizons and capabilities . . . .

To judge a contemporary work of art correctly demands that calm, unprejudiced mood which, while susceptible to every impression, carefully guards against preconceived opinions or feelings. It requires a mind completely open to the particular work under consideration. Only when his work is viewed in this way is the artist fully equipped to go forth into the world with those feelings and visions which he has created, and which he, the mighty ruler of every passionate emotion, allows us to experience with and through him: pain, pleasure, horror, joy, hope and love. We can very quickly and clearly see whether he has been capable of creating a great structure which will endure, or if, his mind working in momentary, unsteady creative flashes, he has caught our fancy with details only, thereby causing us to forget the work as a whole . . . .

—Carl Maria von Weber

(Excerpts from his reviews, as quoted in *Composers on Music*,

an anthology edited by Sam Morgenstern, Pantheon Books 1956)

Every new work of importance will contain elements of strangeness. Audiences of the past enjoyed primarily the very fact that they were recipients of a communication that added something hitherto unknown to their esthetic experience . . . . Haydn had to present new works at every "party" of his employer . . .

If our present-day audiences would approach a new work not with the expectation that it should reaffirm previous impressions, but with the thrill of curiosity for what a composer has to say that is new in his new work, what he is going to give them that they did not have before, then they would react with great spontaneity to the new beauty, however different, and they might find themselves enriched, occasionally, by a great artistic experience.

—Marcel Dick (1950)

The function of the creative artist consists in making laws, not in following laws ready-made. He who follows such laws ceases to be a creator. Creative power may be the more readily recognized the more it shakes itself loose from tradition. But an intentional avoidance of the rules cannot masquerade as creative power and still less engenders it. The true creator strives, in reality, after perfection only. And through bringing this in harmony with his own individuality, a new law arises without premeditation.

—Ferruccio Busoni

Con-tempo: "with the times". Con-tempo music is the most interesting music that ever has been written, and the present moment is the most exciting in music history. It always has been. Nearly all con-tempo music is bad, too, and so it was ever. The "lament of present days", as Byron called it, is as old as the first antiquarian.

Modern: *modernus, modo:* "just now". But, also, modus, "manner", whence "up-to-date" and "fashionable" . . . .

And "new music"? But surely that misplaces the emphasis. What is most new in new music dies quickest, and that which makes it live is all that is oldest and most tried. To contrast the new and the old is a *reductio ad absurdum*, and sectarian "new music" is the blight of contemporaneity. Let us use con-tempo, then, not technically, in the sense that Schönberg and Chaminade lived at the same time, but in my meaning: 'with the times'."

—Igor Stravinsky

(In *Dialogues and a Diary*, with Robert Craft; 1963)

VI. SOME CREATIVE SPIRITS

When I open my eyes, a sigh involuntarily escapes me, for all that I see runs counter to my religion; thus I despise the world which does not intuitively feel that music is a higher revelation than all wisdom and philosophy. (1810)

I love most of all the realm of the mind which, to me, is the highest of all spiritual and temporal monarchies. (1814)

Ludwig van Beethoven

Sublimated in the art works are the narratives of men. Art becomes the artist's true reality and life remains but a sad dream. A merciful muse has shown the artist the way out of his misery: the dark forces of destruction which endanger his psychic existence can be fought through the creative act. Enslaved by his unhappiness, threatened with doom, the artist revolts and sets himself free through work.

Frederick Dorian
from *The Musical Workshop*, 1947

Ode to Igor Stravinsky (APRIL 1982)

*

First published in the Nineteenth Program, Forty-fourth Season of The Cleveland Orchestra, March 22–24, 1962, in honor of Stravinsky's Eightieth Birthday, and occasionally reprinted since. In 1962 it was also published in The Christian Science Monitor. *This, on the occasion of the one hundredth anniversary of the composer's birth, was its final appearance in the pages of the program books.*

*

LET US IMAGINE, for a moment, our world without you.

Some history would have to be rewritten. Would our modern orchestra sound as it does? Would dance, the art of motion, annually flower? Would there have been a neo-classic movement? Would tonal harmony have thus expanded?

Perhaps these things would be; more likely, not. But, if they were, they would be different, and certainly much poorer, weaker; far less fecund, productive, influential. Your numberless disciples, where would they have turned?

Music's peculiar fauna would be drastically altered: The Firebird, the Nightingale, Canard—extinct. Renard the Fox an outcast, Chat asleep forever; the stable of the Circus Elephant is locked; Petrouchka, Pulcinella dance no more. Apollo has resigned as leader of the muses; there is no Agon, and the Card Game falters: The Queen of Hearts who failed the Soldier will do nought to save Tom Rakewell. Les Noces beget no offspring; Mavra laughs unheard. The ancient myths (so utterly alive through you) join Perséphone in Hades, fade with Oedipus. Shall Orpheus or the Furies have the final word?

There is yet Spring; but its great pagan mystery is not perceived, its ritual power ignored. One sings the Psalms in praise, but cannot know the mighty Alleluias from your Symphony. One has not felt the Credo as your Mass believes it. The worshipper, it's true, may sense no need of Jeremiah's Threni, of your Canticum; but if he knew, what would he see and feel? *Laudate Dominum* . . . .

Would mankind miss your books, your trenchant observations? Would we survive without the sure direction of instrumental-vocal enterprise, as your clear beat defines it? Where would be, then, the many records of your music-making?

But most of all, what would we, living, do without the rhythmic god, the wild Dionysus? Where would it pulse, that fierce intoxication, which courses now through every measure? Restrained and tempered by Apollo, it seethes yet below; and if a rhythm does not yet exist, you will invent it. Music, it may well be, expresses but itself; but what is "abstract" in your Ballet Scenes, your Concertizing Dances, your sharp or swinging syncopes? They still belong to man, his heart, his brain, his spirit, speak of his wit, vitality, and joy. At moments, too, the calm serenity of classic marble. Emotion? surely; but more light than heat. Sonatas, suites, concertos, songs and symphonies, all come to us as order out of chaos; of nothing is made something, a hurdle—self-imposed—is overcome, an essence found, a principle confirmed. Com-posing, counter-posing; an inner logic guides each step, establishes the form. Yes, order: clarity, conciseness, elegance; reflection, if you will, of some divine design, in small things as in large. The lessons of the past relearned, not mimicked; tradition as a living force that animates the present. In all, and all the time, a will to fashion: not the fashionable, but the fashion-able; to do what can be done. And also, similar to nature, there is constant change, experiment, mutation, search.

165

Style—yes; the craftsman's fingerprints. But always seeking, finding, shaping. A Protean, Picassoesque ballet, this life of yours!

We have not always followed, would not wish to claim that we have understood completely; perhaps you have not either, have sometimes offered problems as solutions. Forgive us doubt, permit us value-judgments; we exercise them still with Bach, Tchaikovsky, Gesualdo. But that which you have shown us on your explorations—for half a century Magister Artium—might well convince that you have more to show.

Allegiant to many nations, and to none, your home has been wherever you could work. Whatever source you tapped, the ethnic streams joined universal rivers. Like a phenomenon of nature, you have enriched the world, have peopled it with living, lasting things. Not for a long time yet, it is our hope, shall we say *tibi valedico*. But we now join the chorus, Greek or other, that sings *te amabam.*

"A Sip of Scotch" (APRIL 1982)

STRAVINSKY APPEARED as guest conductor of The Cleveland Orchestra six times: the first in 1925, the last in March of 1964, when he was almost eighty-two. On that last occasion, it was the editor's most privileged duty to ferry the great composer to and from his hotel (the Wade Park Manor) and Severance Hall, and to see to his needs at rehearsal time.

In vivid retrospect, it was almost incredible to realize that out of that tiny head on a tiny figure had come *The Rite of Spring* more than fifty years before. His physical frailty was such that one had to wonder how he would ever get from the conductor's room to the stage; and amazement deepened when one watched him miraculously transformed on the podium into a vigorous young man.

Learning that his *The Soldier's Tale* was the favorite recording of my children, Stravinsky graciously autographed the album to them: "To you the children of . . . ." It is now a recording not to be lent to anyone.

Stravinsky had the habit of fortifying himself before rehearsals and performances by a drink or two of fine Scotch from a silver flask. One rehearsal morning, he filled the cap of the flask—but suddenly stopped before putting it to his lips, and with a small bow handed the cap to me for a first sip. It was, without question, the most memorable drink of my life.

Hindemith and Bach (JANUARY 1964)

WHEN PAUL HINDEMITH died a month ago, on December 28, 1963, many of the obituary tributes remarked in passing on the Bach-like character of his approach and workmanship. It had long been a truism to regard him as a twentieth-century counterpart of baroque, renaissance, or even medieval masters, with their solid musical structures full of learned counterpoint, their willingness and ability to do anything asked of them, their sheer professionalism. That Hindemith admired J. S. Bach above all other composers, and consciously patterned some of his works upon those by the Cantor of St. Thomas, had been abundantly attested. Yet in all those commentaries, or at least in those encountered thus far by the present writer, no attempt has been made to show how profound this relationship may actually be, once certain inevitable divergencies have been dealt with. Parallels in the arts can, of course, be pursued ad absurdum, and circumstantial evidence is rarely conclusive. But in this instance, facts speak for themselves, and the history of music may be richer by another symbol of continuity.

What Divides Them

Bach came from an astonishing line of professional musicians, a family unique in history as "seven generations of creative genius". Hindemith had to run away from home before he could follow the artistic career for which he was so richly endowed.

Hindemith traveled the world over; his life was adventurous and complex, and he found himself in the public eye as composer and performer from his twenties on. Bach never left the German-speaking countries; his life was restricted, almost provincial; he was little known as a composer until his last years, known mostly as an organ virtuoso.

Bach was a family man, with twenty-one children by two wives. Hindemith had no children, in his long and otherwise happy marriage.

Beyond his immediate pupils, the eighteenth-century master exerted virtually no influence on the course of music during his life-time; the bulk of his output remained undiscovered for close to one hundred years, although Mozart and Beethoven studied a few of his works with delight and benefit. The twentieth-century composer was enormously influential for forty years, with outstanding pupils counted in the hundreds and elements of his style adopted on a world-wide scale.

Hindemith was intensely interested in the stage, and wrote many operas; Bach was not, and there survives no single stage work from his otherwise indefatigable pen.

Bach spent most of his life in the service of the church; Hindemith taught in conservatories and universities, and appeared as instrumentalist, lecturer, and conductor.

Hindemith wrote voluminously about music, its craft and its philosophy; he was eloquent about the role of the artist in society. Bach, less of an "intellectual" though no less of an intellect, rarely verbalized his thoughts, though he held strong opinions.

The contemporary master was a practicing musicologist, whose programs of "ancient" music were of extraordinary fidelity, perception, and vitality. Bach, though keenly aware of the history of music before him and constantly utilizing its achievements, lived at a time when such research—scholarly or practical—was hardly known.

What Unites Them

Both composers died before they were seventy: Bach at sixty-five, Hindemith at sixty-eight. That they had more to contribute, there is no doubt; but each had in essence completed a lifework beyond which it would be ungrateful to ask more.

Their productivity was enormous, with catalogues of works running into many hundreds of pieces in a vast variety of media, written quickly and for the most part designed to fill specific commissions or needs.

All his life, Hindemith battled for a condition that was natural and self-understood to Bach: a reasonable relationship between the composer and the consumer of music. He asked that the musical needs of the public—whether listener, singer, instrumentalist, or ensemble—were again to become the composer's need and stimulus. The opposite and "romantic" situation—in which a composer produces only what he must even when it may not be wanted or needed—both men consistently subordinated to the other. The term "Gebrauchsmusik" ("music for use" or "functional music"), attributed more than thirty years ago to Hindemith, perfectly characterizes every Bach cantata written for next Sunday's service, every Mozart violin sonata, every Haydn trio. It was done to be used: practical, performable, unpretentious; nothing at all need keep it from being at the same time excellent, or even great.

In this quest for a rapprochement of producer and consumer, Hindemith interspersed his creation of large and demanding works with music for virtually every instrument with piano; he provided, in fact, a modern literature for the making of music, along the lines of a thousand-year-old tradition. These sonatas are for the most part not easy, or "commercial", or even "teaching pieces"; they are important, satisfying and often beautiful music. Bach's sonatas for woodwinds with harpsichord served exactly the same purpose.

Hindemith was able to do this so fluently because he could play almost every instrument passably well himself, in addition to being a competent pianist and a virtuoso on viola and violin. Bach's knowledge of instrumental possibilities was likewise extensive, and personally acquired.

Both men were craftsmen of the highest order. Their technical skills were immense, their workmanship spotless. Both demanded flawless execution of their music, impatient with shoddiness, self-indulgence, and laziness. Both drove themselves mercilessly to accomplish their tasks as "artisans", resulting finally in blindness for Bach, a circulatory ailment for Hindemith.

Germans both, they were dreamers as well as doers. The "anti-romantic" label commonly affixed to Hindemith is largely nonsense, based on his early and necessary rebellion against post-romantic excesses in orchestration, form, and "feeling". Almost all his work, early and late—to anyone who really knows it—is suffused with mystery, wonder, a sense of beauty and human warmth. It has been possible also to see Bach, as Pablo Casals sees him, as a great romantic, with his soaring structures, the depth and expressiveness of his human communication, the charm of his detail, and his mysterious horizons.

Both were sublime melodists. Many of us can sing Hindemith's melodies with the same degree of affection we bring to Bach's; they spring from the most vital of lyric impulses, are inevitably "right" in shape, pleasing and memorable in expression. There are literally dozens that leap to mind.

It was in part because of their great melodic fertility that both Bach and Hindemith became masters of counterpoint, accomplished architects of vast polyphonic edifices, designers of tapestries woven from many independent and interdependent strands of tone. Like all composers who work easily in contrapuntal media, they fell occasionally into facile routine, into a spinning-forth of threads without further musical compulsion, into the motoric rhythms of an engine. But this is comparatively rare with both, when measured against the usual inspiration by which their many-voiced textures were conceived and developed. Both believed in the integrity of the line over harmonic considerations, the linear over the vertical; their logic was inexorable, and sometimes severe. Both worked out "methods" from their practice, only to hand them on to their pupils while they themselves went on to discover new applications of their principles.

Hindemith taught with pleasure and utter devotion, concerned with the elementary as well as the advanced; he believed it his duty to perpetuate in others his knowledge, his craft, his skill. He wrote textbooks and manuals, and to perform music of all periods with him was learning at its best. While Bach for the most part passed along his technical skills without writing them down, his basic attitude toward study and teaching appears to have been the same: tradition as a living force.

Both Hindemith and Bach, in fact, were almost compulsively didactic, always instructing others as to proper artistic conduct and personal ethics. Both masters had a profound *mystique* of art, convinced of the ethical powers of music, the moral potentialities of sound, the mystery of musical and even numerical symbolism, the unswerving demand upon an artist to bring his inner vision to sounding life and then to share it; yet a delicious sense of humor usually preserved them from pomposity.

Both men were argumentative, dogmatic, intolerant of what they considered as demeaning to themselves and to their art. Both were profoundly religious; and while Hindemith—born a Lutheran—concerned himself for decades with the great medieval saints of the church (St. Francis, St. Anthony, St. Augustine, and others) and finally turned to Catholicism itself, the Lutheran Bach showed the degree of his desire to unify the faiths by so supra-Christian a work as the *B minor Mass*, set to the pre-Reformation text of the Latin ritual.

There is much more that brings the two composers together across the centuries. Most significant, perhaps, is the fact that they were both conservatives in the best sense. It is a complete misinterpretation nowadays to call Hindemith a reactionary as it had been for J. S. Bach's sons to refer to their father as "the old fogy". In his last decade of life, Bach was still writing fugues, while few others were. New trends in music had already become dominant, but he cared little that he was "passé" in the eyes and ears of his students and contemporaries. Perhaps he knew how advanced his work essentially remained. Hindemith too, in his youth an artistic radical, found himself at fifty overtaken by events and style, regarded with some condescension by the avant-garde. But his place was already secure, his contribution to the regular repertoire a solid fact. Whether the works of both composers' final years have a vitality equal to those of their earlier periods may be questioned; but it is possible that their "past mastery" was yet deeper, greater, if less outwardly "effective".

With Bach's death in 1750, the so-called "baroque" period officially ends; we ascribe to 1950 and its environs the close of the "neo-classic period". But it may well be, and music history has much to support such an assumption, that just as the legacy of Bach's music was in due course re-discovered and proved to contain more substance than that of his more successful contemporaries, so Hindemith's own renaissance will yet come, after a period of relative quiescence. When many of the experiments of today have turned into curiosities of history, we may find in the work of Paul Hindemith some of the deepest values—both esthetic and human—that have been given sounding shape in this century.

Bach's last name as used by him
at the close of *The Art of Fugue*.
(B-flat is B in German, B-Natural is H.)

Béla Bartók in Cleveland (MARCH 1987)

*

This followed the annotation for a performance of Bartók's Second Piano Concerto *by Peter Donohoe, with Simon Rattle as guest conductor.*

*

WHAT THE GREAT CRITIC Lawrence Gilman said about the *First Concerto* in 1927 is surely relevant also to the Second. The Bartók of today, he wrote, was "acrid, powerful, intransigeant; the musician of darkly passionate imagination; austerely sensuous, ruthlessly logical, a cerebral rhapsodist: a tone-poet who is both an uncompromising modernist and the resurrector of an ancient past." Bartók's dynamism, wrote Edwin Evans at the same time, was "the time-spirit at work", and he recognized "a suggestion of the melancholy that is the undercurrent of the ubiquitous dynamism of today." It is fascinating to speculate how—or whether—the times have really changed in the last sixty years.

When Béla Bartók played his *Second Piano Concerto* at Severance Hall in 1940, reaction from the press was decidedly mixed. To quote from the reviews of the time is not intended at this time to prejudice anybody in one direction or another, but merely to serve as a historical sidelight—perhaps to illuminate the changes in artistic attitude, if any, that may have taken place since those days, just before World War II directly involved the United States as well.

Bartók's arrival in Cleveland was widely heralded, with considerable coverage also in the local Hungarian press. Surprisingly, the story by Elmore Bacon in the *Cleveland News* announcing his appearance dealt largely with his accomplishments as a scholar and collector (with Zoltán Kodály) of indigenous Hungarian folklore, while misinterpreting these efforts as "dressing up the Magyar folk tunes in modern attire". And he continued by saying that "the distinguished musicologist was making his Cleveland début" at the concerts of December 5 and 7, 1940. But when he had heard the concerto in performance by The Cleveland Orchestra under Artur Rodzinski's baton, Mr. Bacon reported that "those who went to the concert expected to hear Pianist Bartók express himself in the tuneful and charming Magyar folk song of which Composer Bartók is master, were mistaken. What they heard was ultra modern music, barbaric thunderings, savage syncopation, pastoral pipings and bewildering modulations and rhythm shifting . . ." The performer, "equipped with a prodigious technique, had little opportunity to display expression or offer a well-turned thematic discourse. He was too busy with the pyrotechnics." Mr. Bacon considered the possibility that "the barbaric tumult of the final movement might be considered in a way to express conditions of world thought. The savage brilliance and unrelenting forward fury of the music could be indicative of today's selfishness, hate, despair and discord . . ." Yet the reviewer had to acknowledge the fact that Bartók "won highly enthusiastic applause, and a beautiful bouquet of flowers, presented by two equally lovely young women in Hungarian native attire."

In *The Plain Dealer* of December 6, 1940, Herbert Elwell wrote that the audience "had the disquieting experience of listening to some contemporary music of uncompromising individuality . . . The work must have given rise to some perplexity, though it also evoked some enthusiasm." And after describing the musical events, Mr. Elwell summarized his own response by saying that "this music partakes of the bitter protestation engendered by the moral climate of the last World War [1914–18]. It is nothing if not the work of an independent thinker, who realizes his intentions with ascetic severity, by rejection of everything pretty or plastic in the way of melody and, not infrequently, by extraordinary intuitive discoveries in novel sonority and purely dynamic effect. It has a certain kind of fortitude and integrity in its scorn for the refinements of tradition. But it gave me the impression of being more cerebral than barbaric, more naïve than sophisticated . . . It provokes a speculative question as to whether the times have not already overtaken this kind of pioneering in modernism which was so popular at international festivals in the 1920s." This last point of Mr. Elwell's was of special relevance in view of the fact that the very next concert pair featured the Cleveland premiere of the *Violin Concerto* by Alban Berg, a totally different example of "modernism" indeed.

Arthur Loesser, writing in *The Cleveland Press*, was most favorably inclined. (Some years later, he was to make a marvelous recording, with Beryl Rubinstein, of Bartók's *Sonata for Two Pianos and Percussion*—a disc still available through The Cleveland Institute of Music.) "Bartók Concerto Full of Life, Wins Applause", read the headline; and the subhead said, "Power of Composer Impresses Audience". Mr. Loesser called the occasion "a privilege and opportunity" for Clevelanders to hear "the foremost Hungarian composer" in performance: "Mr. Bartók did not have to proceed very far in his performance before the listeners were aware that they were in the presence of an uncommonly strong personality, and were receiving a communication from a highly original and forceful musical mind. This is not to pretend that many people 'liked' or 'enjoyed' the concerto in any passive manner. Gentle adjectives like 'charming', 'pleasing', 'attractive' or 'witty' could hardly be applied to it. Yet the power of its conception could not fail to impress.

"The concerto seems to combine an elemental, barbaric, almost brutal rhythmic dynamism with an intellectual approach to thematic development, and some occasionally rather remarkable sophistications of tone color. . . . The delicate sustained resonances achieved by modern piano manufacture are fairly well wasted on this concerto; it might almost be executed on a set of super-xylophones . . . . Yet, as I said, the work produces a powerful impression, that is, as long as the muscles can tingle with its rapid and changing pulsation and the ears be struck with unusual splotches of tone-color . . . ."

Having arrived in Cleveland on December 1, Bartók was interviewed by all newspapers. He recalled a visit to Cleveland in 1928, when he was "taken to a small Hungarian restaurant by some friends, and they served red wine just like in Hungary—it was really remarkable, in Prohibition time!" He spoke of enjoying his sessions with Benny Goodman (for whom he wrote his *Contrasts*) and of admiring the work of our jazz musicians such as Earl Hines. The Cleveland weather was not to his liking, Bartók said. "It is nasty. It is uninspiring. Still, you are lucky. You have plenty of fuel and good lodgings. That is more than we have in Europe. I like it here. I am happy." He seemed pleased that critics and public were beginning "to know and to appreciate Hungarian peasant music. This is important because upon this type of music our highest forms of music are based." (Yet it was later reported that the composer was upset to find how little interest in the artistic traditions of the "old country" was shown by his transplanted compatriots, and especially the American-born second generation.)

Mention should not be omitted that Cleveland's customary hospitality to visiting artists was extended also at that time. After the Thursday concert, there was "a small, informal supper party" in honor of the composer, at the home of the late Mrs. George P. Bickford, a trustee of The Musical Arts Association from 1939 to 1982. And after the Saturday concert, there was a reception for five hundred persons at the Wade Park Manor "to shake the composer's hand, eat pozsonyi and dobos torte, hear gipsy music and watch the dancing of the palotas." The event was arranged by the Magyar Club, the Cleveland Chapter of the Hungarian Women's World League, and the Hungarian Civic Club. Municipal Judge Louis Petrash acted as chairman. The affair was attended by members of Hungarian societies, representatives of the city's musical organizations and members of the staff of the Hungarian consulate. Nor, on the other hand, should the fact be glossed over that this composer, who had just received an honorary degree from Columbia University, then went on to find the bulk of his music ignored and even "boycotted" (his own term) in the United States, and that despite a few sporadic successes like the *Concerto for Orchestra* of 1943 he spent his remaining five years of life under conditions approaching abject poverty.

Pierre Boulez: An Appreciation (NOVEMBER 1986)

NO OTHER LIVING COMPOSER has been the subject of so much commentary in print, has generated more lively discussion and healthy controversy, and has become as influential on the musical life of our era. While in his twenties and thirties he was regarded as a revolutionary and iconoclast, he is now widely accepted as an elder statesman of the art of music. He has by no means abandoned his fundamental convictions, strongly-held opinions and pioneering intent, but his stature and accomplishment are such, across the whole spectrum of the art, that a far less confrontational spirit on both sides has been engendered. Mr. Boulez has made an exceptionally important contribution to the cultural life of the twentieth century; he has, in fact, helped to alter the course of musical history itself.

Pierre Boulez has been a major force not only with his own compositions since the premiere of his *Le marteau sans maître* in 1955, but also as a teacher and mentor of numerous younger (and older) composers; as a conductor whose presentations of twentieth-century music are regarded not so much as "interpretations" but as illuminations of exceptional clarity; as a prolific author of books, essays and polemics; as an administrator deeply concerned with music's place and purpose in life; as a public teacher whose illustrated lectures have been models of stimulation and insight; as a guiding force in the integration of musical art with the new potentialities of electronic technology; and not least as a personality of apparently limitless intellect balanced by innate modesty, courteous directness, artistic integrity, human warmth, and captivating charm.

Mr. Boulez made his debut as guest conductor of an American orchestra leading The Cleveland Orchestra in Severance Hall on March 11–13, 1965; he subsequently served here as a regular guest conductor, became Principal Guest Conductor in 1969 at the invitation of George Szell, and Musical Advisor from 1970 to 1972. During his Cleveland years, he directed more than one hundred works from three centuries, including thirty first performances in Cleveland or at these concerts; at Blossom Music Center, he conducted twelve concerts. At Severance Hall, he initiated a series of "Informal Evenings" with the participation of both audience and Orchestra, presenting and discussing the works of Olivier Messiaen, Edgar Varèse, Alban Berg and Igor Stravinsky. He made four recordings with The Cleveland Orchestra, two of which (Debussy's *Images* and Stravinsky's *Le Sacre du Printemps*) were Grammy Award winners for "best classical performance". Of his own works, only two have thus far been heard at these concerts: the U.S. premiere of his *Figures, Doubles, Prismes* (March 11–13, 1965), and *Rituel, In Memoriam Bruno Maderna* (October 7–8–9, 1976, Lorin Maazel conducting).*

---

* In the first program of his two-week engagement in 1988, Mr. Boulez included his *Notations I-IV,* and in the second program he led his *Pli Selon Pli,* "Portrait de Mallarmé".—Editor.

In 1977, he became director of IRCAM, the *Institut de Recherche et de la Coordination Acoustique/Musique* in Paris, a section of the Georges Pompidou National Center for Art and Culture, also known as the Beaubourg Center. There, he has concerned himself largely with avant-garde phenomena, including electronic and computer-produced music; composers and musicians from all over the world have come to IRCAM to work with him and the distinguished staff he has engaged.

With the support of the French government, he has established an orchestra specifically for new music, the Ensemble InterContemporain, thirty musicians available full-time to rehearse and perform compositions of the twentieth century. With that ensemble, he has recently visited the United States in a wide-ranging tour, performing in Los Angeles, San Francisco, Chicago, Boston and New York, and featuring his adventurous new work, *Répons*. His guest-conducting and recording schedule in a wide repertoire during the last decade testifies to Mr. Boulez's unflagging energy and commitment.

Boulez's *Notations I-IV* (november 1986)

*

To interpret is to describe a structure as a function of its expressive power.

I have never understood why a musician, in particular a composer, should have as his first duty the relegating of his intelligence to the warehouse of dangerous accessories . . . A sensibility which catches cold at the slightest intellectual draft seems to me pretty feeble.
                                                                                  —Pierre Boulez

*

A MUSICAL SCORE is a blueprint that must be realized in actual sound. Just as the architect and the engineer construct their buildings and machines from detailed blueprints or designs, the conductor or performing artist brings to life the symbols and directions specified on paper. In the process, the end results will invariably differ from the original intention, depending upon a host of circumstances. In architecture and machine technology, changing conditions and materials will influence the final outcome; in music, interpreters will arrive at different conclusions most of which will be justifiable. Ensembles, performing spaces, audiences and even specific circumstances will affect the outcome. Even the twelfth century cathedral does not remain exactly what it was when new: the builders were not able to visualize adjoining buildings, roads and parking lots that have altered the image substantially.

While, as a conductor, Pierre Boulez has always represented the score or musical blueprint with utmost fidelity and clarity, as a creative artist he has always been suspicious of the "masterpiece" as an unchangeable entity, as a finished and immutable product. "Composition," he wrote more than a quarter century ago, "would be immeasurably boring if one demanded nothing more, so to speak, than organized guided tours with prearranged stops." As a result of that thinking, he has always been ready to leave a work "open-ended", "unfinished" in the sense that it could be expanded or contracted, added to or subtracted from. "The art work," he wrote, "is no longer that predetermined architecture which extends from a beginning through rather certain developments to the end. Rather, the boundaries are voluntarily erased and the duration is no longer determined exactly in advance—time structures, so to speak, arise. This leads to a conception of the creative process in which the definite no longer rests within the power of the author. Chance forces its way into the art work, chance, which is never definite. . . . I am ever more convinced that if one wishes to formulate creative inspiration, one must really come to grips with it, even more, must organize it. . . ."

It is that attitude also which has made it possible for Boulez to take up some pieces of music written at twenty and reshape them, at the age of fifty-three, into new structures, in a new medium and in an expanded form. What were "notations", sketches, essences, now become something else. If, for Boulez, an artwork is not forever engraved in its time and space, then it can grow, change, and become a process rather than a monument. From the beginning of his career, Boulez was a "contemporary" composer, concerned with where music was now, rather than with what and where it had been. Among his major sources were the serial methods of Schoenberg, Berg, and especially Webern, as well as the new sounds and rhythms of his teacher and mentor, Messiaen. Thus the material of his keyboard "notations" of 1945 was still capable thirty-three years later of being utilized and transformed, with all of the composer's mature technique brought to bear on them. And, to be sure, no more than Ravel's *Valses* just performed is this "orchestrated piano music".

Witold Lutoslawski: An Introduction (MARCH 1988)

On March 3-4-5, 1988, Lutoslawski appeared in the "Composers of Our Time" series, conducting The Cleveland Orchestra in three of his works; the mayor of Cleveland proclaimed the week in his honor.

"NO GREAT COMPOSER," said Aaron Copland, "ever left the language of music exactly as he found it." This is clearly one of the major accomplishments of Lutoslawski: to have extended the range of musical language, not by invalidating that which had been previously spoken, but by enlarging the vocabulary, the grammar, the syntax and the semantics of the art. Listening to his music may extend *our* range, our sense of the possible, and of the musically desirable. This composer's art uses the language of music, ultimately, not as phonetics, as sound *per se*, but as aesthetic (and therefore expressive) communication. As he has said, he does not wish to convince, but to find kindred minds and hearts. What, factually, was the road he took—or had to take—in that quest?

Born in Warsaw in 1913, Lutoslawski began to study music when he was six, and composed his first notated work at nine. At thirteen, he started the study of the violin; at fourteen, he attended classes at the Warsaw Conservatory, but did not remain there long. He became a private pupil of the respected composer Witold Maliszewski, a former student of Rimsky-Korsakov and Glazunov, and took piano lessons from Jerzy Lefeld. After some study of mathematics at the University of Warsaw, he returned to the Conservatory for further studies with Maliszewski and Lefeld, and took degrees in 1936 and 1937. In his twenties (the 1930s) he served for a year in the Polish army. Having begun to make a name for himself as a composer, he found himself caught up in the turmoil of World War II, seeing action at Cracow and being taken prisoner at Lublin. After escaping and walking back some two hundred and fifty miles to Warsaw, he made a precarious living as a duo-pianist with fellow composer Andrzej Panufnik. Having escaped from Warsaw after the failed uprising of August 1944, he returned at the end of the war to work with Polish Radio. His first appearance as a conductor was with the Polish Radio Orchestra in 1946. His *First Symphony* was enthusiastically received in 1948, but the infamous cultural (or, better, "anti-cultural") decree promulgated in Moscow in 1948 had its effect on Polish music as well. While occupying himself with so-called "utilitarian" music, he continued to work on his own and develop his musical language. The splendid *Concerto for Orchestra* was premiered in 1954 and contributed to his growing reputation.

With the *Musique Funèbre* of 1958 (dedicated to the memory of Bartók), Lutoslawski captured the attention of a worldwide public. In the 1960s, he encountered some music by John Cage, and realized that he could apply some of the American composer's ideas and techniques to his own work. His use of "chance" or "aleatory" elements, however, has been of quite a different nature: it does not involve improvisational activity on the part of players within an ensemble, as far as pitches, form and dynamics are concerned, but it allows a certain freedom of rhythm and timing in the process of performance. Certain musical events now take place with a new flexibility, and result also in a somewhat different notation of scores. The considerable number of compositions produced by Lutoslawski in the last quarter-century is marked by ever-increasing ingenuity of design, but never at the price of direct and powerful communication.

Continuing to reside in Warsaw, he became one of the leaders of the remarkable avant-garde movement that flourishes in present-day Poland, and remains as an example of personal and artistic independence and daring under any and all conditions that seem to make them difficult or inadvisable. Thus the composer's style has moved from a partially neoclassic, partially folkloristic idiom into regions which are at the same time "up-to-date" and deeply indebted to the values of the past. His works thrust into areas of sonority and form not yet fully explored, while cherishing principles and traditions that are intrinsically immutable. Lutoslawski's music is always "dramatic", but not overtly theatrical; there is a powerful sense of momentum and of contrast, and even an audience not attuned to unfamiliar music tends to find itself fascinated, impressed, and often moved. It is, in addition, challenging and interesting to play, as performers everywhere have attested.

Hans Werner Henze: A Brief Introduction (APRIL 1985)

SINCE THE END OF WORLD WAR II Hans Werner Henze has been considered a composer of exceptional gifts, and is now one of the leading creative personalities on the musical scene. His work has passed through some drastic changes of style, from radical "post-Webern" tendencies and "atonal stridencies" toward a music that has been called "Mediterranean-ized". In recent years, he has allied himself with the political left-wing, writing several works with polemical and even revolutionary intent. He has visited the United States several times since 1963, as composer-conductor (Chicago, Boston, New York, etc.) and has also directed some nineteenth-century works for recording. At his request, the world premieres of his operas *The Young Lord* (Berlin, 1965) and *The Bassarids* (Salzburg, 1966) were conducted by Christoph von Dohnányi.

The author of a dozen ballets and as many operas, seven symphonies and much chamber and vocal music, Henze is difficult to classify as belonging to any "school"; as the Italian writer and classical scholar Franco Serpa has said of him, he has rejected any form of stylistic dogmatism, and has "reaffirmed his ties with the whole European tradition, which is French and Italian as well as Germanic, and proceeded to assimilate the heritage of the twelve-tone Viennese school, the rhythmic style of Stravinsky, the lyric cantabile lines of Italian music, and the French taste for irony and intellectual refinement." Henze himself does not see his purpose as that of a synthesis, but rather as that of eclecticism, which is defined as "the method or practice of selecting what seems best from various systems". He accounts for this by paraphrasing Goethe: "An eclectic is one who, out of what surrounds him, out of what goes on about him, applies to himself that which conforms to his own nature." From inside, from that nature, he contributes an extraordinary sense of fantasy, an uncanny "ear" for orchestral possibilities, and a desire to express and to communicate. He blends tonal and atonal elements, sweetness and acerbity, heat and coldness, love and hate. He is regarded as having struck a balance between the Dionysian and the Apollonian approaches to art, to have matched the reputed conflicts of passion and logic, of heart and mind. Even in the works that date from his early twenties, one feels the intent of combining the irresistible rhythm of Stravinsky with the impassioned lyricism of Berg, of finding the river in which would merge the streams known as classicism and romanticism, or their "neo" manifestations. There is little question that Henze is the most productive and significant composer for the theater in our time, with the number, extent and impact of his works for the stage matching those of his late great friend, Benjamin Britten.

An artist of deep social consciousness and strong convictions about the purposes of art in society, Henze has not shied away from conflict and confrontation; some of his works and actions have provoked censure and even an occasional scandal, which he has accepted as the price of doing and saying exactly what his principles demanded.

From many standpoints—personal, artistic, and political—the composer is a contro-versial figure; but then, so were Beethoven, Berlioz and Wagner. Ultimately, it will be the music that counts, and it will be interesting to see at the end of this century whether Henze's attempt at expressive communication with as wide a public as possible will have gained a more secure place in the repertoire than the hermetic and often forbidding work by some of his leading contemporaries. Henze has always believed that music must speak to people—whether it pleases or angers them, whether it moves or provokes them. As the music of the last quarter of the twentieth century has rediscovered the values of tonality and personal expressiveness (with the once iconoclastic Penderecki as a striking example), so we find that Henze has been in the vanguard of that trend all along, and has thus been genuinely "ahead of his time".

Henze's versatility in the world of the arts is phenomenal. A fine pianist, he is also a conductor of much experience, and not only of his own music; a brilliant writer, he has documented his life and works with frankness and insight. As Gerhard Koch has observed, "for Henze, composition, interpretation, action and reflection, all belong together." Several new books by Mr. Henze have recently been published, one of them a detailed "work diary" on his recent opera, *The English Cat*. He has also been very active as a teacher and in public educational ventures. Between 1976 and 1978 he directed an unusual community festival and workshop in the Italian mountain town of Montepulciano, involving many leading composers and performers and creating a stimulating artistic climate. He is now engaged in a project in the Austrian town of Deutschlandsberg, enlisting the talents of numerous gifted artists of high school age.

(On October 18-20, 1990, Christoph von Dohnányi and The Cleveland Orchestra presented a complete concert performance of Henze's opera, *The Bassarids*, at Severance Hall, with chorus and soloists. On October 27, these artists performed the work at Carnegie Hall, New York. Mr. Dohnányi has continued to champion this composer's music in his performances here and elsewhere. In April 1985, Henze had appeared for two weeks as composer-conductor in the "Composers of Our Time" series at Severance Hall.)

Aaron Copland's Eighty-fifth Birthday
(NOVEMBER 1985)

*

Aaron Copland died in December 1990 at the age of ninety.

*

ON THURSDAY, NOVEMBER 14, 1985, the world of music celebrated the eighty-fifth birthday of the great American composer, Aaron Copland. Born in Brooklyn on that date in 1900, Copland has been a major presence in American music for sixty years, since the mid-1920s. In honor of this anniversary, some two hundred works by him were scheduled for performance across the country during this season; The Cleveland Orchestra was among the first to initiate the festivities, with a performance of the *Clarinet Concerto* last August 2 at Blossom Music Center, with Franklin Cohen as soloist and Jahja Ling conducting. An extended excerpt from Copland's ballet, *Appalachian Spring*, was performed in the "Key Concert" of November 3, Christopher Wilkins conducting.

In November of 1974, Aaron Copland was the first to be honored by the Orchestra in its "Composers of Our Time" series, with a program of his music under his own direction. The program consisted of the *Fanfare for the Common Man*, *El Salón México*, *Inscape*, the *Piano Concerto* (with Leo Smit as soloist), and the *Third Symphony*. Over the decades, the following works by Copland, under many different conductors, have been played at Severance Hall and Blossom Music Center in addition to the pieces already listed, and often in repeat performances: Suite from *Appalachian Spring*, *Variations on a Shaker Theme* from that ballet, Suite from *Billy the Kid*, *Danzón Cubano*, *Letter from Home*, *A Lincoln Portrait*, *Nonet for Strings*, *Orchestral Variations*, *Quiet City*, Suite from *The Tender Land* and excerpts from that opera, *Dance Symphony,* and the *Old American Songs* for voice and orchestra. Mr. Copland himself has appeared as guest conductor of the Orchestra four times, at Severance Hall in 1965 and 1974, and at Blossom Music Center in 1968 and 1970.

Mr. Copland has been an all-round musician of exceptional versatility: composer, conductor, pianist, teacher, organizer of events, administrator, cultural ambassador, music critic and commentator, polemicist, writer of numerous books and essays, concert narrator (in his *Lincoln Portrait*), mentor and champion of younger artists and colleagues, and "star" of television documentaries. Copland's influence on the musical scene has been of incalculable effect; perhaps more than any other artist, he has represented the best in American music to the world, and in his own country has helped to make "classical" music respectable and in the best sense popular.

Copland's voluminous writings include *What to Listen for in Music,* a basic guide for the layman or beginning student; *The New Music 1900–1960* (revised and enlarged edition); *Music and Imagination* (the Norton lectures at Harvard 1951–52), and *Copland on Music,* an extensive collection of essays. Published by St. Martin's Press is the composer's autobiography, in two volumes, written in collaboration with Vivian Perlis; the books cover the periods 1900 to 1942 and 1943 to 1985. Copland has always been an exceptionally fluent and lucid writer; his books, most of them now available in paperback, are in the great tradition of literature by composers, and stand comfortably with such classics as the writings of Berlioz, Schumann, Wagner, and Busoni.

Here are a few excerpts:

> Change in music, like change in all the arts, in inevitable. After all, why should I or any other composer living in a time like ours write music that reflects some other period? Isn't it natural for us to try to develop our own music? . . . . The whole history of music is a history of continuous change. There never was a great composer who left music exactly as he found it.
>
> *The New Music*

> My love of the music of Chopin and Mozart is as strong as that of the next fellow, but it does me little good when I sit down to write my own, because their world is not mine and their language is not mine. The underlying principles of their music are just as cogent today as they were in their own period, but the essential point is that with these same principles one may and one does produce a quite different result.
>
> The uninitiated music lover will continue to find contemporary music peculiar only so long as he persists in trying to hear the same kinds of sounds or derive the same species of musical pleasure that he gets from the great works of the past. When approaching a present-day musical work of serious pretensions, one must first realize what the objective of the composer is and then expect to hear a different treatment of the elements of music—harmony, melody, timbre, texture—than what was customary in the past.
>
> Why is it that the musical public is seemingly so reluctant to consider a musical composition as, possibly, a challenging experience? When I hear a new piece of music that I do not understand I am intrigued—I want to make contact with it again at the first opportunity. It's a challenge—it keeps my interest in the art of music thoroughly alive.
>
> But I've sadly observed that my own reaction is not typical. Most people use music as a couch; they want to be pillowed on it, relaxed and consoled for the stress of daily living. But serious music was never meant to be used as a soporific. Contemporary music, especially, is created to wake you up, not put

you to sleep. It is meant to stir and excite you—it may even exhaust you. But isn't that the kind of stimulation you go to the theatre for or read a book for? Why make an exception of music?

What to Listen for in Music

Whatever form of new music is contemplated, one thing is certain: without generosity of spirit one can understand nothing. Without openness, warmth, goodwill, the lending of one's ears, nothing new in music can possibly reach us.

From "Are My Ears on Wrong?" A Polemic,
The New York Times Magazine, March 13, 1955

A Program Note on the String Symphony of Marcel Dick (MAY 1988)

*

Marcel Dick died on December 13, 1991, at the age of ninety-three. A book of essays in his honor was published in 1990 by the Edwin Mellen Press.

*

MARCEL DICK, whose ninetieth birthday was celebrated in 1988, has been a major force on the musical life in the Cleveland area for forty-five years. He received his earliest formal music training at the Royal Academy in Budapest, where he studied violin with Joseph Bloch and Rezsö Kemény and theory and composition with Victor Herzfeld and Zoltán Kodály. He was awarded his degree in violin in 1915 and became Professor of Music in 1917; further studies were interrupted by World War I. Before emigrating to the United States in 1934, Mr. Dick had a distinguished career as a violinist with the Budapest Opera and Philharmonic, as assistant concertmaster of the Vienna Volksoper, and principal violist of the Vienna Symphony, 1923–34. Noted as a chamber music player, in 1924 he co-founded the famous Kolisch Quartet with which he toured widely. In the same year, Arnold Schoenberg invited Mr. Dick to play in the première of his *Serenade, Op. 24*; he was to remain Mr. Dick's mentor, colleague and friend for many years.

In the United States, Marcel Dick performed as a member of the Detroit Symphony and of the Stradivarius Quartet. In 1943, he was appointed principal violist of The Cleveland Orchestra, serving until 1949 when he became head of the department of graduate theory and composition at The Cleveland Institute of Music. Other teaching experience has included positions at the Royal Academy, the Municipal School of Music in Vienna, Kenyon College and Case Western Reserve University. Renowned as a teacher, Mr. Dick has had many notable students. While at CIM, until his retirement in 1973, Mr. Dick conducted the Institute Orchestra; he has several times appeared on the podium of The Cleveland Orchestra. In 1962 Mr. Dick was the recipient of the Music Award of the Cleveland Arts Prize, and in 1978 he received an honorary degree of Doctor of Musical Arts from CIM. With his American-born wife, Ann, formerly an accomplished singer,

Marcel Dick has long resided in Cleveland Heights. They have a daughter, Suzanne, who is married to Orchestra cellist Harvey Wolfe, two granddaughters, and two great-grand-sons.

*

In the program book for the Minnesota Orchestra's premiere of his *Symphony for Two String Orchestras*, Mary Ann Feldman wrote that "as a composer, Mr. Dick identifies himself with the twelve-tone tradition of Arnold Schoenberg that emerged in Vienna during the time that he was so integral a part of its musical life. His *Symphony for Two String Orchestras* . . . is a thoroughly dodecaphonic work. Though he has graciously provided some insight into the structure and essence of the Symphony, Mr. Dick warns against the assumption that a description of the tone row that generates the music might be pertinent to its understanding. 'Just as it would be of no interest to give detailed information of the construction and functions of the C major scale of a piece in C major, I do not find that any significant purpose would be served in elaborating on the relations of the tones within the row and its governing functions. These should reveal themselves through the music.' Elsewhere Mr. Dick, an articulate teacher and spokesman for this tradition, has observed that in the history of music each prevailing technique or style has been processed within the principles of an organized grammar and syntax. His own happens to be that of twelve-tone serialism. The frame of reference for this expressionistic Symphony, then, is the language of twelve-tone technique, already known to the orchestral audiences through the works of its chief exponents, Schoenberg, Webern and Berg."

The program included the following letter, which Mr. Dick had written to Ms. Feldman as an introduction to his work:

> I composed the *Symphony for Two String Orchestras* in 1964. It is dedicated to my former student Linda Allen as appreciation for her *First Symphony*, dedicated to me. It is in three movements, a phantasy-like first movement in varying tempi and moods, a somewhat stormy second movement, resembling in its formal distribution a scherzo and trio, and a slow, perhaps introspective finale, except for its middle section almost like silence expressed in sounds.
>
> Although contrasting greatly in expression as well as in the technique of realization, the three movements have one thing in common, which after completion almost persuaded me to give the *Symphony* a subtitle: "Three Reflections," in the multiple sense of the word. Whether the images are reflected by a calm, or by a turbulent surface, or by an urge to recapture experiences that were once alive, they will never be quite the same if relived through the eyes and remembrances of one who shaped them and then was transformed by them. Nor are they the same in this music. In the specific application of the arch form at a certain point of each movement, all its features proceed in reverse order, continue in their reflections, as it were. But never literally. Sometimes distorted, sometimes, perhaps, beautified. Yet in another aspect does human experience manifest itself: an image, while giving way to its reflection, still might go on through its own momentum in association with the mirrored one into which it eventually dissolves.

Reviews of the first performance were exceptionally cordial. In *The Minneapolis Star*, John K. Sherman wrote, "The new composition . . . was one of the most exquisitely winning, to my mind, of the contemporary works we have heard lately. . . . Cast in serial idiom, its three movements spoke in intimate, almost secret terms, refined yet communicative in expression. Long planes of sound, in chords and unisons, stretched out in 'horizontal' fashion, ruffled now and then by flickering figures. The midway scherzo had nervy textures, with jabs, points and exclamations increasing and decreasing the tonal density. . . . The finale reached subtly but intensely to an inner spiritual center and finally to the shores of silence. A most original and poetic work."

In the *St. Paul Pioneer Press*, John H. Harvey observed: "Marcel Dick is a man of vast practical experience in the string medium, having played viola in leading orchestras and in three world-renowned string quartets. . . . The significant things about the three-movement piece were not what building methods the composer used but the obvious sturdiness of its structure and the expressiveness of its content. It is predominantly lyrical, though its middle section raises considerable stormy tension, and its last movement, elegiac in character, is deeply moving. Not the least of the work's distinctions is its masterly handling of the strings and the delicacy and variety of timbres evoked from the instruments as an integral part of the design."

Among the major contributions of Marcel Dick to the Cleveland musical scene have been the local premieres of many important works under his direction; these include Schoenberg's *Pierrot Lunaire* and *Ode to Napoleon*, Webern's *Symphony* and Stravinsky's *Les Noces* and *L'Histoire du Soldat*, to mention only a few. On the occasion of the Cleveland Orchestra premiere of Schoenberg's *Second String Quartet* (orchestrally performed), Mr. Dick wrote for the program an illuminating essay on the work.

Eulogy for Marcel Dick at the Memorial Service, The Cleveland Institute of Music, January 31, 1992

THERE WAS A BOOK published recently, entitled *The End of History*. Its thesis is controversial. When we think, however, about the passing of Marcel Dick, we realize that here a segment of history did come to an end. History, as someone wrote, is not events but people. Marcel's life, spanning almost the entire twentieth century, was living history in the most vivid sense. The splendid book of essays in his honor, published in 1990, tells his story and that of his era. Not only did he have two careers of distinction, one in Europe and one in the United States, but he was deeply involved in the major currents of artistic as well as political history. He worked with the leading figures of creative musical life on both continents; he took part in the crucial explorations of the art, not as a bystander but as a protagonist. He not only was a witness to the music of our century, he helped to make it. And such disciples as Hale Smith, Donald Erb, Linda Allen and Anne Trenkamp will carry his legacy into the twenty-first century.

Marcel Dick was blessed with an extraordinary array of talents: A masterly violist, as soloist and as orchestral and chamber music player; an accomplished conductor; an inspired and inspiring teacher; a superb and significant composer. He championed and generously promoted all that was new and fresh, cherished and nurtured all that was old and worth preserving. As a good friend wrote to Ann a few weeks ago, Marcel was on all accounts a giant among musicians. Add to this his gifts as a raconteur and essayist, and as a man of profound general culture; most important, add his gift of friendship, his ability to make and sustain relationships with people whom he loved and who loved him.

Marcel was the recipient of at least one other blessing not given to everyone who reaches his nineties: although his body was failing his mind remained sharp and clear to the very end. Ten days before he left us, our dear and loyal Ann and I sat with him and listened to the Budapest Quartet playing late Beethoven string quartets. He was with it all the way, asked for the movements he wanted, gave cues and indicated dynamics with his hands. The music was in him, and he was in the music.

To his friend and mentor, Arnold Schoenberg, Marcel paid a final symbolic tribute. We know that Schoenberg was superstitious to a high degree; in July of 1951, at the age of almost seventy-seven and fatally ill, he fretted about surviving Friday the 13th. Marcel could have left this world on December 5, the two hundredth anniversary of Mozart's death; he was ready; but he decided to remain with us until the moment was right: the late evening of Friday, December 13, exactly forty years and five months, virtually to the hour, after the passing of the man he revered above all other musicians in this century, Arnold Schoenberg. It was a final bow of respect and homage, and, by its timing, became in itself a work of art—for which, along with so much else, we thank him.

Arnold Schoenberg rehearses with the Kolisch Quartet. Drawing by B. F. Dolbin, c. 1926, from the collection of Marcel Dick. Left to right: Joachim Stutchevski, cello; Marcel Dick, viola; Schoenberg; Rudolf Kolisch (who held the bow in his left hand) and Felix Khuner, first and second violins.

VII. ON STAGE AND BEHIND THE SCENES

This pianist possesses an extraordinary technique which permits him to surmount the easiest pieces with the greatest difficulty.

Hans von Bülow

What is good execution? It is simply the art of conveying musical ideas adequately to the ear.

Johann Sebastian Bach

The interpreter is not able to increase the worth of a work; he can merely diminish it occasionally, since the best that he can give is simply a rendering on a par with the real value of the work.

Felix von Weingartner

The Liking Is in the Listening (JANUARY 1975),
by Lorin Maazel

*

Lorin Maazel served as Music Director of The Cleveland Orchestra from 1972 to 1982, a decade characterized by a Board of Trustees farewell resolution as "lively, exciting, and imaginative". There were many incandescent performances to remember, notably the 1973 concert performance of Strauss's Elektra. *Among Mr. Maazel's many valuable contributions was a series of concerts by the Orchestra with massed high school choruses in Public Auditorium, and another series designed for area college students. In 1974 he initiated the "Composers of Our Time" series, which continues to this day, and he devised and directed a series of chamber orchestra concerts entitled "Music of Today". At the program office's request, the conductor contributed a number of stimulating personal essays; this one was originally written for the Carnegie Hall program.*

*

THE QUESTION of audience preparedness is an intriguing one. The danger of carrying the thought to an extreme is present in every proposal made by self-defined elitists. Nevertheless, it is also true that the performing artist is thrilled to communicate through his art to an audience well versed in its subtleties. Exposure to and participation in the function of music at an early age is one method of achieving that kind of listenership. Through recordings, a child of average intelligence and sensitivity can become as familiar with the "Sanctus" of the Berlioz *Requiem* as with "Silent Night", as struck by the thundering "Dies Irae" as by the theme song of his favorite TV thriller. By playing a simplified version in a school band of the "Dies Irae", he can develop tactile contact with the mechanics of the piece. Later on as an adult, the child so exposed will hear the *Requiem* in detail and depth. Extramusical associations will slip away, leaving a sense of familiarity with the terrain, exquisite to the senses. Anything can become familiar—"the only things we really hate are unfamiliar things" (Samuel Butler: *Life and Habit*). Prejudicial preconditioning? Yes, if the exposure is limited to Schuetz, Schubert, or Schoenberg—hearing all manner of music provides perspective and teaches discrimination.

And those who come to the *Requiem* "late in life"? How fortunate they are! How envious we professionals can be of the music lover who hears a masterpiece for the first time! I can empathize as the listener is drawn into the "Introitus" by the ascending scales—Berlioz, with restraint and a noble strength, pleads for eternal rest—the thought of God's wrath germinates slowly to burst forth upon us in crimson cascades of brassy lava—the acrid ochre of the satanic sepulchre; then, death defeated. I breathe with the listener as Berlioz, the penitent, sings his tears of contrition, of supplication ("Quid sum Miser"). The mass unfolds—and I leave the listener to make his way towards the final pluck of God's Lamb ("Agnus Dei"), alone in the peopled solitude of a shared experience.

"We professionals": a concept replete with pejorative connotations of routine, sterile superiority, desensitizing through repetition. In fact, the professional musician is forever being resensitized through the act of listening whilst performing. A performance is an occasion which also heightens the artist's response.

A recent Occasion of Occasions was mine on July 27, 1974, at the first performance in recorded history of the Berlioz *Requiem* in its original orchestration: four brass orchestras (thirty-eight players in all) placed at the four corners of the choir (four hundred and fifty voices) and an orchestra of one hundred and fifty musicians. The setting: Orange, in the South of France, in a Roman amphitheater, gloriously intact, compact of acoustic, the ultimate *son et lumière* spectacle. At the dress rehearsal, the Mistral, that gritty wind which once maddened Van Gogh not far away at Arles, spun sheaves of notes about the stage. The choired voices swirled, deflected and enraged by the brazen breeze. The brass blazed its "Dies Irae", the massed stones withstood the fiery test, the tenor and his angels intoned the "Sanctus", subduing Mistral and man. The experience was so total, my senses so liberated, that the following evening I felt somehow released from the performing of the work to the extent of my being able to listen whilst conducting, and to become one with the twelve thousand eight hundred people gathered under a starry cupola. The Mistral was no longer evident, a few crickets and a music-loving bird, a festival mascot who, from its mysterious perch in an archway, accompanies all performances most appropriately with antiphonal warbles and a discreet low whistle, exquisitely timed. I have no real memory of having conducted that evening, but I remember everything I heard. I hope to continue to learn how to listen by listening. The liking is in the listening. Keep listening, friends.

Arthur Rubinstein (JANUARY 1983)

Arthur Rubinstein died on December 20, 1982, in Geneva, at the age of ninety-five.

ARTHUR RUBINSTEIN, one of the greatest pianists in the history of music, made his official debut in Berlin when he was 12, in 1899; the conductor was Joseph Joachim. His American debut took place in Carnegie Hall, New York, on January 8, 1906, with the Philadelphia Orchestra. He made his first appearance with The Cleveland Orchestra on November 25–27, 1937, in Brahms's Second Concerto, Artur Rodzinski conducting. He returned to Severance Hall for eleven further concert pairs and five sets of special concerts, one of the latter including all five concertos of Beethoven. In a final single Pension Fund Benefit concert on March 29, 1976, Lorin Maazel conducting, he played Beethoven's *Emperor* Concerto. He also appeared with Mr. Maazel and the Orchestra in Paris on October 1, 1975, during the ensemble's European tour of that fall, playing the Schumann *Concerto*. His total number of concerts with this Orchestra was, if the record is correct, thirty-five.

Mr. Rubinstein's repertoire with the Orchestra included nineteen different works: the five Beethoven concertos; the two of Brahms; Mozart's K. 453 (G major), K. 466 (D minor), and K. 488 (A major); Tchaikovsky's No. 1; Rachmaninov's No. 2 and *Paganini Rhapsody*; Saint-Saëns's No. 2 (which he played in Berlin under Joachim as early as 1900); Schumann's *A minor Concerto*; the two of Chopin; Liszt's No. 1, and Szymanowski's *Symphonie Concertante* (dedicated to him).

The artist's ties with Cleveland were most cordial; in addition to his Cleveland Orchestra appearances, he gave solo recitals in Public Music Hall at least nine times. George Szell, with whom he appeared as soloist as early as 1933 in the Netherlands, was a close friend, as was his keyboard colleague Arthur Loesser. Eunice Podis studied and coached with him extensively, and regards him as a profound and lasting influence on her artistry.

Arthur Rubinstein was in the truest sense a citizen of the world; and there is not a major musical center anywhere that does not recall this extraordinary man and artist with vividness, admiration, gratitude, and love.

It is not so good, in a musical way, to overpractice. When you do, the music seems to come out of your pocket. If you play with a feeling of "Oh, I know this," you play without that little drop of fresh blood that is necessary— and the audience feels it.

Don't tell Hurok, but I would play the piano for nothing, I enjoy it so much.

At breakfast I might pass a Brahms symphony in my head. Then I am called to the phone, and half an hour later I find it's been going on all the time and I'm in the third movement.

I knew Picasso before he was Picasso and I was Rubinstein.

At every concert I leave a lot to the moment. I must have the unexpected, the unforeseen. I want to risk, to dare. I want to be surprised by what comes out. I want to enjoy it more than the audience. That way the music can bloom anew. It's like making love. The act is always the same, but each time it's different.

Happiness is to live. It is the only happiness possible.

—Arthur Rubinstein

During most of the twenty-four-year tenure of George Szell in Cleveland, a visiting pianist, violinist, or singer was listed on the program page as "Assisting Artist". One day there was an emphatic phone call from Mr. Szell: "Arthur Rubinstein says he is not an assisting artist. He is a soloist. Please designate him as such from now on."

Fine Arts Magazine, January 1968
Dea ex Machina: Enter a Celestial Soprano via Jet

*

In reviewing the Saturday (December 30, 1967) Cleveland Orchestra performance of Handel's Semele, Alice Flaksman stated that Robert Shaw must have felt at times that he was directing a "who dunnit". Here the editor unravels some of the mysteries.

*

THIS SEEMS to be the season at Severance Hall when the sopranos are called upon to prove that they are not only possessors of beautiful voices, but musicians as well. In the November 27 issue of *Fine Arts*, we reported the remarkable feat of Judith Raskin, who found herself suddenly having to give performances of Berlioz songs with The Cleveland Orchestra in keys not in her natural vocal range. In the December 28–29–30 series of concerts, we encountered another "operatic heroine" in the person of Phyllis Curtin.

She was, in fact, the second singer to be challenged by an unexpected assignment. The first had been Helen Vanni, the attractive blonde mezzo-soprano who had come to Cleveland to sing the role of Ino in Handel's opera, *Semele*, with Robert Shaw conducting in his first and welcome return engagement. When Elaine Bonazzi, who was scheduled to sing Juno, was advised not to attempt the Thursday evening performance because of a throat ailment that had troubled her for several days, Miss Vanni assumed both roles, and projected them vividly. ("Ino that Juno"?)

On Friday morning, another complication arose. Although Miss Bonazzi was ready to return (and sang with exciting drama in the Friday and Saturday evening performances), the ensemble lost its leading lady when Beverly Sills decided that the state of her voice would not allow her to appear again, and departed for her home near Boston. Although the noted coloratura soprano of the New York City Opera had given a spectacular account of the title role on Thursday night, and almost nobody could have observed anything amiss, she had been concerned about an increasing laryngitis—which was not appeased by the inhospitable Cleveland weather.

The whole production was in imminent danger of being cancelled. So an urgent call went out to the distinguished soprano of the Metropolitan Opera, Phyllis Curtin, who had sung the part—three years before, and in a different and abridged edition—with the Amor Artis Chorale and Orchestra in New York. At four o'clock in the afternoon, Miss Curtin arrived at Severance Hall, had a piano rehearsal and a bite of supper, and walked on stage at eight-thirty—as beautiful and poised as one recalled her from her three previous appearances in this series (Verdi's *Requiem*, Foss's *Time Cycle*, and Haydn's *The Seasons*).

She did of course have to rely on the score more than usually, was forced to omit some numbers that simply could not have been brought off without a full rehearsal, sang the part "straight" without all the extra ornamentation that fits the style, and actually had to accomplish a bit of "public sight-reading". Withal, her presentation of the demanding role was assured and impressive, her blend with the ensemble sensitive and flawless in timing. Long known for the keenness and reliability of her musicianship, Miss Curtin gave hardly a hint of the fact that less than twelve hours earlier she had had no idea of what she would be asked to do. In the opera, Semele is not content to be a mortal, though beloved by Jupiter; one would gladly have seen the status of "La Divina" awarded at least to the diva.

The story was not over, for on Saturday afternoon Miss Curtin had to honor a contractual obligation to the Metropolitan to "stand-by" in a *Traviata* performance. So she flew back to New York in the morning, waited until the last act of the Verdi opera had safely begun, and winged back to Cleveland, arriving late in the afternoon—in time to eat and change for the Saturday night performance of *Semele*. Although tiredness showed in her face, it did not in her voice; the performance was again more than estimable—and of course by now "rehearsed", thanks to the Friday presentation!

Here once more was an example of professionalism at its best, an instance of a "good trouper" who not only accepts an extraordinary challenge but discharges it with admirable skill, grace, and artistic communication.

Fine Arts magazine was published in Cleveland between 1956 and 1973 under the editorship of Alla Wakefield.— Editor.

Remarks in Observance of the
Twentieth Anniversary of
the Death of George Szell
(June 7, 1897 - July 30, 1970)

*

This talk was given on Saturday, July 14, 1990, at Blossom Music Center, for the trustees and members of The Musical Arts Association.

*

EVERY GREAT INDIVIDUAL leaves a powerful impress on those around him or her, an aura that does not diminish in time but gains in vividness. Many of us became not only acquaintances or colleagues of Mr. Szell, but his students and disciples. I shall not claim to have been his friend, as Frank and Martha Joseph were, and Percy and Helen Brown, and Alfred and Clara Rankin, and as Dorothy Humel Hovorka was. Yet he was for the most part friendly to me, and kindly disposed; he not only expected me to do my job decently, he wanted me to do so. I think I came to understand him, and learned to respect him as a man as well as an artist.

If I now share with you my first impressions of him, it is only because they give you instantly a flavor of his personality, and set the tone of the relationship we had for over twelve years, from 1958 to 1970. So many of you will have similar stories to tell. And I have many more.

We first met one evening in October of 1957, in the conductor's room, after the third concert of the season, which concluded gloriously with the Brahms *Second Symphony*. A. Beverly Barksdale, the esteemed orchestra manager, introduced me to Mr. Szell as the person who was being considered for the vacant post of program annotator. I expected, at that moment, the usual pleasantries along the lines of "are you comfortable at your hotel, did you enjoy the concert," etc. What he said, however, was this: "Ah yes, nice to meet you. I have long wanted to ask you how you came to the conclusion that the second subject in the first movement of the *Eroica* is this one (and he hummed it) rather than the more commonly accepted that one (and he whistled it)." Now I had written the liner notes for the Orchestra's recording of the symphony for the Epic label a couple of years before, from Boston, so I had under the circumstances only the vaguest idea what he was talking about. I lamely defended my viewpoint, and Mr. Szell responded: "Yes, yes, that is one possible way to look at it. Well, thanks very much, and I'll see you tomorrow at lunch." As I staggered out of the room, I realized that here was a person who had no time or inclination for small talk, but was concerned with making every moment count with what he considered matters of substance.

*

In Mr. Barksdale's helpful and solicitous company, we met the next day at the Wade Park Manor. Mr. Szell outlined to me the nature of the position, and what his expectations were. "I must tell you frankly," I said, "that there are things here I have never done before; I am likely to make my share of mistakes." His answer will be forever indelible in my ear and mind, as if it were on a recording. Looking virtually through me with those ice-blue eyes of his, he said: "It is a good thing for a young man not to be entirely convinced of his own infallibility." I thought to myself that it was a good thing for a man of any age, but made sure not to verbalize the thought. Mr. Szell took a chance and offered me the job; Mr. Joseph signed me up, I made my share of mistakes as predicted, and somehow survived the next dozen years.

They were stormy ones, occasionally at the edge of disaster; but there were also times of shared enjoyment, of witty exchanges, of caring, and even of affection. For let it never be forgotten: George Szell may have prized infallibility, and the word "compromise" was conspicuously missing from his artistic dictionary; but when it was a matter of a player's or colleague's personal misfortune, Mr. Szell's innate humanity rose to the fore and led to many a kindly act, a generous gesture. It will interest you to know that in the current issue of *Symphony* magazine, the journal of the American Symphony Orchestra League, our long-time Orchestra cellist Donald White is quoted on George Szell's enlightened views and progressive decisions in the area of minority hiring; the article also relates the conductor's sympathetic responses at moments of stress.

Most of all, those who worked with him *learned* something every day. His comments on any subject whatsoever, freely dispensed whether requested or not, were almost always insightful and valuable. He was in his way a great teacher, and one was well advised to take his counsel seriously while retaining a sense of independence and individuality.

For that was not always easy. Mr. Szell, like many Europeans of the old school, was a *Besserwisser,* one who knows everything better. And most of the time, he really did! Yet that drive for knowledge, for mastery, that "divine dissatisfaction", had its inevitable price. When it came to musical or other professional performance, there could be no trace of sloth or disorganization. The fact that perfection had to be fought for unceasingly was a *sine qua non* of George Szell's existence, and therefore by necessity of his associates. That among *fallible* people this created tension and sometimes fear cannot fairly be denied. But it also meant that he demanded of others no more than he demanded of himself, and it tended to bring out in us a desire to do the best we could, to exceed our normal capacities. A review of a Cleveland Orchestra performance some twenty-five years ago said, "The players performed as if their very lives depended on it." Let me assure you, they did! And everyone understood that Szell's commitment to the art was total; as he said in an interview, "I love music more than myself."

*

But it was in this way, through such a rigorous regimen and Olympian standard, that George Szell made of a very good orchestra a great one, that he shaped a nationally renowned ensemble into one internationally acclaimed. As he liked to say, "Where others stop playing, we begin to rehearse." I do not need to recount for you the story of this rise to pre-eminence, in which so many people proudly took part—administratively as well as musically, in support groups as well as in actual performance by our magnificent musicians, and in the tangible expressions of enthusiasm from those who loved and believed in the Orchestra. The world came to know Cleveland through this Orchestra. But as always in history, it required the vision and indeed the genius of one person to provide the spark for such "magic fire music". In a message published in tonight's program book, Robert Shaw focuses on the essence of that genius with surpassing insight and eloquence.

*

The unshakable pride that the members of this Orchestra have always taken in their quality as an ensemble is a direct legacy of Mr. Szell. Unquestioned dedication to the art is what he taught by example, and it remains one of his lasting gifts to us. It is tradition, not as rote observance of established patterns, of "this is the way we have always done it", but as a living and vital force. Dorothy Humel Hovorka recently shared with me a transcript of Mr. Szell's remarks to the Orchestra in 1962, just before the first rehearsal of its concert in the inaugural week at New York's Lincoln Center. "I am sure," he said, "you are all aware of the significance of this occasion which is indicative of the enviable station you have reached in the musical life of the nation. This is due not only to your superb artistry but to your attitude toward your work which is part of this artistry, to your artistic responsibility, discrimination and sound self-criticism. . . . Whenever I am away from you—I want to say this without getting sentimental—I am missing you . . . no matter with what other orchestra I am making music; and while I am away, I always imagine in my inner ear how beautiful it sounds when you play. . . ."

Those who have succeeded George Szell on the podium of this Orchestra have cherished that sound, that flexibility, that unfailing sense of quality. However different their own approach, they have known that such standards were permanent and of the essence. Our present music director, Christoph von Dohnányi, has often spoken of the great inheritance that fell to him when he came to us in 1984: an ensemble of matchless refinement whose technical standards had been decisively upheld in the fourteen years that followed Mr. Szell's death. Recently, Mr. Dohnányi spoke to a German journalist about that legacy. When he was growing up as a musician, Mr. Dohnányi said, "Everyone knew that The Cleveland Orchestra was something special. Like all of us, I was of course a great admirer of George Szell. He had a way of making music that pointed to the future. . . . An incredibly intense and completely devoted musician, who deserved our respect." And in another interview, he was quoted to say, "You can be a different conductor from Szell, but you cannot be a better one."

*

Music-making that points to the future—how interesting. It implies clarity, scholarship, fidelity to the text and to the intentions of the composer. It also means that loving the past does not forbid coming to terms with the present, nor cherishing hopes for the future. Such hopes include the seeking-out and engaging of promising young soloists and guest conductors, the training and nurture of gifted podium assistants. And it means a fair balancing of the repertoire.

This is a good moment to dispel a persistent and pernicious allegation against Szell, and that is that he was not interested in the music of our time. Utterly untrue. While he was highly critical and selective, he still programmed an enormous literature of twentieth-century music. He conducted some thirty world premieres and countless first performances in the United States and in Cleveland. Of course his "standard repertoire" included the "modern classics" such as Stravinsky, Hindemith, Bartók, Kodály, Prokofiev, Bloch, and Janáček; he gave wonderful performances of works by Berg and Webern; he championed the creations of William Walton and Henri Dutilleux; he presented new works by Bohuslav Martinů and Benjamin Britten; he conducted the symphonies of William Schuman and Peter Mennin, also on tour; he recorded music by Schuman and Samuel Barber; he sought out music by young Americans such as George Rochberg and Easley Blackwood and Benjamin Lees, and programmed these works also in the Orchestra's Carnegie Hall concerts.

Whenever living composers came here, they were amazed at his knowledge of their scores, his comprehension of their intent, and his unswerving devotion to giving them their best possible exposure. When there were pieces and styles for which he did not personally care but which he thought worthy of a hearing, he would ask Robert Shaw or Louis Lane or guest conductors to program them. And let it be remembered that it was he who brought Pierre Boulez to Cleveland in 1965 to conduct his own music in his United States orchestral debut, and soon thereafter appointed him principal guest conductor.

George Szell was a musician who took his responsibilities seriously, and among these was the firm conviction that the creation of music did not stop in the year 1899.

*

There was one quality of George Szell's that was really infallible: and that was his taste. Never did I hear him exaggerate a phrase, lapse into emotional bathos, do anything for show. That impeccable taste, that crucial sense for the artistic fitness of things, stood him in good stead for the re-creation of the classical repertoire. His Beethoven, Haydn, Mozart, and Brahms were supremely "right"; one could do them differently, but players as well as listeners could not find his way with them other than convincing and exemplary. One could always trust George Szell to give an interpretation that was thought-out and thought-about, solid, and honest; and when he was at his best it was inspired.

In 1964 (a year before the National Endowment for the Arts was established), President Johnson sent a message to Cleveland paying tribute to George Szell on his fiftieth anniversary as a conductor, and "to express the warm appreciation of a grateful nation and world for his contributions to the preservation and enrichment of culture." Indeed, George Szell gave to his orchestra and this community the entire second half of his life as a mature musician. The acoustical renovation of Severance Hall in 1958 resulted from his relentless stimulus. He could still take pride in the building of the incomparably beautiful festival facility, Blossom Music Center, in the conception and planning of which he had been intimately involved. He conducted here exactly twenty-two years ago, in the inaugural season of the Center, and again the following year, 1969.

*

To a person concerned with language, the words "record" (as a noun) and "record" (as a verb) should be of particular interest. They come from the Latin *recordari*, which means to inscribe in the heart, and thus to remember. George Szell, like many a great artist of historical stature, has left us a record of his music-making in three ways: through the orchestra he refined and exalted, through the recordings he made for us to possess, and through the memories he inscribed upon our hearts.

Immortality is largely memory. We may have a physical object—like a cathedral, a statue, a golden coronet, or a compact disc—to tell us of the past, and of who made them. An object such as a recording or a photograph or a film may bring to life the music-making and the appearance of a person no longer physically with us. Artists, particularly, are fortunate in being able to leave such records of their lives—so that they can always be among us, become in fact "immortal".

When you hear tonight Johannes Brahms' *A German Requiem*, superbly conducted by Mr. Szell's friend and colleague and disciple, Robert Shaw, you will note in the seventh and closing movement music built around these words: "Blessed are the dead . . . . Saith the spirit, that they rest from their labors, for their works do follow after them." In theology, "works" is to be taken as "deeds"—deeds good or bad. George Szell's good deeds, his works, are alive today, and he lives through his works.

George Szell—A Personal Vignette (MAY 1980), by Kurt Loebel

*

Kurt Loebel has served as a member of this Orchestra's violin section since 1947, George Szell's second season. One of the ensemble's senior members, he has made a distinguished contribution to the Cleveland musical scene, also as a long-time faculty member of The Cleveland Institute of Music.

*

GEORGE SZELL died in the evening of Thursday, July 30, 1970, while The Cleveland Orchestra was playing a concert at Blossom Music Center under Pierre Boulez. At intermission, as we were waiting for Mr. Boulez to mount the podium, word was passed to the Orchestra to assemble backstage after the concert for an announcement. Most of us sensed what it was about. Louis Lane announced that Mrs. Szell had asked that the Orchestra be the first to know that Mr. Szell had passed away.

Two evenings later, we opened a Blossom concert with a conductorless performance of Bach's *Air*, in his memory. One listener was overheard to say, "It's like a prayer!" At that very moment, the structural supports of the Pavilion shell—which in those days produced a booming noise resulting from the change of temperature at night—responded to the music with a sound resembling the slamming of a door. One might fantasize that it symbolized the door being shut on the life of George Szell, whose life and work were primarily identified with The Cleveland Orchestra.

None of us suspected that the performance of Beethoven's *Eroica* in Anchorage, Alaska, on May 29, 1970—in the final concert of the 1970 tour to the Orient and played in an unglamorous high school auditorium—would be Szell's final conducting appearance. In response to a letter from the Orchestra Committee expressing get-well wishes during his illness in June, he responded: "Your kind letter was read to me over the phone, has moved me, and I want to thank you most warmly for the sentiments you voice. I was keenly aware of the help every orchestra member gave me during the tour. Without this help, I could not have got through the tour at all."

*

Szell was a complex person, full of contradictions; it is likely that he would have succeeded in any intellectual endeavor. He had great physical strength and mental ability. His encyclopedic knowledge on many varied subjects was impressive, although his "know-it-all" attitude was sometimes hard to take. In spite of the scholarliness of his music-making, he was also motivated by the need to project his personality. He understood, perhaps from his early days as an operatic conductor, that he had to be an actor and showman as well, within the framework of artistic restraints. His repertoire emphasized the Classic and Romantic periods. He performed little contemporary music, referring to it sarcastically as "temporary music".* He also objected to Muzak, which pursues all of us in hotel elevators and shopping centers, and called it "wallpaper music".

He spoke fluent German, French and English, but seemed reluctant to admit to his knowledge of Hungarian, the language of his father. (His mother had been Slovakian, and he had no hesitation about Czech.) He wanted to know everything, asked detailed questions of anyone, whether it was about the workings of a car engine or about a cut of meat. He would tell orchestra members how to have their glasses adjusted, what color socks to wear and how to take a nap. On one of his forays through Severance Hall, he might even tell a cleaning lady how best to handle a mop. He enjoyed showing off his knowledge of a score, by identifying a single note in a measure of an inner voice part, while asking that the rest of the score be covered with a piece of paper. He would take a player to task after a chamber music concert, when a single note had been accidentally misread. Yet I had seen him panic, not knowing where to deposit the coin in a Coke machine.

Szell could be charming or difficult, all at the same time. He was relentlessly pursuing his goals in rehearsal, and we often felt overrehearsed and reaching a point of mechanical perfection. Once, as we approached a difficult passage, he shouted excitedly, "Look out! The last time you played it, it was perfect!" He would rehearse the National Anthem, "Happy Birthday" played on the occasion of Arthur Rubinstein's birthday, a comedy routine with Jack Benny—all in utter seriousness. Nor was he reluctant to ask a principal player to his home on a Sunday, to work on his conception of an interpretive detail. Not having attended public school during his child-prodigy days and with his pedagogical habits based on a nineteenth-century Austro-Hungarian educational approach, his methodology and psychology reflected both the positive and the negative, which he either consciously or unconsciously transmitted to the Orchestra.

He was always compulsively teaching, but he was not devoid of a sense of humor. Sometimes his sophistication was counteracted by a surprising naïveté. When the Cleveland Indians won the World Series, we decided to greet Szell's appearance on the podium with a rendition of "Take me out to the ballgame!" He was dumbfounded, being unacquainted with the tune or its meaning.

Curiously, many of our best performances took place during the more tension-free Thursday morning dress rehearsals. Someone jokingly remarked: "He even rehearses the inspiration!" The press often criticized him for being cold and too calculating. My feeling was that underneath that forbidding exterior he was a highly emotional man, who had difficulty controlling his strong feelings and especially his temper. An insight into the warmer side of his character was expressed in a tribute written for the memorial service for Arthur Loesser on January 11, 1969: "Arthur was not only a great old friend, but a unique personality, whose character, artistry, culture and knowledge were rooted in better bygone times. Both as an exponent of that disappearing world and as his irreplaceable self, he will remain unforgotten."

Being childless, he perhaps pictured us as his children. Before a tour he would say, "Don't eat in any questionable joints." On the day of our last concert in Anchorage, he watched me trying to dial a room number directly from the house phone in the lobby. He insisted that I had to go through the operator at the desk. When he saw that I was wrong and he was right, he said: "See, always listen to Papa!"

He worked untiringly, pushing himself to the limits of endurance, agonizing over music and demanding the same from others. It was said of him that he was his own worst enemy—until Rudolf Bing of the Metropolitan Opera retorted, "Not as long as I'm alive!" His musical dogma was clarity, precision, and rhythmic vitality—an approach he preferred

* The word "contemporary" should be taken here as only signifying "avant-garde"; not music of the twentieth century as a whole. It is still widely believed that Mr. Szell was uninterested in and unsympathetic to the music written after World War I; that is not correct.—Editor.

to sensuous sonorities or coloristic effects. He was a fine pianist. When he played a Mozart concerto, conducting from the keyboard, he was afflicted with the natural problems of one who suddenly has to perform rather than tell others what to do.

This week's program, observing the tenth anniversary of George Szell's death, reminds us of the important contribution he made during a quarter-century of the Orchestra's history. In looking back, we realize the even greater importance of looking forward as well, in the hope of ever-increasing public support and enthusiasm for one of Cleveland's greatest assets.

George Szell's Last Tour,
by Eugene Kilinski (MAY 1972)

*

This article was published in The Plain Dealer Sunday Magazine *on August 22, 1971, a little more than a year after Mr. Szell's death. Mr. Kilinski, now retired, was associate chief librarian of The Cleveland Orchestra, a violinist and conductor, and a former concertmaster of The Cleveland Philharmonic Orchestra. The article is here reprinted by kind permission of the author and of* The Plain Dealer, Cleveland.

*

GEORGE SZELL must have suffered considerable and increasing physical pain during the last few months of his life. But he continued in characteristic fashion to give of himself completely in conducting supreme, masterful performances with his great Orchestra. During its tour of the Far East The Cleveland Orchestra, if anything, outdid itself in the quality of its playing under Szell, as attested by huge ovations before large audiences and wildly enthusiastic reviews.

Only to those who had occasion to work with him at close range did it become apparent that he was weakening during the later stages of the tour, weakening but not faltering. Knowing he had to conserve his failing strength for each performance, he declined invitations to many recreational activities such as grand sightseeing tours which had been specially arranged for him in Japan.

On the other hand, he refused to give in to his illness, and so continued all of his musical activities, including, when the occasion demanded it, that of being the ever-compulsive coach and teacher of his players. A case in point occurred prior to the beginning of one concert as players were milling about and practicing backstage. Szell stood in the wings ready with baton in hand, absorbed in his own thoughts, when suddenly he lifted his head and stared at one of the violinists who at that moment was innocently playing through the opening theme of the Mozart *G Minor Symphony*, scheduled for that evening's concert. Perhaps the maestro heard something questionable in the rendition, for he swiftly walked over to the player and engaged him in earnest discussion in an undertone, emphasizing his points with small but vigorous conducting motions. The violinist, somewhat caught short and looking a bit glassy-eyed, nodded his head slowly in acknowledgment of the unexpected lesson.

On another occasion, Szell was overheard to greet a wind player backstage most cordially with an inquiry after his good health, after which he added: "By the way, do you remember the last time we played the——Symphony, I think it was a week ago? What happened to you twelve bars before letter K in the slow movement?" There followed some remark about the player's lack of *tenuto* and a reminder concerning attention to harmonic balance. Or, arriving at the hall in a rush for another concert, he would shout to one of the managers, "Tell So-and So I want to see him in my dressing room—with his instrument!"

An incident in Sapporo bears out the perpetual surveillance which George Szell exercised over his forces. In keeping with modern practice, the Mozart *Symphony No. 40* is played with a reduced string section. One of the bass players who had not rehearsed or played the work for this particular series of performances on the Far Eastern tour was asked by the personnel manager at the last moment to fill in in the Mozart work for one of the other bassists who was ill. The substitute player afterward described to me his nervousness during the performance because "The Old Man kept staring at me like an owl during all the difficult passages, but during the easy parts he never looked my way once." The roving, penetrating eye of the conductor, unencumbered by the presence of a score, was, of course, a familiar and sometimes chilling experience felt by many in the Orchestra.

*

For the most part, such prodding was regarded as a normal (if uncomfortable) condition to Cleveland Orchestra routine. Actually, the greatness of the conductor was matched by the high integrity and exceptional ability of the players themselves. The Orchestra members knew tacitly that their prime obligation was to live up to the standards of their director in every way. One might imagine that the players, most of whom were visiting the Orient for the first time, would be tempted to go sightseeing on a grand scale and thereby reduce their individual practicing and preparation to a bare minimum. After all, they were fine musicians, well trained, and they knew the tour music thoroughly, so why should they not permit themselves to relax a bit and enjoy their new exotic surroundings? However, such thinking was not in evidence. I believe that John Mack, our first oboe, expressed the prevailing orchestra attitude quite positively when I met him one morning in a Tokyo hotel elevator.

"Well," I asked airily, after we had nodded greetings, "have you been doing much sightseeing here in Japan?" He looked at me almost pityingly as he replied, "Are you kidding? As far as I'm concerned this is strictly a job. I have all I can do to keep my reeds in shape, practice a bit, and rest before each concert. After all, I have all those solos to play every evening. I have no time for sightseeing."

William Brown, a member of the violin section and therefore not called upon to play solos in the orchestra, was equally conscientious. Bill and I had had some exciting excursions during days off to Osaka Castle, the Temmangu Shinto Shrine, and through the teeming Oriental back streets near the Umeda railroad station in Osaka. But when I proposed an additional early afternoon visit to the Atsuta Shrine in Nagoya on a concert day, Bill politely declined with, "Thanks, Gene, but you'd better count me out. If I don't get to the hotel to rest a bit and to practice, I won't be in any shape for the concert tonight."

Concertmaster Daniel Majeske did his sightseeing from the windows of his hotel rooms—while practicing. At the Hotel New Japan in Tokyo his windows opened onto a Japanese garden, complete with miniature stream, stepping stones, and a lovely hillock atop of which was a tiny Shinto shrine. It was here that Dan, standing at his window with violin and bow in hand, witnessed a Japanese wedding in progress one afternoon. He regretted being unable to observe this colorful ceremony at close hand because of the necessity for practicing and going over some concertmaster solos for the coming evening's performance.

*

The perfectionist attitude of Szell and his refusal to compromise his artistic standards in small as well as in large matters were fully revealed during his rehearsal of the Japanese and Korean national anthems. These were pieces on a par with "America, the Beautiful" in difficulty, which undoubtedly any junior high school orchestra could have sight-read adequately. Nonetheless, Szell insisted on having at least a run-through of these hymn-like tunes prior to their public performance. Unfortunately, the parts had arrived too late in Osaka, after Szell's rehearsals for the tour had been completed; the two remaining practice periods had been reserved for Pierre Boulez's three concerts in Osaka and Tokyo. However, Boulez graciously invited Szell to take fifteen minutes of his own first rehearsal for playing through the anthems. During this brief period The Cleveland Orchestra's musical director carefully drilled his instrumentalists for balance, attack, phrasing—in short, all of the elements he would pore over in a serious composition, and he made those nondescript, watery hymns sound like real music. Then, as an ultimate gesture of respect to the Japanese people, Szell, having spent a concentrated fifteen minutes of study on the task in his dressing room that evening just before the concert, conducted his first performance of the Japanese national anthem from memory.

Perhaps the most meaningful testament to his genius was given by a young woman, a stranger who appeared backstage shortly before intermission of The Cleveland Orchestra's second Tokyo concert. I wondered about the identity of this extremely attractive dark-haired woman, an Occidental, who had smiled vaguely in my direction once or twice. Then as the music towered to its climax and thundered to its close she approached me directly, and with eyes shining, ecstatically exclaimed, "Oh, I can't believe it. I have never in my life heard anything like this. What a great orchestra! I have never heard such a great performance of the Schumann *Fourth Symphony*. What a magnificent conductor! Oh, perhaps I should introduce myself," she continued, her English betraying a slight central-European accent. "My name is Frau Spirer. My husband is one of the concertmasters of the Berlin Philharmonic." She went on to explain that her husband's orchestra had just finished its own tour of Japan and was about to return to Germany.

*

The great successes of The Cleveland Orchestra on the Far East tour were a repetition of the triumphs that had been part of the Szell legend for decades. But to witness the first overt signs of the great maestro's illness was a poignant and heartbreaking thing. For me the first ominous indication occurred at the end of the Nagoya concert, halfway through the tour. There had been several curtain calls, one encore, and a continuing roar of applause when the conductor turned to the manager backstage and remarked that he would like to take just one more bow and then call it an evening. Mr. A. Beverly Barksdale, the manager, not realizing how great was the maestro's fatigue, suggested a wait-and-see attitude. But after his next curtain call the conductor went straight to Barksdale and said desperately, "Look, I simply cannot go on. I am completely exhausted." It was a genuine cry of distress. The manager quickly urged him to retire after his next bow, of course, and Szell brought the Orchestra offstage with him the next time out. Afterwards, as I followed Szell, who was walking slowly to his dressing room, he seemed a bone-weary and bent old man.

Thereafter, encores were always cut to one, after which the Orchestra was motioned off the stage with the conductor after a few brief curtain calls, a drastic change of procedure for one who in the past seemingly never knew the meaning of fatigue and who was known to be most generous with encores on foreign tours. Although it was not known to me at the time, I later discovered that he conducted the entire tour with a fever. And yet, despite the crushing weariness he must have felt after each concert, he was never heard to utter a word of complaint. He remained the personification of imperious dignity throughout. It was not for nothing that he was tagged by his own solo horn player, Myron Bloom, as "the last of the great aristocrats among conductors."

In Sapporo, his secretary had arranged for him to see a doctor on the afternoon of his concert there, but Szell, who at first acquiesced to the idea, later changed his mind. "No, I don't want to see him after all," he said. "If he examines me he will only tell me not to conduct tonight. Cancel the appointment." The secretary later explained that the sponsors of the Sapporo concert, early in the preliminary negotiations, wanted a guarantee that Szell would conduct because they felt that without him they would be unable to sell the concert in this relatively unsophisticated, northern frontier island of Japan. Szell knew this and felt he could not let them down.

That evening the conductor was his usual iron-willed self, controlling his forces with that great sense of drama and towering drive for which he was so famous—for all except the final two movements of the concluding work, the Sibelius Second Symphony, when he suddenly seemed to go slack, bowing his head and gripping the right side of his chest with his left hand, and barely able to indicate the beat with but the feeblest of stick motions.

The last concert George Szell ever conducted in his life was at Anchorage, Alaska, the final one of the tour. Listed on the program, among other works, was the Walton *Variations on a Theme by Hindemith.* However, in mid-afternoon Szell rather mysteriously ordered the *Mozart G Minor Symphony* substituted for it. The seemingly practical reason he gave for this move was the indisposition of his first trombonist (there is much heavy brass in the Walton opus), but was this the real reason? Did he have some premonition that this might be his last concert ever? If so, would he not want to perform the music he loved best, music which in the eyes of the world he conducted greater than anyone else within living memory? It seemed most fitting that the last composition George Szell conducted, the closing work in Anchorage, was the *"Eroica" Symphony,* Beethoven's hymn to heroism.

George Szell: A Tribute (JUNE 1990), by Robert Shaw

*

In June 1990 Robert Shaw wrote a brief tribute to George Szell printed in the Blossom Music Center program of July 14, 1990, when he conducted the Brahms Requiem, observing the twentieth anniversary of Szell's death.

*

EVEN TO HIMSELF, George Szell must have been something of an enigma. I often have wondered if he ever let his right hand (of command) know what his left hand (of compassion) was doing. Long after the act, one would hear rumors of his charity or personal generosity—but, to his face, one would not dare to accuse him of the indiscretion of sentiment.

His disciplinings, however abrupt, were tolerable—first, because they were not motivated by self-pity. (He was distressed not for himself, but for the composer.) Second, we knew that he clearly demanded many times more from himself than he required of us. And third, almost always, when the right arm of authority descended it was followed quickly and demonstrably by an improvement in the product.

It is not the function of a "conscience" to be comforting—and for many of us George Szell was the conscience of our profession. Above all was his insistent advocacy of the composer's prescription and intent, as versus a performer's personal "style" or "interpretation".

In direct line from this were judicious performance practices that favored structure over color, clarity over sonority, temporal stability over eccentricity, remote control over balletic ecstasy, and right notes over best wishes.

Always he elected elegance over extravagance. And, if asked to choose between the intellect and the emotions, he would have declared the mind to be itself the sun.

For me and, I think, for most of us who were privileged to make music in his time and presence, his recorded performances reveal a seldom-approached blend of solo instrumental virtuosity and ensemble disciplines. But even more remarkable is that which is missing: those emphases and excesses—some, perhaps, even unintentional—that too often in this age make up a performer's trademark or "image".

When it came to making music, George Szell's enigmatic sort of self-awareness was sufficient to eschew personal caprice and idiosyncracy. Earlier than might have been expected, those who came to watch him perform ended by listening to the music.

To the ends of our days we will be grateful.

A Bouquet for Louis Lane (1992)

ONE OF THIS WRITER'S most esteemed colleagues during his tenure at Severance Hall was Louis Lane, the distinguished American conductor. Mr. Lane was a member of the conducting staff at Severance Hall for twenty-six seasons, from his appointment as Apprentice Conductor to George Szell in 1947 to successive posts as Assistant and Associate Conductor, and finally Resident Conductor. He returned as guest conductor in 1973–74, 1975–76, 1978–79, and appeared most recently of many times at Blossom Music Center in July of 1991.

During these more than three decades, Louis Lane conducted The Cleveland Orchestra hundreds of times, in the subscription series, the Pops concerts at Cleveland Public Auditorium, the educational concerts, special and tour concerts, and in numerous recordings both with the Cleveland Summer Orchestra and the Cleveland Sinfonietta as well as the Orchestra itself. He served as musical director of Lake Erie Opera Theatre from 1963 to 1970, conducting memorable performances.

One of Mr. Lane's most noteworthy contributions was a repertoire of exceptional breadth and imagination, which included over the decades some seventy-five Cleveland premieres, of which over fifty were twentieth-century compositions from Cage to Lutoslawski and Schoenberg, and twenty-five were lesser-known works by earlier composers from Arriaga to Leopold Mozart, from Berlioz to Berwald. It is an astonishing list, an example of daring program-making for which the conductor has been widely honored nationally.

Mr. Lane has served as principal guest conductor of the Dallas Symphony and the Atlanta Symphony, and has widely appeared internationally. Several of his recordings have won major awards. In recent years he has been closely associated with The Cleveland Institute of Music, as conductor and musical advisor, leading numerous concerts of the school's superb symphony orchestra and chamber orchestra. Last year, he participated in a recording of works written by George Szell in his youth, an album produced by the Institute for its benefit and now available.

When Louis Lane appeared at Cleveland Orchestra concerts in October 1973, he conducted the *Turangalîla-Symphonie* of Olivier Messiaen, with the composer present. Following the performances, Mr. Messiaen wrote the following on the title page of Mr. Lane's score (as translated from the French): "Great, indeed very great conductor, so precise, so dynamic, so profoundly a musician and possessor of a technique so assured, who conducted this work with such perfection and impassioned commitment—in all affection and admiration."

Louis Lane is one of the most knowledgeable and insightful musicians I have ever encountered and worked with. His taste—like that of his erstwhile mentor, George Szell—is flawless, and his cultural erudition is deep as well as wide. When requested, he can write brilliantly, and he can deliver an extensive lecture without a note before him. It should not be forgotten, furthermore, that Mr. Lane's steady hand and sound judgment continued to be of crucial significance to the life of The Cleveland Orchestra after the death of George Szell in 1970. Collaborating as Resident Conductor with Musical Advisor Pierre Boulez, Louis Lane played a major role in maintaining the standards and upholding the morale of the Orchestra during those years of transition.

Christoph von Dohnányi and the Music of Our Time (1992)

IF THERE IS such a thing as "guilt by association", there must also be something we may call "glory by association". There is, in fact, a very justifiable pride that orchestra musicians, staff members, concert patrons, and friends may feel about being associated with what is widely considered to be "the best" in the world of symphony orchestras. "In my view," wrote a critic of *The Christian Science Monitor* from New York in 1989, "The Cleveland Orchestra has earned the title of America's premier symphony ensemble—in terms of sheer virtuosity, versatility, and overall musical commitment." During the Orchestra's European tour of 1990, the critic of the Vienna *Kourier* observed: "The musicians from Cleveland came to Salzburg after a long absence. Christoph von Dohnányi is their conductor and together they are virtually unbeatable." And in 1991, the critic of *The Boston Globe* commented after the Orchestra's guest engagement at Tanglewood that "it will take some doing to excel the standards of execution the Cleveland has developed under Christoph von Dohnányi and the individual and unmistakable artistic profile he has sculpted for the ensemble."

Yes, it is a music director who sets and maintains such standards, and for that he must obtain and maintain the total cooperation of the extraordinary community of musicians he faces daily. Their work is achieved by genuine and willing collaboration rather than by imposed authority, and it is leavened by integrity both personal and artistic. It is the joint commitment and shared ability of all performers that makes possible, concert after concert, week after week, season after season, playing of such unexcelled quality and captivating inspiration.

*

This is not a book of encomia for performers, a collection of rave reviews. But it is one that is founded on the continuity of excellence which this Orchestra has provided for its city, its country, and the entire musical world, for so many decades. The contribution that Christoph von Dohnányi has made to this living tradition, since his accession to the post of Music Director and Conductor in 1984, is by now a historical fact, and provides the celebration of The Cleveland Orchestra's seventy-fifth anniversary with a special luster and radiance. It is now our good fortune, as announced in November of 1992, that he has agreed to remain at the helm of the Orchestra into the next millennium.

It is valuable to have so many of the Orchestra's performances not only in memory but "on record"; this most recorded of American orchestras today has by now produced a veritable library of musical literature, from virtually all eras of the existing orchestral repertoire.

*

As we look at the history of great orchestras, we find again and again that they were in the forefront of musical creativity, the seeking-out and presentation not only of what was "classical" and therefore "safe", but of what was new and therefore challenging. Think of the Chicago Symphony under Theodore Thomas and Frederick Stock, offering its public such "moderns" as Wagner and Brahms, Strauss and Mahler; think of the Boston Symphony under Serge Koussevitzky, when living American music found an ardent and indomitable champion, from Ives and Ruggles to Copland and Piston and Harris and Hanson and Bernstein. The Cleveland Orchestra's history is no less distinguished; all its music directors have known what a great ensemble's responsibilities to its own time really are.

And so it is today: from the moment that Christoph von Dohnányi first appeared on the podium, in 1981, he has made it clear that there are *three* centuries of orchestral music, with our own—now drawing to a close—meriting "equal time". It is as a matter of course that Mr. Dohnányi has brought us, in fair balance with Mozart and Brahms, with Haydn and Bruckner, the European classics of our century: Bartók, Janáček, Lutoslawski, Stravinsky, Schoenberg, Berg, Webern, Henze, and many others. But he has also sought out the music of the United States, and seen to it that assistant and resident conductors choose their own examples for presentation. Here is a listing of those American works which Mr. Dohnányi has himself conducted, and in many cases took on the Orchestra's tours for multiple performances. It is an impressive list, and one that is sure to be augmented in years to come:

CHARLES IVES: *Three Places in New England; The Unanswered Question; Fourth Symphony.* CARL RUGGLES: *Sun-Treader; Men and Mountains; Angels.* EDGARD VARÈSE: *Amériques; Ecuatorial.* DONALD ERB (Cleveland): *Concerto for Brass and Orchestra.* FRANK WILEY (Kent): *Abstracts.* DENNIS EBERHARD (Cleveland): *The Bells of Elsinore.* MARCEL DICK (Cleveland): *Symphony for Strings.* JOHN ADAMS: *The Wound Dresser.* ELLEN TAAFFE ZWILICH: *Oboe Concerto.* JAMES OLIVERIO: *Timpani Concerto.* PHILIP GLASS: *The Light.* JOSEPH SCHWANTNER: *New Morning for the World.* SHULAMIT RAN: *Concert Piece for Piano and Orchestra.*

*

It was for that kind of dedication to the living art of our time that Christoph von Dohnányi was honored in August 1989 with a special citation from the Cleveland Arts Prize. In a ceremony at Blossom Music Center, the conductor was honored *"for his committed support and championship of twentieth-century music as a vital and challenging part of the Orchestra's repertoire."*

As an example of the imaginative and often daring program-making brought to us by the conductor, and of his consistent eagerness to try unusual and thought-provoking approaches, we recall the following musical "happening" of 1985, a striking and memorable event.

AN ORCHESTRAL PROGRAM AT CHRISTMAS-TIME: Severance Hall, December 19–20–21, 1985, Christoph von Dohnányi conducting MOZART, *Symphony No. 40* in G minor; VARÈSE, *Ecuatorial for Baritone and Orchestra* (Günter Reich, soloist); Intermission; SCHOENBERG, *A Survivor from Warsaw,* for Narrator, Men's Chorus and Orchestra (with Günter Reich and The Cleveland Orchestra Chamber Chorus); followed without pause by SCHOENBERG, *Friede auf Erden* ("Peace on Earth") for Mixed Chorus; followed without pause by BEETHOVEN, *Leonore Overture No. 3.*

This program of December 1985 was one of the most unusual Christmas-time selections ever given in Severance Hall. It was evident that Christoph von Dohnányi wished to make the audience think about as well as celebrate the season. It was felt that the challenge posed by a program so remarkably chosen and structured would benefit from some introductory comments:

AN INTRODUCTION TO THIS PROGRAM: A program book for an opera performance usually begins with (or contains) a brief synopsis of the action. The present symphonic program, while remaining in its framework as concert rather than stage music, still exhibits a certain dramatic structure, design and progression.

For Mozart, the key of G minor was almost always one of agitation and highly personal expressivity. In the *Symphony No. 40,* he speaks to us of tragedy; but, being

Mozart, he does so beautifully, and with classic perfection of form. Beethoven's *Leonore Overture No. 3*, which closes the program, provides the balancing counterweight, rounds out the arch. It begins on a grand unison G, and fights its way through to a radiant C major, a hymn to liberty and to the "Freude" which the composer so eagerly sought.

Varèse's *Ecuatorial*, which closes the first half of the program, is an intense and powerful invocation, an ardent plea for the sustenance of life and the preservation of peace. It is a ritual of the Maya, a great pre-Columbian civilization. The disappearance of that culture tells us that the prayer was not answered; yet its message is universal, and speaks also for the yearnings of our time and of our all-too-fragile civilization.

The second half of the program is a "symphonic collage". We move, as it were, *dall' inferno all' paradiso*—from hell to paradise. (Mahler had thus designated the finale of his *First Symphony*, heard here earlier this season.) At the close of the year, we muster the courage to look at the tragedy fully revealed forty years ago. In a few searing minutes, Schoenberg brings us face to face with humanity at its lowest and at its highest, with what Paul Henry Lang once called, in speaking of Beethoven's *Eroica*, "catastrophe and triumph at one and the same moment". *A Survivor from Warsaw* is an art work that does not call for the usual audience response of approval or degrees of it; thus its symbolically abrupt close is followed at once with another prayer for peace, for harmony among men, for reconciliation. *Friede auf Erden*, written forty years before the *Survivor* and seven before World War I, gives us a vision of hope—without which, after all, we cannot live. And Beethoven's overture symbolizes for us humanity's will to overcome the direst obstacles, to be free of oppression, and to prevail.

Thomas Carlyle wrote, "see deeply, and you see musically." The arts by nature deal with essence, not with surface. Great art is never merely attractive superficially. In this holiday season, "we look at the shadow as well as the light", and our celebrations cannot be without reflection, memories, insight, and compassion.

POSTLUDE

What's past is prologue.
William Shakespeare
from *The Tempest*

At the Close, an Editorial Confession
(MAY 1988)

AS THE CURRENT EDITOR'S TENURE with The Cleveland Orchestra draws to a close, it may be appropriate to mention one linguistic and literary idiosyncrasy which has over the years raised many an eyebrow. The issue is, of all things, punctuation.

This writer has, from the beginning in 1958, carried on a private rebellion against American usage in the placement of quotation marks. The first of many inquiries came from the late George Szell. After some conversation and dispute, he said: "Well, if you feel so strongly about it, go ahead." And so our department did, and we have found to our pleased surprise that some other local media have over the years adopted the device, at least occasionally.

What is the fuss all about? The most recent letter, from Mr. Clark West of Orange Village, Ohio, puts the matter very clearly, and we are grateful to him for his interest and courtesy. Mr. West cites various definitive sources in support of the rule that "all periods and commas must go inside the end quotation marks." The editor has no problem with placing the period and the quotation mark where they were, in that last sentence. But he *would* have a problem with a brief proverb or a saying like "a sadder and a wiser man", or the name of a musical composition.

Mr. West, a former teacher of journalism and associate of *The Wall Street Journal*, explains his—generally accepted—stand on the matter: "This rule originated in the early days of printing, when all type was hand-set. Periods and commas tended to fall out of the chases into which type was locked in the form for printing. If memory serves me, Ben Franklin was one of the first to insist that periods and commas all ways [*sic*] be placed within end quote marks." Exactly; are we now in the "early days of printing", or has that technical problem long since become an irrelevancy?

A newspaper or magazine article says, "last night, the Met performed 'Rigoletto,' to the evident delight of the audience." Is that the name of the opera? Or: "The Met last night performed 'Rigoletto.'" Again, we thought the name of the opera was "Rigoletto". It's that simple. The long-standing custom has been that colons and semi-colons go outside the quote marks: "Rigoletto": and "Rigoletto"; but would one believe that in recent years, *The New Yorker*, that paragon and pace-setter of style, has begun to put semi-colons inside while leaving colons outside? There, it is "Rigoletto;"—than which nothing looks sillier. Of course, exclamation points and question marks remain outside, even in *The New Yorker*, unless the sentence or the quote actually includes them. For names of pieces, italic type without any quotation marks would obviate the problem, but that is not always available.

What Mr. West considers an avoidable mistake that has long marred our programs is, in fact, an intentional attack on a long-ingrained and unfortunate custom, based only on an odd bit of typographic history and not on linguistic logic. Some newspapers in England have adopted American usage, but 95% of all print media in Europe and else-where have not. *Der Spiegel*, the outstanding German-language news magazine, recently reviewed a new biography of Oscar Wilde; one sentence reads: *Sein Roman, "Das Bildnis des Dorian Gray", der 1891 erschien, machte ihn schliesslich zum Skandal.* Naturally; the name of the protagonist is "Dorian Gray", not "Dorian Gray,".

Whether or not such a quixotic assault on a powerfully entrenched grammatical habit has any chance of outliving the tenure of this particular Don Quixote is highly doubtful. Tilting at windmills is always dangerous, and usually has the same result. But it was worth the try, for thirty years. Ah yes, we just found a label from a German beer bottle, distributed in this country. The sentence, in English, reads: *Beck's is brewed in strict accordance with the "Reinheitsgebot", the German purity law of 1516.* So there; purer than that we cannot get. Perhaps the solution to the whole problem would be to adopt the ear-splitting and side-splitting "phonetic punctuation" developed and demonstrated by Victor Borge, most recently at Severance Hall on May 8, 1988.

*

Speaking of language, its history and meaning, the semantics as well as the syntax: Many of us have long wondered about the derivation of "English horn", which is of course neither English nor a horn, but an alto oboe. The instrument's body used to be slightly curved, somewhat like a horn, or angled, therefore *anglé*; the English, or *Les Anglais*, are said to have valued that instrument as early as the 17th century. But it is our own English horn player, Felix Kraus, who may recently have discovered the most probable (or at least the most charming) derivation of all. In Mahler's Fourth Symphony, the poem in the finale has a line, "Wir führen ein englisches Leben", which means "we lead an angelic life". "Englisch" here is a contraction of "engelisch", which has nothing to do with England. So that's it! Mr. Kraus's instrument, therefore, is an "angelic horn" not only because of how it sounds and how it is played, but because it is likely to be—along with the harp—the instrument of paradise itself.

—K. G. R.

*

THE MUSICAL ARTS ASSOCIATION presents, in observance of his 30th anniversary as program annotator and editor, a concert of chamber music by KLAUS GEORGE ROY. Performers will be Cleveland Orchestra members CAROLYN GADIEL WARNER and STEPHEN WARNER, JOELA JONES and RICHARD WEISS, JEFFREY KHANER, JOHN RAUTENBERG, THEODORE JOHNSON, JOHN MACK, FELIX KRAUS, DONALD MILLER, and ROBERT BOYD, with guest artist CHRISTINA PRICE, soprano. Mr. Roy will provide spoken program notes. The concert takes place in Reinberger Chamber Hall on Sunday afternoon, April 10, 1988, at 3:00. Tickets at $5 are now available at the Severance Hall ticket office.

About the Author

*

KLAUS G. ROY was born in Vienna in 1924. At fourteen, soon after the Austrian *Anschluss*, he began to study English, and in 1939 emigrated with his parents to England. In 1940, the family came to the United States and settled in Boston. After graduation from The Cambridge School of Weston in 1941, he attended Boston University before joining the United States Army in 1944, serving 1945–46 in Tokyo as Information-Education Officer; he returned to Boston University in 1946, studying musicology with Karl Geiringer. After receiving his Mus. B. in 1947, he went to Harvard to study composition with Walter Piston and took courses in music history with Archibald T. Davison, A. Tillman Merritt, and others; he earned his M. A. degree in 1949. Between 1948 and 1957, he served as music librarian and instructor at Boston University, and also was a regular contributing music critic of *The Christian Science Monitor*. In 1958, he began a thirty-year tenure as program annotator and editor of The Cleveland Orchestra. From 1975, he taught a music course at the Cleveland Institute of Art. Since his retirement from the Orchestra in 1988, he has continued to teach and lecture on the faculties of the Cleveland Institute of Music (which awarded him an honorary doctorate in 1987) and Case Western Reserve University. While at Severance Hall, he gave more than seven hundred pre-concert talks and other programs including several concert narrations, and served as intermission host for the Orchestra's broadcasts originating with WCLV. He has given lectures in Boston, Cambridge, Minneapolis, San Antonio, Toronto, Washington, D.C., throughout Ohio, and in Nebraska, Georgia, and other states.

Since the 1940s, numerous artists have performed Mr. Roy's music including Cleveland Orchestra conductors Robert Shaw, Louis Lane, Lorin Maazel, Michael Charry, Robert Page and Matthias Bamert. Artists long associated with the Orchestra such as cellist Lynn Harrell, violist Abraham Skernick, oboist John Mack, pianists Eunice Podis and Arthur Loesser, and many other Orchestra members have generously participated in performances over the decades. Among other artists of international renown who have performed his music are conductors Sarah Caldwell, Yoshimi Takeda and Samuel Adler, pianist Theodore Lettvin, soprano Penelope Jensen, bass-baritone John Shirley-Quirk and his wife, the oboist Sara Watkins, and organists Karel Paukert and Daniel Pinkham. Mr. Roy's compositions have been performed, in addition to Cleveland and at Blossom, in Boston and at Tanglewood, in New York, Chicago, San Francisco, Washington, D.C., Dallas, Saint Louis, Birmingham and Milwaukee. Internationally, his music has been heard in London, Paris, Rome, Berlin, Lisbon, Madrid, Rio de Janeiro, Jerusalem and Warsaw.

Mr. Roy's catalogue of one hundred and forty opus numbers and three hundred smaller pieces includes two operas, the first premiered in 1957 over WGBH-TV, and the second—a children's opera with a libretto by Leonard M. Trawick—in 1983 at the Cleveland Zoo. A number of his compositions are recorded. He has written incidental music for three Shakespeare plays (Cleveland 1973, 1975, and 1979), and an orchestral piece performed by twelve orchestras nationwide including The Cleveland Orchestra under Lorin Maazel. During the 1991–92 season, over thirty different works of his were performed. A sizeable proportion of his catalog is published and he has received many commissions, including those for his two operas. His most recent commission, from The Singers' Club of Cleveland, was premiered in Severance Hall in 1993.

Mr. Roy has written program notes for some two hundred recordings since 1951, on ten different labels. He has been a contributing editor and critic of *Stereo Review*, and now writes regularly for *Stagebill* magazine. He continues to give concert previews for The Cleveland Orchestra, the Ohio Chamber Orchestra, and the Cleveland Institute of Music. Much of his light verse has been published over the years, and newspapers have presented political and social commentary under his byline. In the 1980s, he was a frequent commentator on the WVIZ "Signature" series. With his wife Gene he has escorted nine music festival tours to Europe as well as across the United States and Canada.

He is an honorary member of Phi Beta Kappa and the Fortnightly Musical Club; upon his retirement in 1988, the Ohio Senate passed a resolution of recognition for his career, and in 1990 he won the Ohioana Library Citation for Distinguished Service in Music to the State of Ohio. Feature articles about his work have appeared in *The Cleveland Press, The Cleveland Plain Dealer,*

Northern Ohio LIVE, and *Symphony Magazine*. Mr. Roy has been active on numerous boards and committees, and has long been regarded as a cultural activist. In 1960, he proposed the establishment of the Cleveland Arts Prize.

Mr. Roy's hobbies include table-tennis, swimming, chess, astronomy, and wide reading in science. Had he his life to live over again, he would convert his enthusiasm for playing as well as watching tennis into serious amateur competition, and would study voice to become a respectable bass-baritone. Yet, as a noted philosopher has observed, there is no conditional in history.

1958 photo by Robert Carman

1988 photo by Dan Milner

The Program Annotators of
The Cleveland Orchestra, 1918 to 1993

DONALD TWEEDY—1918–1920

ARTHUR SHEPHERD—1920–1930

HERBERT ELWELL—1930–1935

ARTHUR LOESSER—1936–1941

GEORGE H. L. SMITH—1941–1957 (also program editor)

KLAUS G. ROY—1958–1988 (also program editor)

TIMOTHY D. PARKINSON—1971–1989 (associate program editor)

JAMES R. OESTREICH—1988–1989

ERIC SELLEN—from 1989 (program editor)

PETER LAKI—from 1990

Cleveland Visual Artists Who Contributed Their Works for
Orchestra Program Covers

VIKTOR SCHRECKENGOST
JOHN TEYRAL
FRANCIS J. MEYERS
JOSEPH McCULLOUGH
JULIAN STANCZAK
JOHN CLAGUE
H. C. CASSILL
NORMAN POIRIER
GEORGE GOSLEE
RALPH MARSHALL

JOSEPH JANKOWSKI
MARGARET K. DUFF
EVELYN M. PIRA
DEBORAH J. KIMSEY
JESSE POIRIER
ROGER COAST
DANIEL C. BROWN
MELISSA E. ROY
JULIE BUBALO
MARTIN LINSEY